Hiking Shenandoah National Park

Fourth Edition

Bert and Jane Gildart

FALCONGUIDES

GUILFORD, CONNECTICUT
HELENA, MONTANA
AN IMPRINT OF GLOBE PEQUOT PRESS

For our children and their children: May you always find
enchantment and beauty in places such as Shenandoah

To buy books in quantity for corporate use
or incentives, call **(800) 962-0973**
or e-mail **premiums@GlobePequot.com.**

FALCONGUIDES®

All interior photographs by the authors unless otherwise noted.

Project editor: Heather Santiago
Layout: Sue Murray

TOPO! Explorer software and SuperQuad source maps courtesy of National Geographic Maps. For information about TOPO! Explorer, TOPO!, and Nat Geo Maps products, go to www.topo.com or www.natgeomaps.com.

ISSN 1556-7958
ISBN 978-0-7627-6464-8

Printed in the United States of America

10 9 8 7 6 5 4 3 2 1

Contents

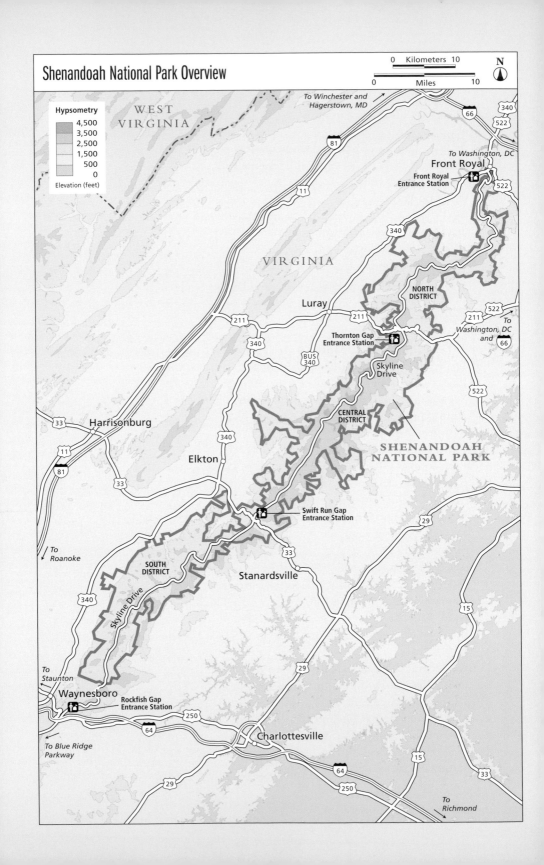

Shenandoah National Park Overview

Hypsometry

4,500
3,500
2,500
1,500
500
0
Elevation (feet)

Kilometers 10

Miles 10

N

WEST VIRGINIA

To Winchester and Hagerstown, MD

VIRGINIA

To Washington, DC

Front Royal

Front Royal Entrance Station

NORTH DISTRICT

Luray

Thornton Gap Entrance Station

To Washington, DC and

Skyline Drive

Harrisonburg

CENTRAL DISTRICT

SHENANDOAH NATIONAL PARK

Elkton

Swift Run Gap Entrance Station

To Roanoke

SOUTH DISTRICT

Stanardsville

Skyline Drive

To Staunton

Waynesboro

Rockfish Gap Entrance Station

Charlottesville

To Blue Ridge Parkway

To Richmond

Acknowledgments

No book is ever written and completed without the help of others, and this guide is no exception. First, we'd like to thank Steve Bair (retired) and Melissa Rudacille of the staff at Shenandoah National Park, who reviewed the book and provided much valuable information. We attempted to incorporate all their thoughts, suggestions, and ideas and hope we have interpreted their comments correctly. In addition, we'd like to thank Greta Miller, director of the Shenandoah National Park Association, who aided with initial logistics and helped us establish just what direction our work would follow. Dan Hurlbert, map specialist, was an invaluable help as well.

Along the trails we met the South District Trail Crew, who offered much good trailside chat and helped explain evolving Shenandoah backcountry policy. Thanks as well to former ranger and adventurer Buck Hisey, now of the Shenandoah Valley, and his wife, Fran (also an adventurer extraordinaire), for their spontaneous friendship, meals, and long night sharing information about Shenandoah.

We want to thank Bill Schneider, founder of Falcon Publishing, Inc., who initially got us to Shenandoah in 1998, and Jess Haberman of Globe Pequot Press, who got us back in 2010. Last but not least we want to thank our special friends Susan and Adam Maffei, who hiked virtually all the trails with us again.

Introduction

> I only went out for a walk, and finally concluded to stay out
> 'til sundown, for going out, I found, was really going in.
>
> —*John Muir*

Located in the Blue Ridge Mountains of northern Virginia, Shenandoah National Park is both a hiker's challenge and a delight. Hiking the park is a challenge because of its generally precipitous nature, but a delight for the same reason. Long and narrow, this 197,411-acre park straddles a ridge crest that courses over 100 miles north and south, embracing rolling hills, quiet hollows, meandering streams, and verdant forests. More than 79,000 acres of the park are designated wilderness.

To some, it seems all the trails in Shenandoah either ascend or descend, but not every park trail is steep or rocky. With more than 500 miles of trails, the park offers a wide variety of terrain and insights into the park's past.

The famous Appalachian National Scenic Trail (AT) is a major route through Shenandoah National Park. From Skyline Drive, the AT leads 1,280 miles to its northern end atop Mount Katahdin in Maine. Each year about 150 people trek the entire AT. Not everyone will want to hike from Maine to Georgia, but many who come to Shenandoah do hike the 101 miles that pass through the park, many of which combine the AT with park trails.

Human History of Shenandoah National Park

"Shenandoah" is an Indian name, probably from the Iroquois language. There are several translations of the term, including "river through the spruces" and "big flat place." The most common translation, however, is "daughter of the stars."

The wilderness of Shenandoah National Park never presented much of an obstacle to European explorers. In his book *The Undying Past of Shenandoah National Park,* Darwin Lambert wrote, "For almost two centuries, more than a dozen gaps or passes of the park-land had roads that followed packhorses, which followed Indian paths, which followed elk and bison, which followed mastodons."

John Lederer was the first European trailblazer to explore what is now Shenandoah National Park and leave a record. In 1669, sixty-two years after the founding of Jamestown, this German adventurer—assisted by Monacan and Manahoac Indians—climbed either Hightop or Hawksbill (no one is sure which) and gazed down into the valley below. Other explorers followed, and they were impressed by the valley's rich, fertile land. They wrote favorable reports of the area, and their writings—combined with expanding population pressures—prompted settlement.

◀ *Shenandoah's hikes are an ideal combination of natural beauty and exercise.*

Tractor seats remind hikers that Shenandoah was once home to farmers.

Between 1725 and 1730, settlers established two small villages in the Shenandoah Valley. The earliest settlers farmed the fertile and level land at the mouths of the hollows. As these areas became crowded, later settlers used the marginal farmlands, and immigration eventually stopped altogether. Early settlers grew corn, tomatoes, and beans and raised cattle.

The surrounding forests provided a cash crop of lumber, and sawmills began to emerge. Mountain farmers hitched their mules and dragged oak, chestnut, yellow poplar, and pine to the mills. Realizing that the bark of chestnut, oak, and hemlock, along with the wood of chestnuts, could be used in the process of tanning hides, farmers built roads to transport the bark to market. Today, many of those roads exist as trails. Farmers and settlers also built roads to transport goods from the Shenandoah Valley to outside markets. Many of the roads remain today as well, and are used as fire roads. Two such roads were used by Stonewall Jackson during his Valley Campaign, when he suddenly turned back Union forces at the Battle of Fredericksburg.

The Civilian Conservation Corps, or CCC, helped build Shenandoah's trail system soon after it became a park. Created by President Franklin D. Roosevelt to improve economic conditions during the Depression, the CCC provided work for jobless men between the ages of 18 and 25. At any one time there were six camps and more than 1,000 workers in Shenandoah, building overlooks, walks, and structures along Skyline Drive (completed in 1939), constructing and improving trails, fighting fires, and building park facilities. Soon after Shenandoah was authorized in 1926, the Potomac Appalachian Trail Club (PATC) built the Appalachian Trail and later helped with its relocation. The club still helps National Park Service trail crews with maintenance and construction.

Trail workers weren't the only people living in the park in the 1930s. A few years before Shenandoah became a park, 465 mountain families still lived in the area. With

All of Shenandoah National Park's trails are well marked with distances and arrows for orientation.

special government permission, nineteen families remained within park boundaries in 1940. The last park resident died in 1979. Though overgrown, graveyards and other vestiges of the mountain people remain. Along Shenandoah's trails you'll find stone walls that once stabilized mountain roads, and you'll see old apple orchards now dominated by striped maple and tulip poplar.

Natural History of Shenandoah National Park

Though several key wildlife species such as elk, wolf, and cougar are absent today, much of Shenandoah Park is being restored to a more pristine condition. Now protected inside the park, Shenandoah's forests have recovered dramatically. Hundreds of plant species—including one hundred species of trees—now flourish inside the park. As the forests reestablished themselves, so too did Shenandoah's wildlife. Today, more than 200 species of birds and fifty species of mammals exist in the park. Red fox and beaver populations have increased, as have Virginia white-tailed deer, which were almost wiped out in the region. Managers estimate they numbered somewhere between 5,000 and 7,000 in 2011. Black bears have also returned to the park, increasing their population from an estimated two in 1937 to more than 300 in the mid-1990s (see "Be Prepared: Backcountry Safety and Hazards").

Turkey populations have also rebounded from virtual extirpation. Biologists estimate there are more than 500 in Shenandoah National Park as of 2011. We frequently saw turkeys as we hiked the park's trails and traveled Skyline Drive while researching this guide, particularly in the early morning and late evening. Peregrine falcons have also returned to the park. Keep an eye out for them on Stony Man and Hawksbill Mountains (see Hike 22: Stony Man Trail and Hike 26: Hawksbill Summit).

Seasons and Weather

Th' fog's ah liftin' on the Rag. Hit's ah goin' ter clear.
See th' fog a rollin' down the Rag. Hit's ah goin' ter rain.

*—Unerring method of predicting weather by
turn-of-the-twentieth-century residents
living near Old Rag (still incontestable)*

Leaf detail as seen in fall in many of the Shenandoah National Park's streams.

Weather in Shenandoah changes frequently. In the summer, fog can roll in suddenly and bring cool temperatures. Hail and high winds accompany drenching rains. Fall and spring are two of the most pleasant times to hike in Shenandoah, but they can also be the most awesome. Lightning storms are frequent and can be nerve-racking, as we discovered one day while hiking in Jeremys Run.

Average summer temperatures in Shenandoah vary from the low 50s to the mid 70s (degrees Fahrenheit) between June and August. Fall (September to November) temperatures can be quite variable, ranging from the low 30s to the high 60s. Winter (December to February) temperatures range from the mid-teens to the high 30s, and in spring (March to May) temperatures rise from the mid 20s to the mid 60s.

You can expect to see snow in Shenandoah from November through March and often into April. Rain falls during all months and is usually heaviest from May through October. Fog (and smog) can be really heavy and constant during the summer months and can last from a few hours to a week at a time.

Vegetation begins to green in April, when nights are often still cold and the days warm. Summer brings warm, and often very hot, days. Autumn brings a wonderful show of fall colors and is the busiest time in the park. Winter is a quiet time, bringing ice, snow, and sometimes frigid temperatures. It also brings more views through leafless trees, abundant animal tracks, and solitude. During winter, very few services or park personnel are available. Skyline Drive is usually open all year but does close—sometimes for weeks at a time—after severe storms.

Fees and Permits

There is an entrance fee that varies depending on time of year and type of vehicle. There are no additional fees to hike on any trails. A backcountry permit, which is free, is required for those camping in the backcountry. For the most up-to-date fee information, please contact the park at (540) 999-3500, or consult the park website, www.nps.gov/shen.

Fall is the perfect time to visit Shenandoah National Park, when the leaves take on brilliant hues and lend an underfoot crackle to your hike's soundtrack.

Be Prepared: Backcountry Safety and Hazards

In Shenandoah National Park you must keep your wits about you.

Begin by getting in shape before going on long hikes. If you are out of shape, hot weather and high humidity can worsen your experience. About half the trails in the park begin with easy descents that can lull you into continuing farther and farther down the trail and make you forget about the long homeward ascent.

If you are caught in a lightning storm, seek shelter away from open ground and exposed ridges. Dropping even a few yards off a ridgetop will reduce your risk. In a forest, stay away from single, tall trees. Look for a cluster of smaller ones. Avoid gullies or small basins with water in the bottom. On open ground, find a low spot free of standing water.

During a lightning storm, assume a low crouch with only your feet touching the ground. Put a sleeping pad or pack—be sure it has no frame or other metal in it—beneath your feet for added insulation against electrical shock. Do not huddle together; members of a group should stay at least 30 feet apart so that if someone is hit, the others can give first aid. If you are in a tent, get in the crouch position. Stay in your sleeping bag and keep your feet on a sleeping pad.

Watch for signs of an imminent lightning strike: hair standing on end, an itchy feeling on your skin—one hiker described it as "bugs crawling all over"—an acrid, "hot-metal" smell, and buzzing or crackling noises in the air. Tuck into a crouch immediately if any of these signs are present.

Stay out of shallow caves, crevasses, or overhangs (numerous in Shenandoah—and very inviting). Ground discharges may leap across the openings. Dry, deep caves offer better protection, but it's still best to crouch and not to touch the walls.

If someone in your group is hit by lightning, be prepared to give CPR and first aid for burns and shock. Many victims survive—even direct hits—especially if help is nearby and rescuers can begin resuscitation. There is no danger of electrocution or shock from touching someone who has been struck by lightning.

Most of the park's accidents occur at waterfalls. Each year many people venture too close to a waterfall, slip on wet or loose rocks, and injure themselves in a fall. Avoid wet rocks near steep ledges, waterfalls, and cliffs.

Hypothermia, a lower-than-normal core body temperature, can occur in Shenandoah, especially when it's wet and cold, for these are times when all the factors contributing to loss of body heat are present. Frequently during the summer, fog moves in and is followed by rains that drench the mountains. Other times it hails, and hikers who aren't prepared can experience hypothermia. Temperatures need not be below freezing for hypothermia to be a threat. Most cases occur in windy and wet weather with temperatures ranging between 40 and 50 degrees Fahrenheit.

Shivering marks the first stage of hypothermia. In advanced stages shivering stops, but only because the body is too weak to continue shivering. This stage may be accompanied by slurred speech, clumsiness with the hands, and impaired judgment. At the first sign of hypothermia, take precautions by changing into dry clothes. In more acute situations, place the victim in a sleeping bag with people lying on either side. Feed conscious victims something warm and sweet, but do not give them alcohol. Because acute hypothermia can lead to death, get medical help immediately.

It's often quite hot in Shenandoah in the summer months, so be careful of heat exhaustion. Avoid strenuous hiking in the hottest part of the day—usually midafternoon. Wear loose, light-colored clothes and a hat with a wide brim and some ventilation. But most important, carry and drink lots of water, even before you realize that you're really thirsty. Shade is easily found in Shenandoah. Take time to rest in the shade and keep drinking water.

Poison ivy abounds in Shenandoah. Learn to identify it, avoiding plants with shiny leaves in groups of three. (Heed the old adage: "Leaves of three, let it be.") In the fall, poison ivy turns a beautiful orange and the plant produces a white berry (see Appendix B: Further Reading for a recommended field guide to Shenandoah's plants).

We recommend you wear long pants and long sleeves while hiking in Shenandoah. Trails are sometimes narrow, and it's easy to get poison ivy oil on your skin and clothing. Use care when selecting where to dig "cat holes" for bodily waste. Rashes on the genitals can be particularly troublesome and may require medical attention.

If you have or may have touched poison ivy, wash the area immediately with water. Washing within the first ten minutes often can prevent irritation. Ideally, you should place suspect clothing in plastic bags until it can be thoroughly washed to remove irritating oils. If a rash appears, apply calamine or Caladryl lotion. Persistent rashes may require something stronger, such as a salve containing cortisone. Extreme cases may require medical treatment.

Most waters in Shenandoah appear refreshing but may contain a microorganism called *Giardia lamblia,* which can cause severe diarrhea and dehydration in humans. Mammals—especially beavers—spread this nasty parasite through their feces. Water can be rendered safe by boiling it for at least five minutes, or by passing it through a filter system with a mesh no larger than 5 micrometers. According to some experts, iodine tablets and other purification additives are not considered effective against the parasite. Any surface water supply is a potential source of this organism, and hikers who drink directly from streams and springs risk contracting "beaver fever" and its painful symptoms.

Biting insects— mosquitoes, gnats, and flies—can ruin a trip. Be prepared with an effective repellent that you have tried ahead of time. It is too late to discover that the repellent is more irritating than the bugs when you are already on the trail. DEET is the active ingredient in most repellents. However, prolonged overuse of a solution of 30 percent DEET can cause some negative reactions, particularly in children.

In Shenandoah the incidence of Lyme disease, caused by a parasitic microorganism carried by ticks, is low. Ticks, however, are numerous, and contact with them makes it possible to contract Lyme disease, Rocky Mountain spotted fever, and human granulocytic ehrlichiosis infection. Ticks can appear any time of the year at temperatures above 50 degrees Fahrenheit—even in January and February. When they attach to the skin, ticks secrete saliva that thins the blood and they begin to feed. At the same time, they may inject a disease-carrying parasite. General symptoms of tick-borne diseases include fever with shaking chills and severe muscle pain. Lyme disease may produce a rash on the palms and soles of the feet, which later spreads to the whole body.

The best way to keep from getting the disease is to prevent ticks from attaching to your skin. Wear long pants and tuck them into your boots or bind the bottoms with a loose rubber band. Wear long-sleeve shirts. Consider applying a spray containing

DEET to your skin and clothing. Some manufacturers sell a tick spray (for clothing only), and it seems to work well when sprayed on pant legs and boots. At the end of the day, conduct a tick search, and don't panic if you find one. The process of transmitting the disease takes hours.

To remove a loose tick, flick it off with a fingernail. If the tick is firmly embedded, use tweezers to pinch a small area around the tick's mouth and pull it out. Try not to squeeze the tick's body as this increases the risk of infection. Finally, clean the area with an antiseptic.

Rattlesnakes are common in Shenandoah, but during the months we spent gathering information for this book, we encountered only two. You should always remain alert to the presence of snakes. If you've never heard a rattlesnake rattle, don't worry—the sound is unmistakable. Rattlers strike when they're angry, and someone in Shenandoah has been bitten every few years, although no deaths have been reported. Snake venom is relatively slow acting, a fact that allows victims time to get medical help.

Learning to avoid snakes and their bites is relatively simple. Watch where you step and where you sit down, particularly in rocky areas. Avoid hiking at night. Snakes generally hole up by day, then bask on sun-warmed rocks or sand when temperatures cool in the evening. They generally hunt at night, so it is best to sleep in tents with sewn-in floors and zippered doors.

Before hiking in snake country, become familiar with first-aid treatment for bites. Commercial snake-venom extractors are great if used within the first three minutes. Victims—if alone—should walk slowly to the trailhead and seek immediate medical attention. If you are accompanying a snakebite victim, anticipate and treat for shock as needed.

Copperheads, the other venomous snake species in Shenandoah, are said to be common, though we never saw one. They usually have yellow spots with black markings that tend to make them fade into their surroundings in mottled light. (See Appendix B: Further Reading for a recommended field guide to snakes.)

Use proper precautions to avoid trouble with black bears in Shenandoah National Park. Never keep your food in your tent. In the backcountry, string it from a high branch, ideally in sealed containers. When you obtain your free backcountry permit, park officials will give you specific height and distance requirements for hanging food. Never cook in your tent.

If you encounter a black bear while hiking, do not run. Black bears are generally intimidated by noise and an upright stance. Clap and shout to let the bear know where you are. If the noise doesn't scare the bruin, quietly back off from a potential encounter. For more information on coexisting with bears in the backcountry, see Globe Pequot Press's *Bear Aware,* by Bill Schneider.

Shenandoah rangers say falling trees pose a greater risk than they have for many decades. Gypsy moth infestations and violent storms have resulted in rotten roots and dead trees ready to topple in many locations in the park. Be watchful of dead trees when you're on the trail—especially in high winds—and be careful where you pitch your tent.

Plan hikes within your group's physical ability. Do not attempt hikes or backpacking segments that are longer than you and your group can safely accomplish in daylight. Know the terrain. Before departing, study the maps. Hiking after dark is not only uncomfortable but also dangerous, especially if you are not familiar with the topography and trail conditions.

Always leave an itinerary of your hike with someone before you leave. It should include where you will park, a description of your car and license plate number, where you will be hiking, when you expect to complete the trip, and who to contact in case of emergency. If you have questions about the trail, ask park rangers before you leave. If you plan to backpack overnight, make sure you first acquire a free backcountry permit, available from the park's two visitor centers, at ranger stations, and at park entrances.

Parts of Shenandoah can be used by both hikers and horseback riders. Such trails are marked with yellow blazes, and horses have the right-of-way on them. Hikers should yield to all stock and riders. If you encounter stock on the trail, move quietly to the lower side of the trail to let the stock pass. To avoid spooking horses, make your presence known. Hikers-only trails are marked in blue; if you are hiking on the Appalachian Trail, the markers are white.

Backcountry Essentials

Comfortable clothes and footwear will do a lot to make your hike pleasant. In cool weather dress in layers. The first, inner layer should be light, made of a material such as polypropylene that will wick moisture away from your skin. Next, wear a warmer, porous layer that can be removed if necessary. Over that, wear an outer layer that is windproof and rainproof. Layers allow you to regulate your temperature by putting on or taking off layers as the weather and exertion dictate. A good poncho or raincoat is standard backpacking equipment, especially in Shenandoah, where rain, snow, sleet, and hail are frequent and unpredictable.

Hiking boots should be sturdy and supportive and have good soles. Many people wear heavy leather boots, while others prefer lighter-weight boots with breathable, water-resistant fabrics. If you are a beginner, visit your local outdoor sporting goods store and try on different boots. Several good books on hiking equipment, including Colin Fletcher and Chip Rawlins's *The Complete Walker*, are listed in Appendix B: Further Reading.

Backcountry camping is available throughout most of the park. Stays are limited to two nights at any one site or fourteen consecutive nights in the backcountry. All campers must obtain a free backcountry camping permit, available from visitor contact stations during business hours or by writing the park superintendent's office (see Appendix A: For More Information). Include your name, complete address, entry and exit dates of trip, number in party, and trip itinerary. Maximum group size for backcountry trips is ten. Some trails are closed to backcountry camping. Park service officials will let you know which trails are closed, and provide you with other regulations, when you receive your permit. (For suggestions on minimum-impact camping, see the "Leave No Trace" section below.)

Hiking with Children

Hiking with children can be enjoyable for the whole family. Kids see the world from a different perspective—it's the little things adults barely notice that are so special to children: bugs scampering across the trail, spiderwebs dripping with morning dew, lizards doing pushups on a trailside boulder. Kids love to splash rocks into a lake, watch sticks run the rapids of a mountain stream, and explore animal tracks in the sand.

To make the trip fun for children, let the young ones set the pace. Until your children are able to keep up on extended hikes, forget about 30-mile treks to a favorite backcountry campsite. Instead, plan a destination only a mile or two from the trailhead. Children tire quickly and become easily sidetracked, so don't be surprised if you don't make it to your destination. Plan alternative campsites en route to your final camp.

Help children enjoy the hike and learn about what they see. Always point out special things along the trail. Help them anticipate what is around the next bend— perhaps a waterfall, or a pond filled with wriggling tadpoles. Make the hike fun and interesting, and kids will keep going.

Young skin is very sensitive to the sun, so always carry a strong sunscreen and use it on sunny days. A good bug repellent, preferably a natural product, should be a standard part of your first-aid kit. Also, carry a product that helps take the itch and sting out of bug bites. A hat helps keep the sun out of sensitive young eyes. Rain gear is also an important consideration. Children generally have less tolerance to cold than adults, so ample clothing is important.

Parents with young children must, of course, carry plenty of diapers—and pack them out when leaving. Some children can get wet at night, so extra sleeping clothes and a waterproof pad are must-haves. To alleviate extra weight, parents with very young children can pack lightweight and inexpensive dry baby foods to which only water need be added.

Make your children aware of what poison ivy looks like and warn them not to touch it. Be especially watchful for stinging insects—wasps, hornets, and bees—and examine your children carefully and often for ticks.

Children learn from their parents by example. Hiking and camping trips are excellent opportunities to teach young ones to tread lightly and minimize their impact on the environment.

Leave No Trace

Few experiences are more irritating or distasteful than finding aluminum cans, candy wrappers, and other trash along the trail. If you can pack it in, you can pack it out. Some people take an extra garbage bag on hikes just to pick up litter left by inconsiderate trekkers. A clean trail is less inviting to the litterer.

Modern, lightweight camp stoves and lanterns eliminate the need for campfires and the stone fire rings left behind. Open fires, in fact, are prohibited in Shenandoah. Backpacking stoves are ideal for wilderness camping and for brewing a hot cup of coffee or bowl of soup. For more information on minimum-impact hiking and camping methods, ask local rangers.

Hiker's Checklist

The following list serves to suggest the types of items you may want to include in your day pack. For instance, the male partner in this authorial team shows some tendency to swell following bee stings, so he always carries an antihistamine. Most people, in fact, react to bug bites, and since body chemistry changes from year to year, you should always take along some type of antihistamine. Customize the first-aid kit in your day pack and backpack to meet your own specific needs.

- ❏ First-aid equipment and supplies
- ❏ Waterproof plastic bag to hold your entire first-aid kit
- ❏ Bandages
- ❏ Adhesive tape
- ❏ Gauze and/or gauze compresses
- ❏ Elastic bandage
- ❏ Aspirin or other pain medication
- ❏ Antibacterial ointment
- ❏ Antihistamine for allergic response
- ❏ Small packet of meat tenderizer to treat insect stings
- ❏ Mild laxative
- ❏ Antidiarrheal medication
- ❏ Compact snakebite kit that includes an efficient suction device
- ❏ Moleskin
- ❏ Needles
- ❏ Scissors, or a Swiss Army knife with scissors
- ❏ Survival kit
- ❏ Space blanket or large garbage bag
- ❏ Whistle
- ❏ Waterproof matches and/or a reliable cigarette lighter
- ❏ Compass
- ❏ Maps
- ❏ Extra high-energy food bars
- ❏ 10 to 20 feet of light nylon rope
- ❏ Small flashlight

How to Use This Guide

More than 500 miles of trails wander through Shenandoah National Park, and knowing where to start can be difficult. This guide will help you select trails based on your abilities and interests. With that goal in mind, we spent three months hiking nearly all of the trails in the park. We often found that the aesthetics of Shenandoah's incredible natural history, as well as its human history, provided compelling reasons to hike these trails.

Even though we hiked nearly every trail, we did not write about them all. We made as many loops as possible because most hikers won't have drop-offs or pickups. With a good topo map (listed in each hike description) and this guide in hand, you can easily choose your own loops or one-way hikes.

There are mileposts on the west side of Skyline Drive. Because almost all trails originate from this road, it's very simple to find your desired trailhead. Skyline Mile 0.0 begins at the north entrance to the park, near the town of Front Royal. Rockfish Gap provides the site for the last milepost, located at Mile 105 in the south. From there, US 250 and I-64 go west to the town of Waynesboro, at the bottom of the mountain as you leave the park.

Hike descriptions include **Distance** and **Difficulty** entries. *Easy* trails can be completed without difficulty by hikers of all abilities and are generally level and short. Hikes rated *moderate* will challenge novices. *Moderately strenuous* hikes will tax even experienced hikers, and *strenuous* trails, generally those that climb steeply, will push the limits of the most Herculean hiker.

The **Traffic** listing indicates how much use a route receives. Trails receiving light use offer an 80 percent probability of meeting one or two parties in a day. Moderate traffic indicates an 80 percent chance of meeting three or more parties, while heavy-use trails offer an 80 percent probability of seeing five or more other groups. Trails receiving heavy use are usually muddy in wet weather. This is a general assessment; the traffic level will vary by season, month, and even day of the week.

Hike descriptions also list the **Maps** required for the hike and provide **Finding the trailhead** directions.

The Hike section includes geologic and ecological features, fishing opportunities, campsites, and other important information. Photographs have been included to give you a visual preview of some of the prominent features seen along the trail. Knowledge of a few special terms will help you understand the geography of Shenandoah National Park: A gap is a mountain pass, a hollow is a valley, and a run is a small stream or brook.

The **Miles and Directions** section highlights landmarks, trail junctions, and gradient changes. Distances were derived using a planimeter, which measures two-dimensional distances on a topographical map. These distances were then corrected for altitude gain or loss and were further modified when park managers made more precise determinations. Nevertheless, the resulting mileages should be considered conservative estimates because they do not always account for small-scale twists and turns or minor ups and downs.

Where appropriate, elevation profiles accompany trail descriptions, providing a general overview of major elevation gains and losses. Elevation profiles are not included for trails where elevation gains and losses are insignificant. The profiles depict the ups and downs of the hikes, with miles on the horizontal axis and elevation (feet above sea level) on the vertical axis. Elevation increments vary depending upon the hike's steepness. Some short dips and climbs (especially those less than 500 feet) may not show on the profiles. Elevation lines are adjusted to fit onto the graph and do not necessarily reflect the actual trail-slope angle.

If you are trying to estimate the length of time required to complete a hike, remember that most trails in Shenandoah either ascend or descend. On the level a good hiker might average 3 to 4 miles an hour. But not here! Don't figure just an hour for a 3-mile hike—figure two hours. And then add a little more time to smell the roses. Shenandoah is a place of great beauty, and you won't want to rush through. Hike descriptions include an approximate time range to complete your journey.

Use this guide in conjunction with topographical maps or other maps as indicated in the hike descriptions. If you refer to all the information provided, you will be prepared for the pleasures and pitfalls of hiking Shenandoah National Park.

About the Maps

The maps in this book use elevation tints, called hypsometry, to portray relief. Each gray tone represents a range of equal elevation, as shown in the scale key with the map. These maps will give you a good idea of elevation gain and loss. The darker tones are lower elevations and the lighter grays are higher elevations. The lighter the tone, the higher the elevation. Narrow bands of different gray tones spaced closely together indicate steep terrain, whereas wider bands indicate areas of more gradual slope.

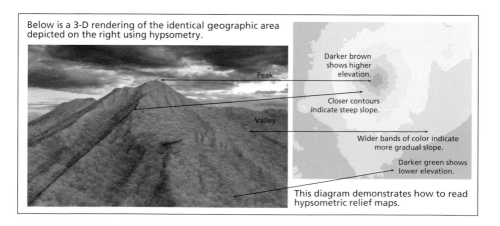

Below is a 3-D rendering of the identical geographic area depicted on the right using hypsometry.

Peak

Valley

Darker brown shows higher elevation.

Closer contours indicate steep slope.

Wider bands of color indicate more gradual slope.

Darker green shows lower elevation.

This diagram demonstrates how to read hypsometric relief maps.

Map Legend

Transportation

≡66≡ Interstate Highway

≡211≡ U.S. Highway

≡230≡ State Highway

≡600≡ Paved Road

= = = = Unpaved Road

▬ ▬ ▬ Featured Trail

- - - - - - Trail

Water Features

Body of Water

Marsh/Swamp

River/Creek

Intermittent Streams

Springs

Waterfall

Land Management

- - - - - State Line

National Park Boundary

Symbols

1 Trailhead

Ranger Station

? Visitor Center

P Parking

▲ Campground

Viewpoint/Overlook

Picnic Area

■ Point of Interest/Structure

Bridge

Lodge

○ Town

Gate

Stable

▲ Peak/Summit

Pass/Gap

∩ Cave

Cliff

Tunnel

→ Direction Arrow

North District

Skyline Mile 0.0 to 31.5

You can easily reach the North District of Shenandoah from Front Royal, Virginia, by leaving US 340 south of town and following the frequent signs to the park's entrance. The park's northern entrance station is less than a mile from US 340. The Dickey Ridge Visitor Center is at Mile 4.6 on Skyline Drive and is worth a stop. The visitor center is the starting point for several trails in this guide as well.

One of the park's first trails provides a commanding view of Massanutten Mountain and several of the various peaks composing the northern end of its range. From Dickey Hill, you can see Signal Knob, a mountain that served as a lookout during the Civil War. The northern portion of the park offers other reminders of the war, and hiking is a good way to step back to that time.

During the Civil War, Marcus Buck watched the Battle of Overall Run from a lookout post in the northern portion of what is now Shenandoah National Park. "It was a very spectacular affair," wrote Buck in his diary, "to look down on men riding, charging and firing their carbines and pistols."

The Appalachian Trail (AT) enters the park along its eastern border about 6 miles south of the entrance station. It first crosses Skyline Drive at Mile 10.4 near Compton Gap and is an integral part of many hikes in this guide.

Shenandoah National Park's Skyline Drive provides 105 miles of pure driving pleasure—as well as access to the majority of the park's trailheads.

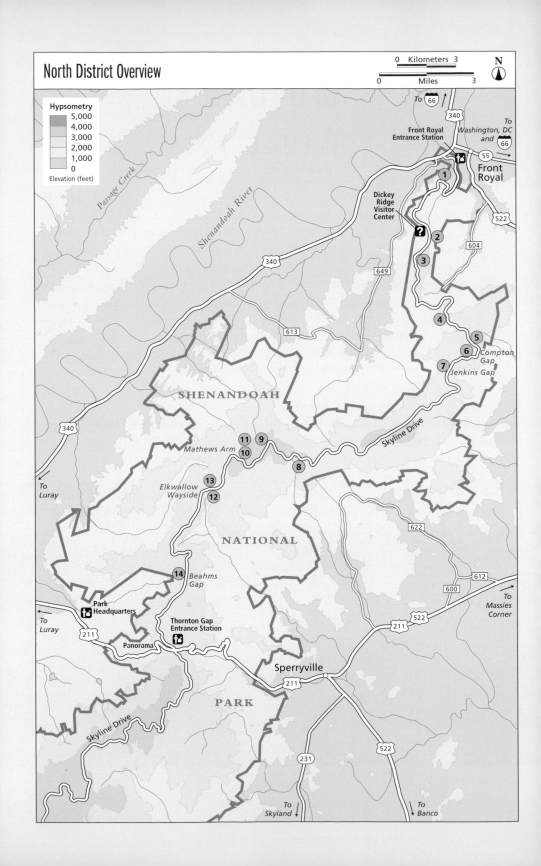

1 Dickey Ridge Trail

The most northern trail in the park, this one-way path leads past old homesteads and a stream, climbs Dickey Ridge, and terminates at Mile 10.4 on Skyline Drive (Compton Gap).

Skyline Mile: 0.05
Distance: 10.3 miles one way. Shuttle needed if entire trail is hiked, though many simply walk until tired and then retrace outbound steps.
Approx. hiking time: 4 to 7 hours
Difficulty: Easy to moderately strenuous
Trail surface: Dirt and naturally occurring rock

Traffic: Light to moderate
Canine compatibility: Leashed dogs allowed
Maps: National Geographic Trails Illustrated Topographic Map 228; Map 9, Appalachian Trail and Other Trails in Shenandoah National Park, North District (PATC, Inc.)

Finding the trailhead: The Dickey Ridge Trail begins on the south end of Front Royal on US 340. As soon as you get on Skyline Drive, but before the park entrance gate, you will see a small parking area on the road to the right (west). The cement post marking the Dickey Ridge Trail stands right beside the parking area. GPS: N38 54.369872' / W78 11.798828'

The Hike

This is one hike where you use your own discretion on the length. If you wish to walk the entire length of the Dickey Ridge Trail, you'll need a pickup at Compton Gap (Mile 10.4). Many people walk on the trail for a few miles, then retrace their steps.

If you are an Appalachian Trail hiker and plan to backpack the entire AT (or portions thereof) from north to south, start at the Dickey Ridge Trail since it connects with the AT at Compton Gap.

The Dickey Ridge Trail begins in what was once an old pasture, which is now covered with new-growth trees and shrubs. After about 0.5 mile, there is a small stream, and you soon come to a left-hand side trail that leads to the entrance station on Skyline Drive. You quickly arrive at a bridge over the stream. For the next 0.75

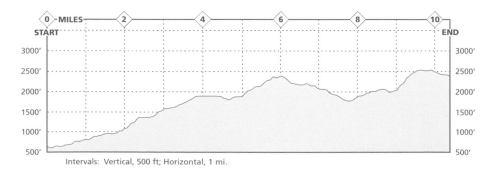

Intervals: Vertical, 500 ft; Horizontal, 1 mi.

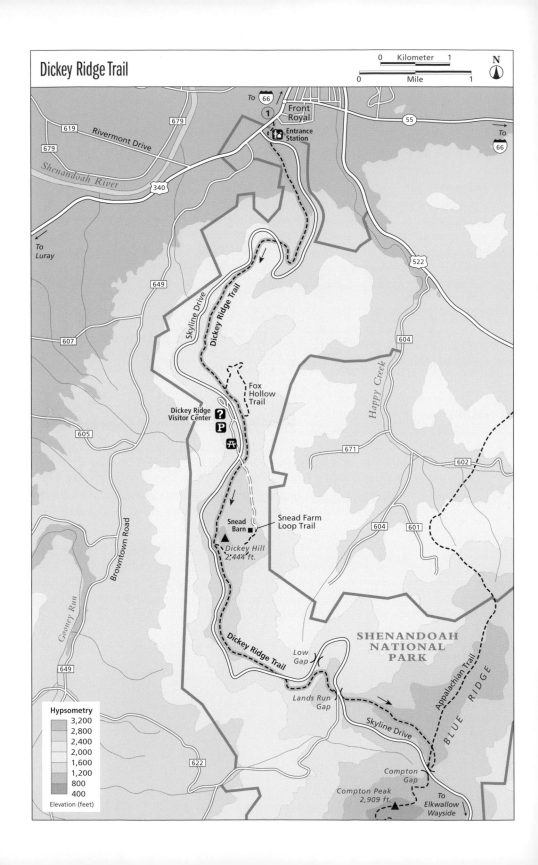

Dickey Ridge Trail

Kilometer

Mile

N

To 66

1 Front Royal

55

Entrance Station

To 66

619 Rivermont Drive

679

679

Shenandoah River

340

To Luray

649

607

605

Skyline Drive

Dickey Ridge Trail

Fox Hollow Trail

Dickey Ridge Visitor Center

Snead Barn

Snead Farm Loop Trail

Dickey Hill 2,444 ft.

522

604

Happy Creek

671

604 601

602

Brimntown Road

Gooney Run

649

622

Dickey Ridge Trail

Low Gap

Lands Run Gap

SHENANDOAH NATIONAL PARK

Appalachian Trail

BLUE RIDGE

Skyline Drive

Compton Gap

Compton Peak 2,909 ft.

To Elkwallow Wayside

Hypsometry

3,200
2,800
2,400
2,000
1,600
1,200
800
400

Elevation (feet)

mile or so, you can see stone walls, paths, and other remnants of old mountain homes.

The trail begins a rather steep ascent as it parallels the Skyline Drive in its climb to Compton Gap. Along the way you encounter the Dickey Ridge Visitor Center, the Fox Hollow Trail, and the Snead Farm Loop Trail at mile 4.6. Low Gap is at mile 7.9, followed by Lands Run Gap at mile 9.2. Detailed signs are posted here and provide appropriate directions at each of the intersections.

At the end of the Dickey Ridge Trail, a route of ascents and short descents, you encounter some beautiful views. The route crosses Skyline Drive several times. Rock hunters will delight in some of the geologic finds along the way.

The Dickey Ridge Trail joins the AT about 0.1 mile from Compton Gap. To complete the hike, turn right onto the AT and hike 0.1 mile to Compton Gap.

Visting Shenandoah National Park in the fall is an added pleasure.

Miles and Directions

0.0   Dickey Ridge Trail begins on the south end of Front Royal on US 340.

4.6   Junction with the Snead Farm Trail.

7.9   Low Gap.

9.2   Lands Run Gap.

10.3   Compton Gap.

2 Fox Hollow Trail

This short and easy loop makes a delightful history hike to an old homestead area. An interpretive pamphlet, available for a small fee at the Dickey Ridge Visitor Center, will enhance the hike. The trail is not rough and is suitable for children. Blue blazes mark the trail.

Skyline Mile: 4.6
Distance: 1.2-mile loop
Approx. hiking time: 1 to 2 hours
Difficulty: Easy
Trail surface: Dirt and naturally occurring rock
Traffic: Light to moderate

Canine compatibility: Dogs not allowed
Maps: National Geographic Trails Illustrated Topographic Map 228; Map 9, Appalachian Trail and Other Trails in Shenandoah National Park, North District (PATC, Inc.)

Finding the trailhead: This trail begins at the Dickey Ridge Visitor Center, about 3 miles south of the Front Royal park entrance. Walk east across Skyline Drive to the park kiosk. GPS: N38 52.307' / W78 12.221'

Reminders of Fox Hollow's residential past are visible along the Fox Hollow Trail.

Long ago, Fox Hollow residents piled rocks to clear space for farming.

The Hike

The park kiosk provides further information about the area and serves as the trailhead.

The trail begins with a slight descent and soon accesses Dickey Ridge Trail to the left. Turn left and follow that blue-blazed trail for 0.2 mile, then turn right (following the blue blazes) onto the Fox Hollow Trail. You will pass piles of rocks reflecting the work once required to clear the forest and prepare it for cultivation.

The trail continues to descend gradually, passing a spring and a mill wheel once used for ornamental purposes. At 0.5 mile the trail passes the Fox family cemetery.

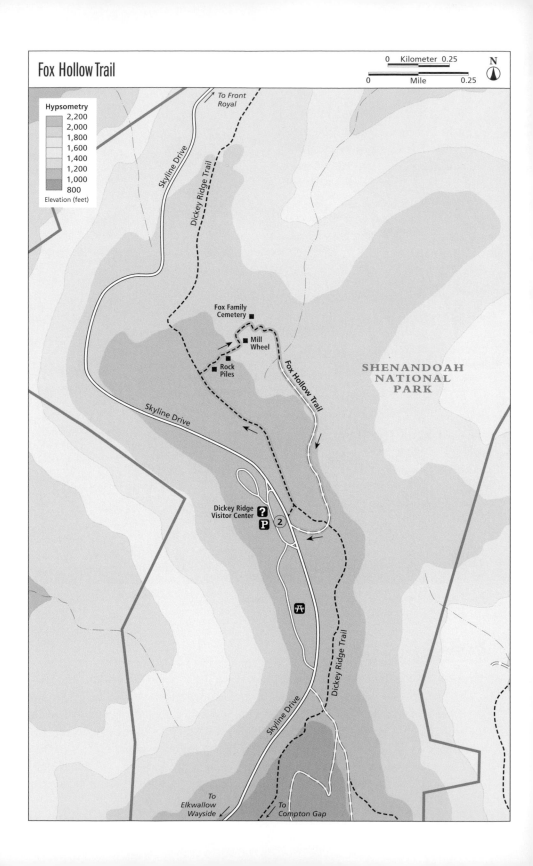

Fox Hollow Trail

0   Kilometer   0.25

0   Mile   0.25

N

Hypsometry

2,200
2,000
1,800
1,600
1,400
1,200
1,000
800
Elevation (feet)

To Front Royal

Skyline Drive

Dickey Ridge Trail

Fox Family Cemetery

Mill Wheel

Rock Piles

Fox Hollow Trail

SHENANDOAH NATIONAL PARK

Skyline Drive

Dickey Ridge Visitor Center

? P (2)

🅰

Dickey Ridge Trail

Skyline Drive

To Elkwallow Wayside

To Compton Gap

The largest stone memorializes Lemuel F. Fox, the son of Thomas Fox, who established the family farm here in 1856. According to the inscription, Lemuel died on May 24, 1916, at the age of 78. The trail continues to cross old pastureland being reclaimed by the forest. Deer have returned to the area and now abound.

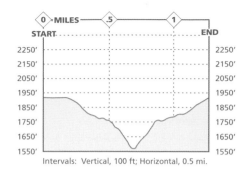

Intervals: Vertical, 100 ft; Horizontal, 0.5 mi.

Shortly after passing the cemetery, the trail begins climbing gradually on its return to the visitor center. Along the way, rock piles and rock fences continue to proclaim that farming once dominated the area. The path is actually an old road that once linked the Fox family with the town of Front Royal.

Upon completion of this short loop, you can extend your hike by following the Snead Farm–Dickey Ridge Trail Loop.

Miles and Directions

0.0 Fox Hollow trail begins at the Dickey Ridge Visitor Center, about 3 miles south of the Front Royal park entrance.

100 yards Cement post. Turn left onto the blue-blazed Dickey Ridge Trail.

0.3 Cement post. Take right fork east onto the blue-blazed Fox Hollow Trail. Encounter the first of many rock piles.

0.5 Fox family cemetery.

1.1 Cement post. Go straight to return to the visitor center.

1.2 Arrive back at the trailhead, completing the hike.

3 Snead Farm–Dickey Ridge Trail Loop

Appropriate for families, this hike takes you to buildings used by the Snead family when it homesteaded in the area.

Skyline Mile: 4.6
Distance: 1.4 miles out and back, or 3.2-mile loop
Approx. hiking time: 3 to 4 hours
Difficulty: Out-and-back hike is easy; loop hike is moderately strenuous
Trail surface: Dirt and naturally occurring rock

Traffic: Light to moderate
Canine compatibility: Leashed dogs allowed
Maps: National Geographic Trails Illustrated Topographic Map 228; Map 9, Appalachian Trail and Other Trails in Shenandoah National Park, North District (PATC, Inc.)

Finding the trailhead: Start at the Front Royal park entrance and go 3 miles south to the Dickey Ridge Visitor Center. The trail begins at Snead Farm Road, an old route with a chain gate that begins across Skyline Drive from the south end of the Dickey Ridge Picnic Area. The trailhead also can be accessed at the south end of the Fox Hollow Nature Trail Loop by turning left onto the Dickey Ridge Trail. GPS: N38 52.294751' / W78 12.153496'

The Hike

Snead Farm was an active, privately owned operation until the 1950s. Its remnants are quite visible. The barn still stands, as does the root cellar. The stone remains of the Carter residence fill an open area. With a little imagination you can recognize the difficulty people had in clearing and farming this land.

After accessing the Snead Farm Road, bear left at the first fork and then bear right at the second fork to gain access the farm complex. Continue along this spur trail to regain access to Snead Farm Road. The walk in to the farm is a pleasant one, since you follow an old farm road. Upon reaching the farm, take time to explore the barn. Peer into the old root cellar; examine the stone foundation of the bunkhouse.

From Snead Farm, either retrace your steps to the Dickey Ridge Picnic Area for an out-and-back hike of 1.4 miles, or continue on the 3.2-mile loop hike by accessing the blue-blazed Snead Farm Loop Trail, which begins at a cement post near the bunkhouse foundation at mile 0.9.

Hike about 1 mile to another cement post at a T junction with the Dickey Ridge Trail. Go north (right) onto the Dickey Ridge Trail. The visitor center is 1.3 miles from this point.

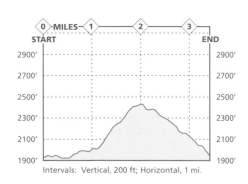

Intervals: Vertical, 200 ft; Horizontal, 1 mi.

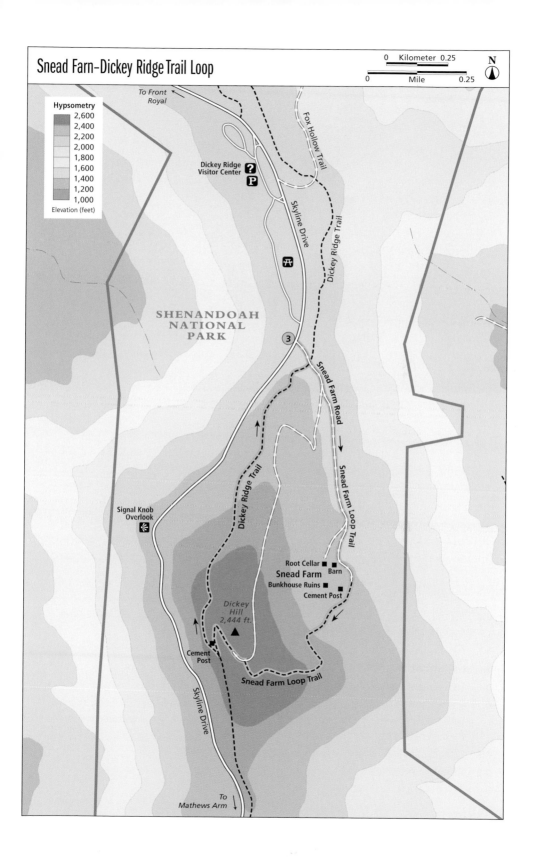

Snead Farm-Dickey Ridge Trail Loop

Hypsometry

2,600
2,400
2,200
2,000
1,800
1,600
1,400
1,200
1,000

Elevation (feet)

To Front Royal

Dickey Ridge Visitor Center

Fox Hollow Trail

Skyline Drive

Dickey Ridge Trail

SHENANDOAH NATIONAL PARK

3

Snead Farm Road

Dickey Ridge Trail

Signal Knob Overlook

Snead Farm Loop Trail

Root Cellar

Barn

Snead Farm

Bunkhouse Ruins

Cement Post

Dickey Hill
2,444 ft.

Cement Post

Snead Farm Loop Trail

Skyline Drive

To Mathews Arm

0   Kilometer   0.25

0   Mile   0.25

N

In addition to this old barn, there's a root cellar, bunkhouse, and stone foundations at the Snead Farm site.

The trail begins a slightly strenuous ascent to the top of Dickey Hill. At the summit, take the spur trail to your right. For a marvelous view of Signal Knob on Massanutten Mountain and the Shenandoah Valley, go left. A hang glider launch area is located just before the path to the viewpoint.

Back on the Dickey Ridge Trail, make another quick ascent. Then the trail begins to descend gradually beneath a canopy of trees. It continues through quiet woods to an intersection with Skyline Drive near the picnic area, thereby completing the loop.

Miles and Directions

0.0 Start at Snead Farm Road, an old route with a chain gate that begins across Skyline Drive from the south end of the Dickey Ridge Picnic Area.

0.1 Fork in road; stay left.

0.3 Fork in road; stay right.

0.5 Fork in road; stay left.

0.7 Remains of the Snead Farm. Retrace your steps for an out-and-back hike of 1.4 miles. If continuing on the longer loop, to return via the Dickey Ridge Trail, pick up the blue-blazed trail at the cement post opposite the stone ruins at mile 0.9. Follow this (the Snead Farm Loop Trail).

1.9 Cement post. Trail junction. Turn right onto the Dickey Ridge Trail.

3.2 Completion of loop. Arrive back at the Dickey Ridge Visitor Center and Picnic Area.

4 Lands Run Falls

An enjoyable jaunt down an old road leads to views of a pretty waterfall.

Skyline Mile: 9.2
Distance: 1.2 miles out and back
Approx. hiking time: 1 to 1½ hours
Difficulty: Easy
Trail surface: Dirt and naturally occurring rock
Traffic: Light to moderate

Canine compatibility: Leashed dogs allowed
Maps: National Geographic Trails Illustrated Topographic Map 228; Map 9, Appalachian Trail and Other Trails in Shenandoah National Park, North District (PATC, Inc.)

Finding the trailhead: The trail begins at the Lands Run parking area, Mile 9.2 on Skyline Drive, at the fire road on the south end of the parking lot. GPS: N38 50.0561' / W78 11.137'

An eager hiker sets off along the trail to Lands Run Falls.

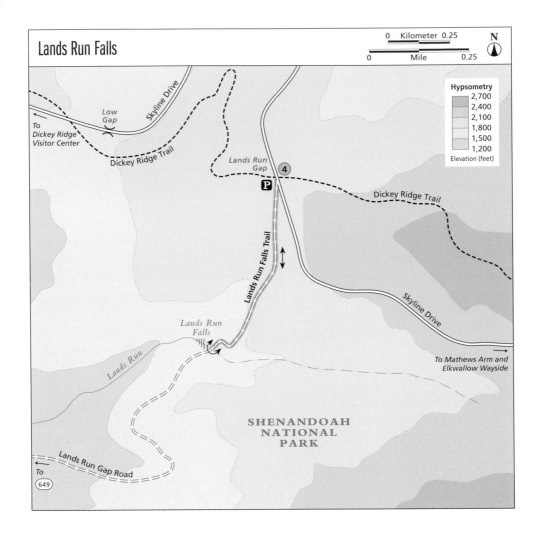

The Hike

Three trails depart from the Lands Run parking area. The Dickey Ridge Trail crosses Skyline Drive at this point. It can be followed south for another 1.2 miles to its end at Compton Gap or taken north for 9.2 miles to the park entrance. The Hickerson Hollow Trail is directly across the road from the parking area. It is 2.2 miles out and back, leads through Hickerson Hollow (once the site of the mountain people's homes), and ends at the park boundary. The third trail is the Lands Run Falls Trail, which is described here.

Lands Run Falls is not especially high, nor can you see the entire falls from the trail, but the setting is lovely and the trek provides a nice leg stretch. The rocks leading out to a viewpoint can be treacherous, so use caution. The woods flanking the trail are dominated by oaks and hickories, interspersed with tulip poplars. Many of the healthiest oaks were knocked down by a tropical storm in 1996; those not denuded by gypsy moths were so heavily laden with leaves that they were easily toppled by the strong winds. In addition to a lovely forest, you will see a great deal of greenstone—volcanic rock exposed by soil erosion—on the uphill side of the road.

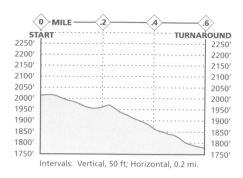

Intervals: Vertical, 50 ft; Horizontal, 0.2 mi.

Follow the fire road/trail, which descends immediately and continues to do so for 0.6 mile. At that point, a stream courses down the hill from the left and passes through a culvert under the road. The falls are on the right. By taking a short spur trail to the right, you can get some inspiring views. The slick rocks and precipitous grade create a potential hazard, so use caution.

The road continues for another 1.4 miles to the park boundary. Unless you have lots of energy to burn, there isn't much point in continuing the hike: The road descends another 600 feet with no viewpoints. Retrace your steps uphill from the falls.

Miles and Directions

0.0   Lands Run Falls trail begins at the Lands Run parking area, Mile 9.2 on Skyline Drive, at the fire road on the south end of the parking lot.

0.6   Stream entering from the left goes under the road. Falls on the right. Retrace your steps after viewing the falls.

1.2   Arrive back at the Lands Run parking lot.

Compton Gap Hikes

Skyline Mile 10.4

Two short hikes—and several spur hikes from these primary routes—depart from the Compton Gap area of Skyline Drive. All are detailed below. The area, including the gap and the peak to the west of the drive, derives its name from the Compton family. The Comptons lived near Indian Run Spring, which can be easily accessed from a junction on the trail to Fort Windham Rocks.

Like other areas of the park, lands cut by these trails are returning to a condition that will soon be a primeval forest. Huge chestnut trees, however, might not ever return, though saplings still grow along trails leading from the gap. Look for the characteristic elongated, pinnately compound leaves with serrated edges.

The area is rich in geology, and the trails course through boulder fields that derive from various geological origins. Lava once intruded into the area, and by investing only a little time you may come to appreciate the expansiveness of the lava flows and the changes that have occurred since these great volcanic outpourings. The Compton Peak Trail also offers views that can orient you to some of the main features in the park's North District.

This lush beauty bush is just one of the many species of flowering plants along the trails.

5 Fort Windham Rocks–Indian Run Spring

This good leg stretcher offers photographic opportunities and insights into local geology.

Skyline Mile: 10.4
Distance: 0.8-mile out and back; 1.2 miles out and back with Indian Run Spring option
Approx. hiking time: 1 to 2 hours
Difficulty: Easy
Trail surface: Dirt and naturally occurring rock

Traffic: Light
Canine compatibility: Leashed dogs allowed
Maps: National Geographic Trails Illustrated Topographic Map 228; Map 9, Appalachian Trail and Other Trails in Shenandoah National Park, North District (PATC, Inc.)

Finding the trailhead: The hike begins at Compton Gap, Mile 10.4 on Skyline Drive. The trail begins on the fire road (which is also the Appalachian Trail) at the northeast end of the parking lot. GPS: N38 49.404364' / W78 10.226611'

The Hike

Begin the hike by walking up the fire road (the Appalachian Trail) to a four-way junction. Turn left onto the Dickey Ridge Trail (blue blazes). The path ascends gently through a new-growth forest that offers ideal habitat for ruffed grouse and other wildlife. Several broods dashed across the trail as we hiked toward the rocks.

As the trail levels, the 45- to 50-foot Fort Windham Rocks appear on your right. Geologists say the rocks are 600 to 800 million years old and are examples of the Catoctin lava formations. A short spur on the right side of the trail leads into the rocks.

On the return, you might want to lengthen the hike by continuing past the cement post (the AT intersection) and dropping the additional 0.2 mile to Indian Run Spring. The spring is off to your left and offers cool water, which should be filtered before drinking. From Indian Run Spring, return to your vehicle.

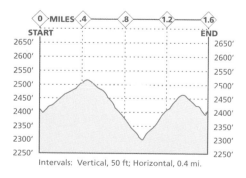

Intervals: Vertical, 50 ft; Horizontal, 0.4 mi.

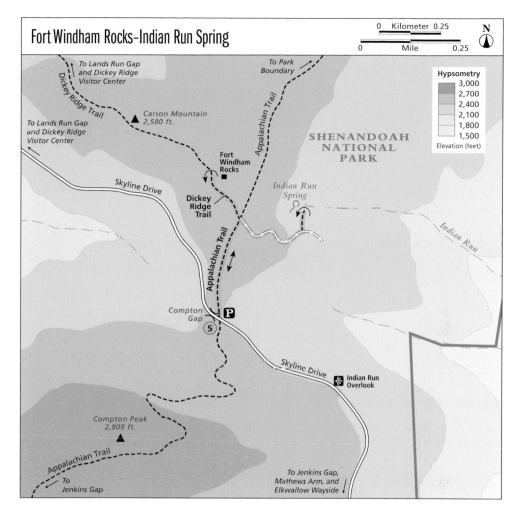

Fort Windham Rocks–Indian Run Spring

To Lands Run Gap
and Dickey Ridge
Visitor Center

To Park
Boundary

Dickey Ridge Trail

Carson Mountain
2,580 ft.

To Lands Run Gap
and Dickey Ridge
Visitor Center

Appalachian Trail

SHENANDOAH
NATIONAL
PARK

Fort
Windham
Rocks

Skyline Drive

Dickey
Ridge
Trail

Indian Run
Spring

Indian Run

Appalachian Trail

Compton
Gap

P

5

Skyline Drive

Indian Run
Overlook

Compton Peak
2,909 ft.

Appalachian Trail

To
Jenkins Gap

To Jenkins Gap,
Mathews Arm, and
Elkwallow Wayside

0   Kilometer 0.25

N

0   Mile   0.25

Hypsometry
3,000
2,700
2,400
2,100
1,800
1,500
Elevation (feet)

Miles and Directions

0.0 Fort Windham Rocks–Indian Run Spring begins on the fire road at the northeast end of the parking lot.

0.2 Cement post, trail junction. Go left on the Dickey Ridge Trail to the Fort Windham Rocks.

0.4 High rocks on right. Retrace your steps and return to the parking lot.

0.8 Arrive back at the parking lot.

Option: To reach Indian Run Spring, go right (downhill/east) from the junction of the Appalachian Trail and the Dickey Ridge Trail for 0.2 mile. Visit the spring, return to the main trail, then retrace your steps to the trailhead. This will add 0.4 mile to the route.

◀ *Pedlar granodiorite is present in the beautiful lava flows seen at the Fort Windham Rocks.*

6 Compton Peak

This out-and-back hike follows the Appalachian Trail and climbs 835 feet to the summit of Compton Peak, where the views are expansive and the geology intriguing.

Skyline Mile: 10.4
Distance: 2.4 miles out and back
Approx. hiking time: 2 to 2½ hours
Difficulty: Moderate
Trail surface: Dirt and naturally occurring rock
Traffic: Light

Canine compatibility: Leashed dogs allowed
Maps: National Geographic Trails Illustrated Topographic Map 228; Map 9, Appalachian Trail and Other Trails in Shenandoah National Park, North District (PATC, Inc.).

Finding the trailhead: The trail begins at Mile 10.4 on Skyline Drive, across the road from the Compton Gap parking lot. GPS: N38 49.487' / W78 10.10251'

The Hike

The hike follows a mile-long segment of the Appalachian Trail, taking you to an intersection. Each fork of the intersection leads to a high point of Compton Peak, both of which are worth seeing. From the intersection, each knob is separated by a distance of only a few tenths of a mile.

The fork to the left proceeds a short distance—probably less than 0.1 mile—and then dips to an unexposed rock face. The face offers both foot- and handholds that you should probably use, particularly if the rocks are wet. The trail continues to a large boulder that stands roughly 18 feet high. Surrounding the boulder are examples of columnar jointing. Some 800 million years ago, extruded lava cooled and cracked into the prismatic columns visible here.

Climb the boulder, for it offers great—on some days magical—views. The boulder's panoramas include the twin peaks of Mount Marshall and Skyline Drive.

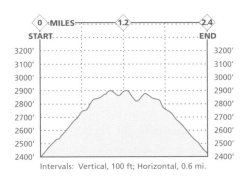

Intervals: Vertical, 100 ft; Horizontal, 0.6 mi.

The Compton Gap Trail provides access to unique geology.

Return to the junction and hike to the other knob, only 0.2 mile round-trip and easy to travel even if wet. This path crosses an almost indistinguishable crest that is Compton Peak and, almost as quickly, descends to a viewpoint. The picture before you includes views of the Piedmont Plateau and Dickey Ridge, which drops down toward Front Royal. Views from both these areas will help orient you to the country's surroundings.

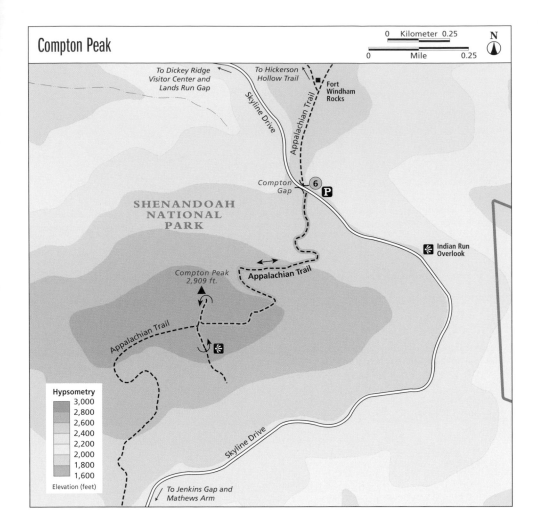

Miles and Directions

0.0 Compton Peak trail begins at Mile 10.4 on Skyline Drive, across the road from the Compton Gap parking lot.

0.2 Huge boulder on left side of the trail.

1.0 Cement post. Choose which knob of Compton Peak to see first.

1.4 Turnaround point after seeing both knobs.

2.4 Arrive back at the trailhead.

7 Mount Marshall Trail and Beyond

A hike along three trails highlights Shenandoah's beauty.

Skyline Mile: 12.35
Distance: 13.4-mile loop
Approx. hiking time: 8 to 11 hours
Difficulty: Moderately strenuous to strenuous
Trail surface: Dirt and naturally occurring rock
Traffic: Light

Canine compatibility: Leashed dogs allowed
Maps: National Geographic Trails Illustrated Topographic Map 228; Map 9, Appalachian Trail and Other Trails in Shenandoah National Park, North District (PATC, Inc.)

Finding the trailhead: The hike begins at the cement post in the parking lot at Mile 12.35 on the west side of Skyline Drive, 50 yards north of the Jenkins Gap Overlook. Follow the white-blazed Appalachian Trail south. GPS: N38 48.420' / W78 10.876'

The Hike

The land around Mount Marshall was once owned by John Marshall, who served as a county judge in the early 1800s.

Follow the Appalachian Trail south, immediately beginning a moderate climb through stands of striped maple taking over an old pasture. The trail is wide and easy on the feet because the ground is dirt rather than rock. In spring wildflowers are abundant. As the trail progresses it levels, then descends toward Skyline Drive. Just before reaching the drive, there's an old Civilian Conservation Corps–built comfort station foundation on the left. It was never completed.

After 1.7 miles, the AT crosses the drive. Remain on the AT and ascend beneath a ceiling of red oak to North Marshall. The trail passes through Hogwallow Flat (2,745 feet), ideal deer habitat. As we hiked the area during the fall, we saw a number of white-tailed deer.

About 0.7 mile after crossing Skyline Drive, the AT comes to an obscure spring off to the left, bordered by rocks. The trail becomes rocky as it approaches the top of North Marshall (3,368 feet), reached after a sharp switchback. Trees obscure the view, but 0.1 mile later a spur trail leads to the right and provides lovely views to the west. On clear days you can see Browntown Valley. To the left are South Marshall, Hogback Mountain, Marys Rock, and Stony Man mountain. To the right is Dickey Ridge. After a short descent, yet another spur trail leads to an even better overview.

The path becomes a brief, steep, and rocky descent but soon levels and widens as it reaches Skyline Drive at Mile 13.9. It's another 1.8 miles to the Bluff Trail. Continue south on the AT and begin climbing South Marshall, where the trail begins an easy ascent. The summit (3,212 feet) provides no views. Descend a short distance to a spur on the right, which takes you to a rock outcropping offering marvelous views to the west. On clear days, the landscape offers superb photographic opportunities.

The trail descends for nearly 1 mile to Skyline Drive and exits at Gravel Springs Gap (2,655 feet). Cross the drive to the parking lot and join the AT at a cement post just south of the fire road. Continue about 0.3 mile through the woods to a cement post. Turn left onto the blue-blazed trail, which picks up the Bluff Trail in another 0.2 mile.

The path descends to a cement post by Gravel Springs. The Gravel Springs Hut is to your right. The area is delightful and provides an ideal spot for a lunch break. The hut is for day use only, unless you're a backpacker with a permit. From the spring, turn left.

Almost immediately you'll see and take the yellow-blazed Bluff Trail, which is to the right at a cement post. In 0.1 mile, pass a cement post and stay straight. Soon the trail makes a sharp switchback to the left at another cement post. Stay left on the Bluff Trail, which becomes a bit rough and rocky as it begins to ascend. Watch out for stinging nettles along the trail; the plants have deceptively beautiful white flowers in the fall. We have also seen lots of recent bear droppings on both the Bluff and Mount Marshall Trails.

At approximately mile 7.4, the Big Devils Stairs Trail merges from the right at a cement post and offers yet more adventure—and more distance—to this excursion. It makes an ideal hike of its own and is described below as an alternative hike. Taking this trail will add 1 mile to your trip.

The Bluff Trail proceeds straight. It is 2.3 miles to the Mount Marshall Trail along a rough, fairly level route. At mile 9.7 the trail encounters a cement post and its junction with the Mount Marshall Trail. Turn left, following the yellow blazes of the Mount Marshall Trail. Cross the four-branched Jordan River (here a small stream) almost immediately, and in about 1.1 miles cross another small creek—the Spruce Pine Branch. Throughout this part of the hike you'll see many dead trees, the result of a gypsy moth infestation. At this point you're walking very near the park's eastern boundary.

The trail nears its end as you begin a descent along an old fire road. Soon the route crosses a third stream (Waterfall Branch), which is narrow with steep sides. After a short distance the trail ascends gently, offering brief views filtered by trees. Wild grape bushes line the trail. At the trail's end, turn right onto Skyline Drive, then walk past the overlook and north to the parking lot.

Options: Three alternative hikes follow portions of the trail described above. The major differences are that the hikes begin at different places along Skyline Drive. The Big Devils Stairs Trail begins from the Gravel Springs Gap parking lot at Skyline Mile 17.6. The Marshall Mountain hikes begin at the parking lot at Mile 15.95 (the Appalachian Trail crossing), at which point one hike proceeds north and the other proceeds south.

Option 1: This strenuous 5.7-mile out-and-back excursion on the Big Devils Stairs Trail begins at the Gravel Springs Gap parking lot at Mile 17.6 on Skyline

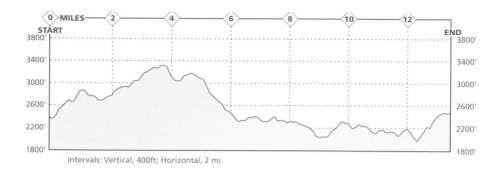

Intervals: Vertical, 400ft; Horizontal, 2 mi.

Drive and begins by following the same route as the more laborious Mount Marshall hike. Follow the Appalachian Trail south (east of the drive). At 0.2 mile take the Bluff Trail to the left. After a 1.5-mile hike on the Bluff Trail, reach a cement post. Turn right onto the Big Devils Stairs Trail, which stays on the north rim, offering inspiring views. We recommend turning around at the viewpoint.

Option 2: Begin this easy hike on North Marshall at Mile 15.95 at the Appalachian Trail crossing. Proceed north on the AT (on the east side of the drive) from the parking lot. The hike is a short one, but it offers ideal wildlife habitat. The trail offers splendid views to the west, though not from the summit (see above). It is approximately 1.2 miles out and back to the summit, with a 300-foot elevation gain and loss.

Option 3: This short, easy hike on South Marshall also begins from the parking lot at Mile 15.95 on the west side of the drive. It's about a 1.6-mile out-and-back trip to the rock viewpoint located 0.25 mile past the summit. This is a more confined view than the one from North Marshall, but it is still quite lovely. The elevation gain and loss is only 300 feet.

Miles and Directions

0.0   Mount Marshall Trail and Beyond begins at the cement post in the parking lot at Mile 12.35 on the west side of Skyline Drive, 50 yards north of the Jenkins Gap Overlook.

150 feet Cement post. Junction with the Appalachian Trail. Go south (left) on the AT, following white blazes. Ascend.

1.2   Trail levels. Begin descent.

1.7   Cement post at Skyline Drive. Cross the drive and continue south on the AT toward North Marshall.

2.4   A spring lies almost hidden on the left. At the same point, note the abundance of rocks placed on the path and around the trees.

3.0   Top of North Marshall. No views at summit due to trees.

3.9   Pass parking lot on the right and cross Skyline Drive to continue on the AT, south toward South Marshall.

4.5   Summit of South Marshall. Descend briefly for views.

5.4   Cement post at Gravel Springs Gap. Cross Skyline Drive, staying on the AT southbound (south end of lot). Do not access the yellow-blazed trail.

Mount Marshall Trail and Beyond

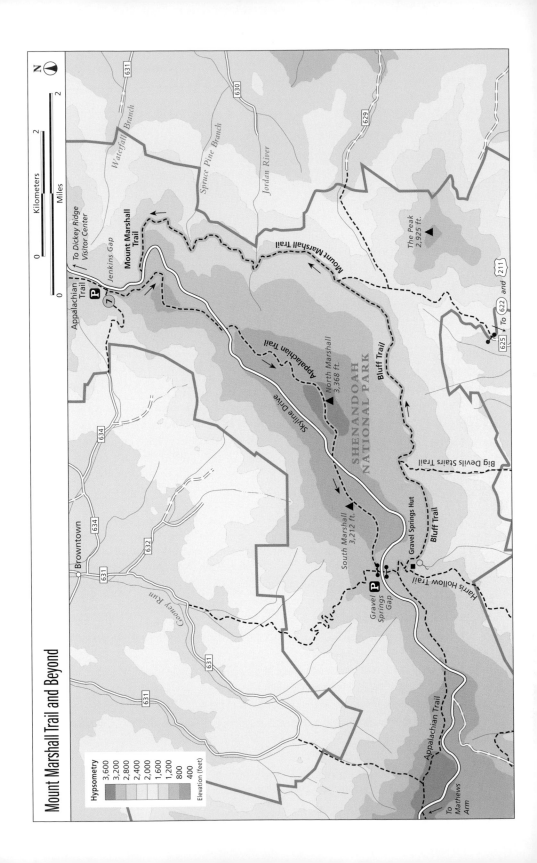

5.7	Cement post. Go left onto the blue-blazed trail that leads to the Bluff Trail in 0.2 mile.
5.9	Cement post at Gravel Springs. Hut on right. Turn left and right, in quick succession. At the cement post, turn onto the Bluff Trail (yellow blazes).
6.0	Cement post. The Harris Hollow Trail converges from the right. Stay straight and follow yellow blazes.
6.1	Cement post at switchback. Stay left on the Bluff Trail.
7.4	Cement post. Stay straight on the Bluff Trail, or turn right for an additional 1-mile spur hike down and back on the blue-blazed Big Devils Stairs Trail.
9.7	Cement post at T. Turn left onto the Mount Marshall Trail (yellow blazes).
9.9	Cross Jordan River, a small four-branched stream. Low water in dry season.
11.0	Cross Spruce Pine Branch, a small stream.
11.9	Cross Waterfall Branch, a narrow stream with steep sides.
13.2	Skyline Drive. Go right, past the overlook.
13.4	Arrive at the end of the loop. Return to your vehicle.

Skyline Drive in the fall is extraordinary.

8 Keyser Run Fire Road–Little Devils Stairs Lariat

Much of this beautiful hike is on a scenic fire road. The final portion climbs through a magnificent wild canyon and gorge.

Skyline Mile: 19.4
Distance: 7.5-mile lariat
Approx. hiking time: 5 to 8 hours
Difficulty: Strenuous
Trail surface: Dirt and naturally occurring rock
Traffic: Moderate

Canine compatibility: Leashed dogs allowed
Maps: National Geographic Trails Illustrated Topographic Map 228; Map 9, Appalachian Trail and Other Trails in Shenandoah National Park, North District (PATC, Inc.)

Finding the trailhead: From Skyline Drive, park at the Keyser Run Fire Road on the east side of the drive at Mile 19.4 and descend at the kiosk. There is ample parking space along the fire road. GPS: N38 45.429' / W78 15.434'

The Hike

The trail passes Bolen Cemetery toward the end of the fire road. The final part climbs through a magnificent wild canyon and gorge that requires boulder hopping and rock scrambling, so wear good boots. The rocks are slippery and dangerous when wet or icy, so use caution.

From the trailhead, walk 1 mile to reach Fourway Junction and a cement post. Continue straight on the fire road. The road descends into a large area of huge, sentinel-like trees that lend an aura of mystery to the woods.

At mile 3.3, the trail passes Bolen Cemetery on the left. A beautiful, peaceful place surrounded by a rock wall, the cemetery contains about forty-five gravestones. Just beyond the cemetery is a cement post. Turn left, still on the Keyser Run Fire Road, marked with a yellow blaze. Still descending, the road winds by remnants of old stone walls from the long-ago farming era. The route then passes near Pignut Mountain and a forest of pignut hickory trees.

Nearly a mile past the cemetery, the fire road ends at the park boundary as it meets CR 614. Go around the chain and turn left, following the gravel road 0.1 mile to a parking lot. The trailhead for the Little Devils Stairs Trail is at the north end of the lot at a cement post.

Follow the blue-blazed trail, which immediately crosses Keyser Run in the form of two small streams. The trail begins a gentle ascent, winding as it passes through the woods. As views of Keyser Run open to the right, look to the far bank for a magnificent rock wall, a remnant of an old bridge. Traces of a road can be seen above the bridge wall, and without too much difficulty you can imagine the backbreaking work involved in clearing the rocks from the land and in building the various structures.

Keyser Run Fire Road–Little Devils Stairs Lariat

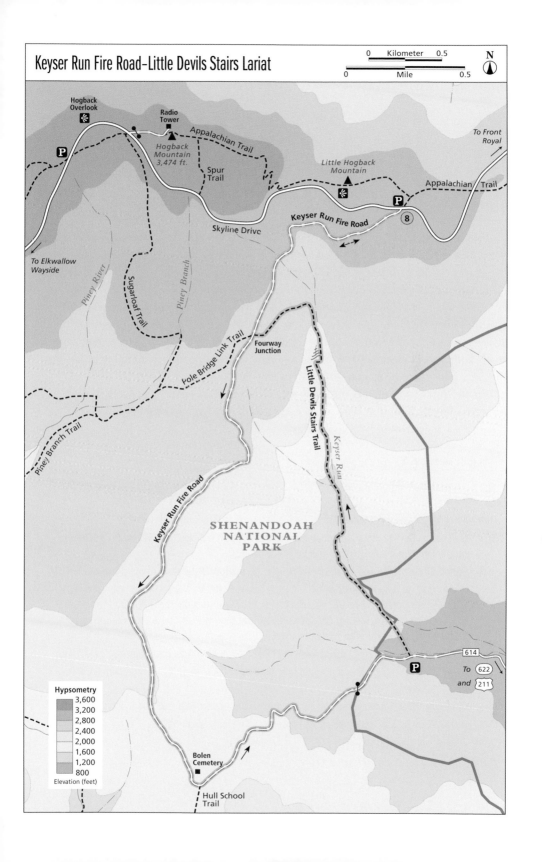

0   Kilometer   0.5

0   Mile   0.5

N

Hogback
Overlook

Radio
Tower

Appalachian Trail

To Front
Royal

P

Hogback
Mountain
3,474 ft.

Spur
Trail

Little Hogback
Mountain

Appalachian Trail

P

Keyser Run Fire Road

8

Skyline Drive

To Elkwallow
Wayside

Piney River

Sugarloaf Trail

Piney Branch

Pole Bridge Link Trail

Fourway
Junction

Little Devils Stairs Trail

Keyser Run

Piney Branch Trail

Keyser Run Fire Road

SHENANDOAH
NATIONAL
PARK

614

P

To 622

and 211

Hypsometry

3,600
3,200
2,800
2,400
2,000
1,600
1,200
800

Elevation (feet)

Bolen
Cemetery

Hull School
Trail

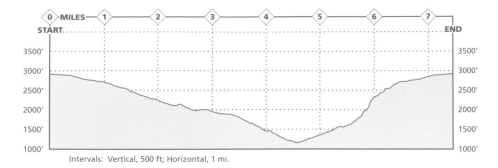

Intervals: Vertical, 500 ft; Horizontal, 1 mi.

The trail becomes rocky, and it will only get worse! Look for the rock piles and walls scattered throughout the woods. We encountered a timber rattlesnake spanning the 4-foot-wide trail; it was in no hurry to move, but it finally crawled to the side, curled up under a fern, and, apparently, went to sleep.

After the rock walls, the trail begins a series of stream crossings. In summer the stream sometimes contains only a trickle. The rocky trail continues climbing and crisscrossing the water on boulders, which you must hop. The trail becomes quite steep, and there is more boulder hopping as the trail enters the ravine. Blue blazes on the trees and rocks guide you through the labyrinth.

At the top of the ravine, after a series of hard switchbacks, you finally emerge at Fourway Junction. At the cement post, turn right and ascend the Keyser Run Fire Road for 1 mile to return to your vehicle.

Miles and Directions

0.0   Keyser Run Fire Road–Little Devils Stairs Lariat begins on the east side of the drive at Mile 19.4.

1.0   Fourway Junction. Continue straight on the Keyser Run Fire Road, descending.

3.3   Bolen Cemetery on left. Cement post just ahead. At cement post turn left, still descending on the fire road.

4.2   Park boundary. Come to gravel road (CR 614). Turn left and descend to the parking lot.
         (*Note:* You can begin hiking here, at the Little Devils Stairs Trail, if accessed from outside of the park. Hike up the Little Devils Stairs Trail to Fourway Junction, turn left onto the Keyser Run Fire Road, follow it down past Bolen Cemetery, then turn left onto the fire road to return to the park boundary and parking lot.)

4.4   At the end of the parking lot, turn onto the Little Devils Stairs Trail (blue blazes).

5.2   Begin a more strenuous ascent, soon to enter ravine. Look carefully for blue blazes on trees and rocks.

6.5   Cement post at Fourway Junction. Turn right onto the Keyser Run Fire Road. Ascend.

7.5   Arrive at the end of lariat hike at the Keyser Run Fire Road parking lot.

⑨ Sugarloaf-Keyser Run Fire Road– Hogback Mountain Lariat

A scenic trek provides spectacular views and an orientation to the area's geographical features.

Skyline Mile: 21.0
Distance: 4.9-mile lariat
Approx. hiking time: 3 to 6 hours
Difficulty: Easy to moderately strenuous
Trail surface: Dirt with naturally occurring rocks

Traffic: Light to moderate
Canine compatibility: Leashed dogs allowed
Maps: National Geographic Trails Illustrated Topographic Map 228; Map 9, Appalachian Trail and Other Trails in Shenandoah National Park, North District (PATC, Inc.)

Finding the trailhead: The hike begins just south of Hogback Overlook at Mile 21.0 on Skyline Drive. Park in the lot on the west (right) side of the drive. The Appalachian Trailhead is located at the south end of the parking lot at the cement post. GPS: N38 45.658' / W78 16.925'

The Hike

Follow the AT north by crossing the Skyline Drive, and descend 0.3 mile from the parking area to a cement post. Turn right onto the blue-blazed Sugarloaf Trail. As the trail descends, mountain laurel lines the path. The woods are fairly open, and there is evidence of gypsy moth destruction. The country here is excellent bear habitat.

The trail crosses Piney Branch, a small stream, then passes several old stone walls. After 1.4 miles, the trail takes you to a cement post in a parklike setting. Go left onto the Pole Bridge Link Trail.

In another 0.5 mile, you arrive at Fourway Junction. Turn left onto Keyser Run Fire Road and begin an easy ascent for 1 mile. Cross the chain at the end of the fire road, then cross Skyline Drive onto the trail on the opposite side of the road. Reach a cement post within 100 yards that directs you back onto the Appalachian Trail. Turn left onto the AT, ascend moderately for about 0.5 mile, after which the trail quickly takes you to a panorama on the right, just down from the top of Little Hogback Mountain. The views of the Shenandoah Valley, Massanutten Mountain, and way beyond are expansive.

From the rock overlook at the viewpoint, begin a descent. Do not access the spur trail, which comes in from the left and descends to Skyline Drive. Instead, stay right at the double white blaze. Descend into a dark wooded area under a heavy canopy of trees, then begin a 0.3-mile steep ascent, with at least ten switchbacks, to the first crest of Hogback Mountain. Some views can be had through the trees near the summit.

A cement post marks a left turn downhill to a spring; stay straight instead. Soon you'll come to a great view to the west. Browntown Valley lies below, and you can

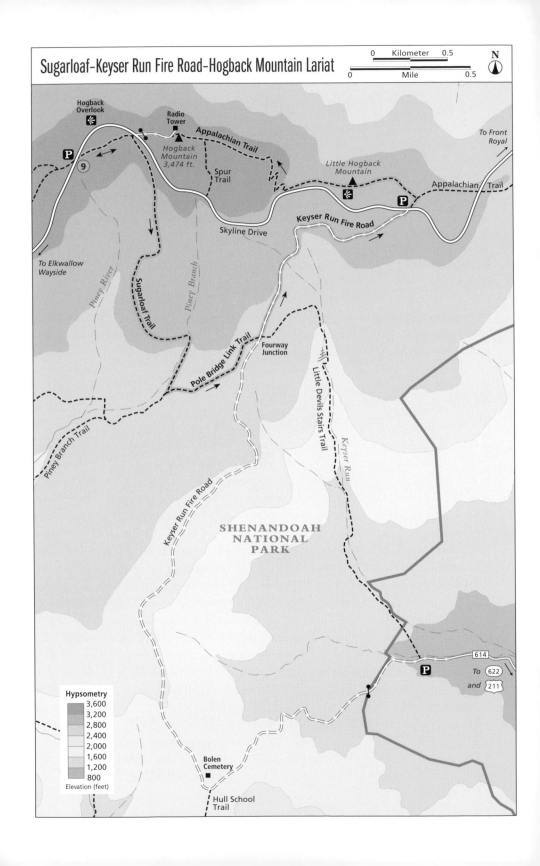

Sugarloaf-Keyser Run Fire Road-Hogback Mountain Lariat

Kilometer 0 0.5

Mile 0 0.5

N

Hogback Overlook

Radio Tower

Appalachian Trail

P

9

Hogback Mountain 3,474 ft.

Spur Trail

Little Hogback Mountain

P

Appalachian Trail

To Front Royal

Keyser Run Fire Road

Skyline Drive

To Elkwallow Wayside

Piney River

Sugarloaf Trail

Piney Branch

Pole Bridge Link Trail

Fourway Junction

Little Devils Stairs Trail

Keyser Run

Piney Branch Trail

Keyser Run Fire Road

SHENANDOAH NATIONAL PARK

614

P

To 622 and 211

Hypsometry

3,600
3,200
2,800
2,400
2,000
1,600
1,200
800
Elevation (feet)

Bolen Cemetery

Hull School Trail

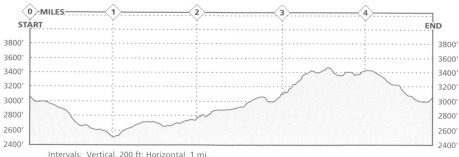

Intervals: Vertical, 200 ft; Horizontal, 1 mi.

see how Massanutten Mountain splits the Shenandoah Valley. To the right lies Dickey Ridge and below it the town of Front Royal. This ledge and grassy area is one of three hang glider launch sites in the park.

The short jaunt to the top of Hogback Mountain's second crest (3,474 feet) now begins as you head for the radio towers at the summit. This is the highest point in the park's North District. Descend toward Skyline Drive on the AT, which parallels and crosses the service road leading to the radio towers. Emerge on the drive. Cross the drive and, again, pick up the AT, following it back to your vehicle to complete the hike.

Option: You can reach both Hogback Mountain and Little Hogback Mountain from just north of Hogback Overlook at Skyline Mile 20.8, where you will find an Appalachian Trail crossing and a service road. Park at the overlook or just south of it, at the Mile 21.0 parking lot on the west. It's about a 0.5-mile out-and-back climb of 115 feet on the AT to the summit of Hogback Mountain and the views. A hike to Little Hogback Mountain and back from this point would add nearly 2 miles and is a somewhat more strenuous hike. The views from both mountains are great.

Miles and Directions

0.0 Sugarloaf–Keyser Run Fire Road–Hogback Mountain Lariat begins near Mile 21.0, just south of Hogback Overlook on Skyline Drive.

0.3 Cement post, turn right onto blue-blazed Sugarloaf Trail.

1.4 Cement post at T junction with the Piney Branch Trail. Go left onto the blue-blazed Pole Bridge Link Trail.

1.9 Cement post at Fourway Junction. Go left onto the Keyser Run Fire Road. The Little Devils Stairs Trail is straight ahead.

3.0 Leave the Keyser Run Fire Road. Cross Skyline Drive to trail directly opposite. Walk 100 yards to the Appalachian Trail and turn left.

3.5 Ascend to the summit of Little Hogback Mountain. View on right. Descend on the AT.

4.0 Spur trail. Do not follow spur left to the drive. Stay straight (right) on the AT and begin ascent to Hogback Mountain.

4.5 Cement post. Stay straight.

4.6 Hogback Mountain. Radio tower. Descend to the drive, then cross the drive to the AT. Go right.

4.9 Parking lot. End of loop.

10 Traces Trail

Take a forest hike along a trail that passes "traces" of mountain folk habitation and natural history.

Skyline Mile: 22.2
Distance: 1.7-mile loop
Approx. hiking time: 1 to 2 hours
Difficulty: Easy
Trail surface: Dirt and naturally occurring rock
Traffic: Moderate

Canine compatibility: Dogs not allowed
Maps: National Geographic Trails Illustrated Topographic Map 228; Map 9, Appalachian Trail and Other Trails in Shenandoah National Park, North District (PATC, Inc.)

Finding the trailhead: The hike begins at the east end of the amphitheater parking lot at the Mathews Arm Campground on Skyline Drive (Mile 22.2). Follow the blue blazes. Note: Gate to campground is closed late fall to mid-May, so you will have to walk to the trailhead at that time. GPS: N38 45.588538' / W78 17.826287'

The Hike

This hike packs a lot into a short distance. It's a great route for a family with small children and for people with an interest in natural and cultural history. What's more, the trail is ideally located for RV campers since it departs from the Mathews Arm Campground, making a counterclockwise circle around the campground.

As you hike on the Traces Trail, you'll see remnants of old rock walls, foundations, and roads. The hike is particularly pleasing in the fall when the leaves are red and gold. It's even pleasing when fog envelops the area and a light rain is falling. Whatever the conditions, don't pass this one up.

The trail is broad and begins beneath a mantle of red oak. Soon the path climbs above the amphitheater. If the trail is wet, it may be slippery, so use caution. Toward the end of the hike, you come to a huge oak that for some reason was spared the ax. If trees could speak, this one could probably relate close to 200 years of history.

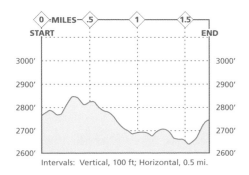

Intervals: Vertical, 100 ft; Horizontal, 0.5 mi.

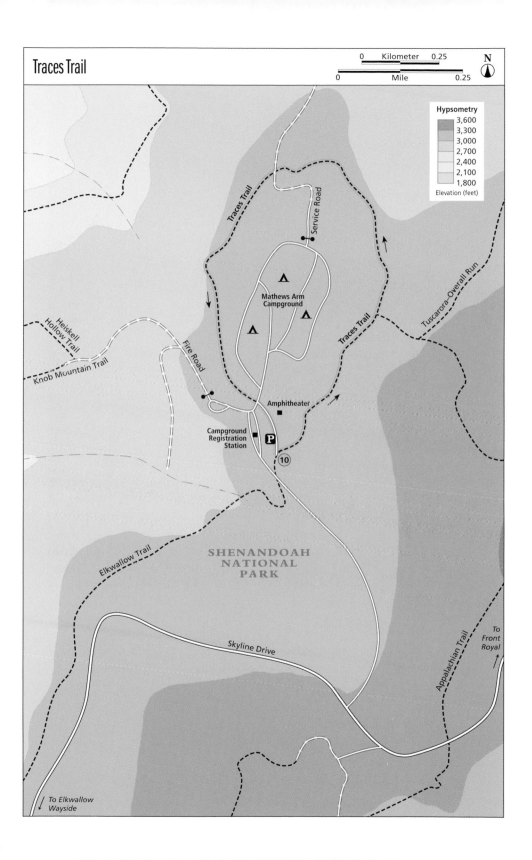

Traces Trail

Hypsometry

	Elevation (feet)
	3,600
	3,300
	3,000
	2,700
	2,400
	2,100
	1,800

N

0   Kilometer   0.25
0   Mile   0.25

Traces Trail

Service Road

Mathews Arm
Campground

Traces Trail

Tuscarora-Overall Run

Heiskell
Hollow Trail

Knob Mountain Trail

Fire Road

Amphitheater

Campground
Registration
Station

P

10

Elkwallow Trail

SHENANDOAH
NATIONAL
PARK

Skyline Drive

Appalachian Trail

To
Front
Royal

To Elkwallow
Wayside

The "Traces" in Traces Trail refers to rock piles and walls that harken back to a bygone era in the park's history.

Near the trail's end, the forest canopy opens slightly, offering hints of other, more lofty vistas. After a 1.7-mile hike, you return to the west end of the parking lot.

Miles and Directions

0.0   Sign and trailhead at east end of amphitheater.

0.4   Cement post. Stay left, descend.

1.0   Cement post. Go straight.

1.7   Arrive at the end of the loop. Cross road to parking lot and vehicle.

11 Tuscarora-Overall Run Trail Loop

This long hike passes two beautiful waterfalls, with several very steep descents and ascents.

Skyline Mile: 22.2
Distance: 9.7-mile loop
Approx. hiking time: 8 to 10 hours
Difficulty: Strenuous
Trail surface: Dirt and naturally occurring rock
Traffic: Moderate

Canine compatibility: Leashed dogs allowed, but not on Traces Trail
Maps: National Geographic Trails Illustrated Topographic Map 228; Map 9, Appalachian Trail and Other Trails in Shenandoah National Park, North District (PATC, Inc.)

Finding the trailhead: The hike begins at Mile 22.2 on Skyline Drive, at the amphitheater parking lot of Mathews Arm Campground. Note: Gate to campground is closed late fall to mid-May, so you will have to walk to the trailhead at that time. GPS: N38 45.461492' / W78 17.161648'

The Hike

It's a good idea to be in shape and have lots of energy for this hike. The trail passes two beautiful waterfalls, but if the season has been a dry one, the falls could be reduced to merely a trickle. The trail also offers views of Massanutten Mountain and beyond. *Note:* On some older maps, the Tuscarora Trail is called the Big Blue Trail.

Begin this wilderness journey at the Mathews Arm Campground, starting on the Traces Trail. Follow the Traces Trail for about 0.5 mile to the first cement post. Go straight to the next cement post and turn left onto the Tuscarora–Overall Run Trail (blue blazes).

For the first 2 miles, the trail gently descends into Bear Wallow, where we saw lots of bear sign. The area is a bit swampy, with lots of tiny streams crossing the path. Rock piles dot the woods, and some blowdown flanks the trail. The route is a good one, although somewhat rocky.

Just before the trail begins a steeper descent to Upper Falls, you enter the designated wilderness. It had rained for three days prior to our hike, so the streams were full and both Upper Falls and Overall Run Falls were spectacular cascades. Soon after Overall Run Falls, you encounter a rock outcropping with a great panorama of Massanutten Mountain and beyond. Many hikers end the hike here and retrace their steps to the trailhead, making a round-trip of between 4.5 and 5 miles.

Beyond the falls the trail drops precipitously. Down in Overall Run, the trail levels but becomes incredibly rocky. Catoctin greenstone is all around. Heading through the open woods, the route begins crossing Overall Run and does so quite often. For well over a mile, the path parallels the stream.

At a cement post at mile 4.6, stay left on the Overall Run Trail and leave the Tuscarora Trail, which goes to the right on its way out of the park. The main trail goes

In the fall, aphids cluster on milkweed pods like this one.

straight and descends under a canopy of trees. Soon the trail widens on what was once an old road. Then it swings a bit away from the run.

At mile 5.2, at a cement post and a double blue blaze, keep left onto the Overall–Beecher Connecting Trail. (The Overall Run Trail once went straight here, leading to the park boundary, but it's abandoned.) Cross the run twice and begin a very steep ascent of the ridge, still on the Overall–Beecher Connecting Trail.

At the next cement post (mile 5.8), turn left toward the yellow-blazed Beecher Ridge Trail. Descend briefly, then begin a moderate ascent. At mile 6.6 turn right toward the Heiskell Hollow Trail. The trail soon descends steeply. Cross the stream two times and come to a cement post. Here, the Heiskell Hollow Trail goes in both directions; turn left for this hike.

The Heiskell Hollow Trail ascends and ascends and ascends for at least 1.7 miles to a cement post at a junction with the Weddlewood Trail. Go right, still on the Heiskell Hollow Trail, still climbing the rocky path. This continues for another 0.8 mile to a junction with a service road. Go left onto the road and follow it 0.5 mile back to your vehicle and the end of the loop hike.

This is a long hike with a series of steep ascents and descents. But don't cut this one short—it's a beautiful trip. Not many people hike past the falls, so if you're seeking solitude and a good workout, go for it.

Miles and Directions

0.0 Starts at Mile 22.2 on Skyline Drive, at the amphitheater parking lot of Mathews Arm Campground.

0.5 Cement post. Stay to right on the Traces Trail. Go 50 feet to another cement post at interpretive sign 9. Turn right, uphill.

0.6 Cement post. Turn left onto the Tuscarora (formerly Big Blue)-Overall Run Trail (blue blazes).

0.7 Huge boulder on left (greenstone).

1.1 Pass through the swampy Bear Wallow. Trail fairly level.

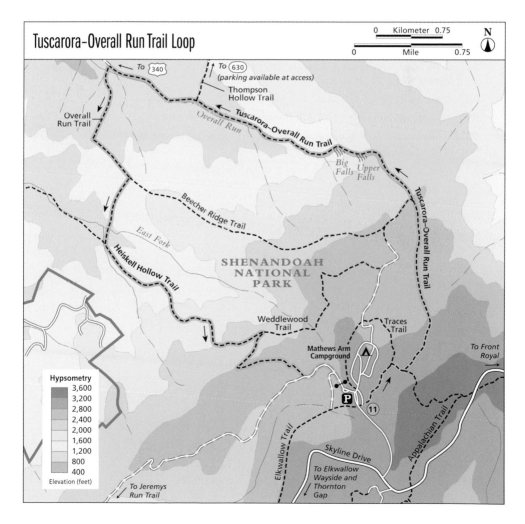

Tuscarora-Overall Run Trail Loop

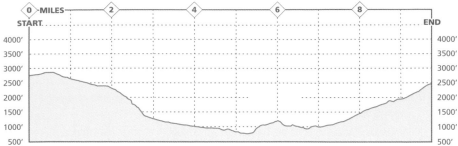

Intervals: Vertical, 500 ft; Horizontal, 1 mi.

2.2 Cement post (three-way junction). Stay straight on the Tuscarora–Overall Run Trail for about 70 yards to another cement post. Turn left, still on the Tuscarora–Overall Run Trail.

3.1 Bottom of Overall Run.

4.6 Cement post. Stay left on the Overall Run Trail (the Tuscarora Trail now branches off to right).

5.2 Cement post. Go left onto the Overall–Beecher Connecting Trail (blue blazes).

5.8 Cement post. Turn left toward the Beecher Ridge Trail (yellow blazes) in order to access the Heiskell Hollow Trail in another 0.8 mile.

6.6 Cement post. Turn right toward the Heiskell Hollow Trail and descend.

8.4 Cement post. Turn left on the Heiskell Hollow Trail, still ascending.

9.2 Cement post at service road. Turn left onto road, follow it to chain, cross chain, make short walk to parking lot.

9.7 Arrive back at the amphitheater parking lot and the end of the loop.

12 Thornton River

Thornton River is a loop hike that descends through some of the park's best bear country. It passes artifacts of the mountain people and meanders along one of the park's most beautiful streams.

Skyline Mile: 24.0

Distance: 10.6-mile loop

Approx. hiking time: 8 to 12 hours

Difficulty: Strenuous

Trail surface: Dirt and naturally occurring rock

Traffic: Light

Canine compatibility: Leashed dogs allowed

Maps: National Geographic Trails Illustrated Topographic Map 228; Map 9, Appalachian Trail and Other Trails in Shenandoah National Park, North District (PATC, Inc.)

Finding the trailhead: The hike begins at the parking lot of Elkwallow Wayside on the west side of Skyline Drive (Mile 24.0). GPS: N38 44.329' / W78 18.499'

The Hike

The Thornton River is named after Francis Thornton, who bought land around 1740 and built a mansion, Montpelier, which still stands. Many other Shenandoah place names honor him, including F. T. Valley and Thornton Gap.

Begin the hike from the Elkwallow Wayside, heading clockwise around the loop. From the parking lot, take the Appalachian Trail north and follow it across Skyline Drive. Follow the trail uphill for about 1 mile, where you encounter a cement post. Turn right and proceed along this trail for only a few yards to another cement post. Turn right onto the Piney Ridge Trail. The left branch is short and leads to the Range View Cabin, operated by the Potomac Appalachian Trail Club (PATC) and available on a reservation basis (see Appendix A: For More Information, and Appendix D: Where to Stay).

Shortly after the cement post, a metal tag on a tree reads BLISTER RUST CONTROL AREA. Blister rust is a disease produced by a spore that attacks white pine trees. Like many diseases, it can be devastating and has wiped out entire forests of white pine. Blister rust control was a major resource protection project in the park in the early 1960s.

At mile 3, the Piney Ridge Trail intersects the Fork Mountain Trail. Bear right. The trail continues to drop. At mile 3.5 there are magnificent stands of tulip poplar. At mile 4.2 you'll encounter another cement post. Turn right onto the Hull School Trail, an old road that winds down and crosses several tiny streams.

At mile 4.9 stands another cement post, at the access to the Thornton River Trail. Turn right, past a number of rock piles. Within a mile, the trail crosses the North Fork of the Thornton River four times in rapid succession. When we hiked this trail in the fall, the colorful leaves, patches of fog, and deer in the mist gave the river a sublime mood.

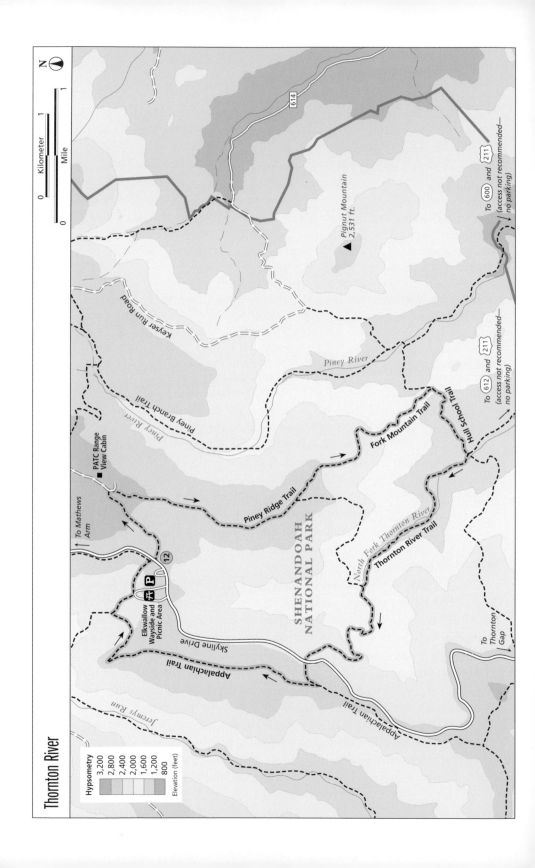

Thornton River

Hypsometry

- 3,200
- 2,800
- 2,400
- 2,000
- 1,600
- 1,200
- 800

Elevation (feet)

N

0   1   Kilometer
0   1   Mile

To Mathews Arm

Jeremys Run

Appalachian Trail

Skyline Drive

Elkwallow Wayside and Picnic Area

12

P

PATC Range View Cabin

Piney River

Piney Branch Trail

Keyser Run Road

Piney Ridge Trail

Fork Mountain Trail

North Fork Thornton River

Thornton River Trail

Hull School Trail

Appalachian Trail

SHENANDOAH NATIONAL PARK

Pignut Mountain 2,531 ft.

614

To 600 and 211 (access not recommended— no parking)

To 612 and 211 (access not recommended— no parking)

To Thornton Gap

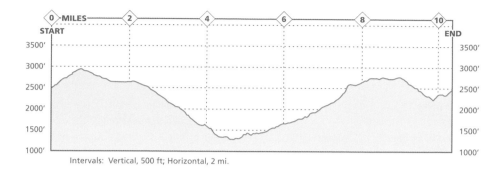

Intervals: Vertical, 500 ft; Horizontal, 2 mi.

At 5.4 miles the trail crosses the Thornton River again. The trail is flanked by a rock wall. The route then swings widely and climbs to a broad ridge forested with red oak. You will find an old rock structure here, perhaps an old chimney. In places, old strands of barbed wire litter the ground. The trail continues a gradual climb.

At mile 6.3 the trail returns to Skyline Drive. Cross the drive and walk left for about 100 yards to where you find the continuation of the Thornton River Trail. Climb the trail for about 0.25 mile, where you'll pick up the AT. Turn right (north) on the AT, which parallels Skyline Drive and returns you back to Elkwallow Wayside.

Miles and Directions

0.0   Starts at the parking lot at Elkwallow Wayside on the west side of Skyline Drive (Mile 24.0).

1.0   Cement post. Turn right onto the Piney Ridge Trail. Reach another cement post almost immediately after mile 1. Turn right onto the Piney Ridge Trail.

1.8   Dense pinewood forest.

3.0   Cement post and intersection with the Fork Mountain Trail. Stay straight onto the Fork Mountain Trail; the Piney Ridge Trail goes north (left).

3.5   Beautiful (magnificent) stands of tulip poplar.

4.2   Cement post. Turn right onto the Hull School Trail.

4.9   Cement post at junction where the Hull School Trail intersects the Thornton River Trail. Turn right onto the Thornton River Trail.

5.4   Fourth crossing over the Thornton River.

5.6   Artifacts of mountain folks.

6.3   Cement post at Skyline Drive. Cross Skyline Drive and hike left along the drive.

6.4   Spur trail to the Appalachian Trail.

6.7   Cement post. Turn right onto the AT.

9.1   Cement post and intersection of the AT with beginning of the Jeremys Run Trail. Turn right, still on the AT.

10.6 Arrive back at the trailhead. Return to your vehicle.

13 Knob Mountain–Jeremys Run Lariat

This full-day hike leads into the wilderness surrounding Jeremys Run.

Skyline Mile: 24.1
Distance: 12.6-mile lariat
Approx. hiking time: 8 to 12 hours
Difficulty: Strenuous
Trail surface: Dirt and naturally occurring rock
Traffic: Moderate

Canine compatibility: Leashed dogs allowed
Maps: National Geographic Trails Illustrated Topographic Map 228; Map 9, Appalachian Trail and Other Trails in Shenandoah National Park, North District (PATC, Inc.)

Finding the trailhead: The hike begins at the lower end of the Elkwallow Picnic Area parking lot, which is just south of the Elkwallow Wayside at Mile 24.0 on the west side of Skyline Drive. Walk down the trail to access the Appalachian Trail (white blazes). GPS: N38 44.460' / W78 18.721'

The Hike

If you are a wilderness buff, this one's for you. You could also make this a backpacking trip, camping at the bottom of Jeremys Run. The trails meander through the designated wilderness areas of Knob Mountain and Jeremys Run. There is a great view from Knob Mountain, and this hike is a long, beautiful trek into the heart of Shenandoah National Park.

Begin by descending north on the Appalachian Trail from the brown signpost at the bottom level of the Elkwallow Picnic Area. Lush grasses line the trail in this forest of tall trees. Soon the path winds by a water pipe on the left.

After about 0.3 mile, you encounter a cement post. Stay straight on the Jeremys Run Trail (blue blazes). Descend through a mature, open forest of oaks and maple—the squirrels love it here!

Descend to a cement post at a three-way junction and turn right onto the Knob Mountain Cutoff Trail (blue blazes). The trail descends, crosses Jeremys Run, then immediately begins to ascend. There is definitely a wilderness feeling to the area, but even so the trail is a good one. Continue the ascent, which is steep in parts and contains many switchbacks. After passing a long rock wall (which bisects the trail at a double blue blaze), a cement post indicates the junction with the Knob Mountain Trail (yellow blazes). Turn left onto the Knob Mountain Trail. From this point, it's about 3 miles to the summit along what is actually an old road.

You are now on a nice, soft ridgetop trail, which begins a steady uphill climb offering occasional views through the partially open forest. When we hiked this route, grouse populations were high, providing food for an assortment of predators.

We came across a huge pile of grouse feathers, as if someone had just plucked the bird. A bobcat may have taken the bird, though owls also prey on grouse.

Not long before you reach the summit of Knob Mountain (2,865 feet), the old road narrows, ends, and becomes a trail once more. There is a cement post just before the top that indicates you have 250 more steep feet to go.

From the top of the mountain stay straight (there's no other way), and begin a descent that will drop 1,600 feet in the next 2.4 miles. The descent begins immediately, at first very steeply through a series of sharp switchbacks. Then the drop becomes much more gradual, along a good, soft trail. Views begin to open to the south and southwest into Jeremys Run and to Neighbor Mountain across the run. On an October day when leaves are in full color, the view is spectacular.

The path keeps descending until it begins to parallel Jeremys Run, on the right. Almost immediately the trail ends by a wood marker. At this point you cross the run for the first (but not nearly the last) time. Look for a yellow blaze on a tree on the far side, as well as a cement post situated right after the crossing. Turn left to another cement post 45 feet away at a fork. Take the left fork onto the Jeremys Run Trail (blue blazes); the right fork is the Neighbor Mountain Trail.

Sycamore trees grow along Jeremys Run, but many were knocked down by the high winds and heavy flooding of 1995. The next run crossing comes very soon, and the trail (a good one) winds slightly upward. Piles of rocks are abundant in the woods, and even though there isn't much of a water flow in dry seasons, the setting is pretty.

The third crossing occurs suddenly, so watch carefully for the blue blazes. The areas here and just ahead offer some possible backcountry camping spots. Look carefully and be sure to abide by backcountry regulations.

The next 4-plus miles negotiate a series of stream crossings with an ascent so gradual that it is hardly noticeable. At approximately mile 11.8, you'll see another cement post. Continue straight and ascend more steeply for another 0.5 mile. The AT comes in here. Stay straight and follow the AT north for the last 0.3 mile to complete the loop at the picnic area parking lot.

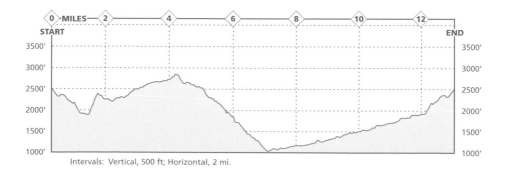

Intervals: Vertical, 500 ft; Horizontal, 2 mi.

Knob Mountain-Jeremys Run Lariat

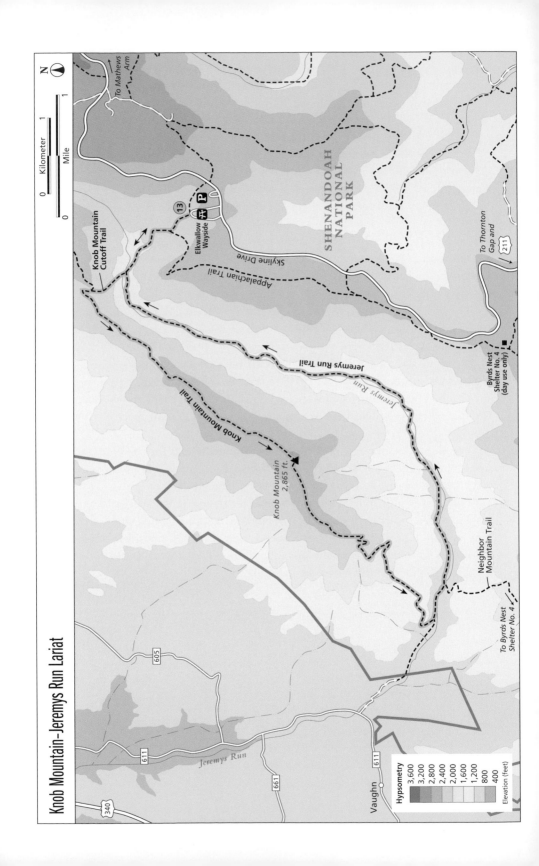

Hypsometry

Elevation (feet)
3,600
3,200
2,800
2,400
2,000
1,600
1,200
800
400

N

0   Kilometer   1

0   Mile   1

To Mathews Arm

Knob Mountain Cutoff Trail

Elkwallow Wayside

13

P

Skyline Drive

SHENANDOAH NATIONAL PARK

Appalachian Trail

Jeremys Run Trail

Jeremys Run

Knob Mountain Trail

Knob Mountain 2,865 ft.

Neighbor Mountain Trail

Byrds Nest Shelter No. 4 (day use only)

To Thornton Gap and 211

To Byrds Nest Shelter No. 4

605

611

661

611

340

Jeremys Run

Vaughn

Miles and Directions

0.0   Start at the lower end of the Elkwallow Picnic Area parking lot, which is just south of the Elkwallow Wayside at Mile 24.0 on the west side of Skyline Drive.

1.6   Cement post. Turn left onto the Knob Mountain Trail (yellow blazes), an old fire road.

3.8   Begin to ascend summit. The road becomes a trail.

4.6   Reach summit of Knob Mountain (2,865 feet). Cement post. No views at summit. Begin descent of approximately 1,600 feet to Jeremys Run.

7.0   At wood post, ford Jeremys Run for the first time. Look for yellow blaze on tree across run. Cement post. Turn left for 45 feet to another cement post at a fork. Stay left onto the Jeremys Run Trail (blue blazes). The right fork leads to Neighbor Mountain.

11.8   Cement post. Stay straight, following blue blazes.

12.3   Cement post and junction with the Appalachian Trail. Take the AT north, staying straight (white blazes).

12.6   Arrive back at the picnic grounds, parking lot, and end of hike.

White-tailed deer, a species seen throughout the park.

14 Byrds Nest Summit and Byrds Nest Shelter No. 4

This fun, tranquil hike leads through a deciduous forest up to one of four day-use shelters in the park.

Skyline Mile: 28.5
Distance: 2.8 miles out and back
Approx. hiking time: 2 to 4 hours
Difficulty: Easy to moderate
Trail surface: Dirt and naturally occurring rock
Traffic: Light

Canine compatibility: Leashed dogs allowed
Maps: National Geographic Trails Illustrated Topographic Map 228; Map 9, Appalachian Trail and Other Trails in Shenandoah National Park, North District (PATC, Inc.)

Finding the trailhead: The trail begins at the Beahms Gap parking area, Mile 28.5 on Skyline Drive. The trailhead is located at a cement post at the north end of the parking lot. GPS: N38 41.7215' / W78 19.199'

The Hike

This short, relatively easy day hike takes you up to a ridge on the Neighbor Mountain Trail and to Byrds Nest Shelter No. 4, a day-use shelter built in 1965. It is one of four shelters in the park constructed with donations from former Sen. Harry F. Byrd Sr. The trek is pretty and tranquil. On clear days you can see beyond Pass Mountain to the east. Once there were views from the shelter, but trees have obscured most of them. The shelter is a large, three-sided stone structure with a huge fireplace and a picnic table.

Begin this hike at the cement post at the north end of the parking lot. Descend 0.1 mile through the woods to a T junction at another cement post. Here the Appalachian Trail runs north–south. Turn north (right) onto the AT. Soon you'll encounter a cement post indicating a spring on the left.

As you trek through a mostly deciduous forest (pretty in the fall), the trees and rocks offset one another's beauty. There are a few short, steep ascents and a few very

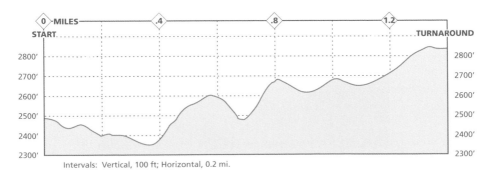

Intervals: Vertical, 100 ft; Horizontal, 0.2 mi.

Author Jane Gildart along the trail to Byrds Nest Shelter.

rocky areas of trail. Sturdy boots are recommended, especially if the trail is wet.

At 0.8 mile you will reach Byrds Nest Summit and a four-way junction of the AT and the Neighbor Mountain Trail. Turn east (right) onto the Neighbor Mountain Trail. In 0.1 mile another post is encountered. Stay straight on the Neighbor Mountain Trail for 0.5 mile more to Byrds Nest Shelter No. 4.

You'll find the shelter in a pretty setting, one that inspires a picnic. A field lies in front, and flowers give color in the summer. Pass Mountain rises to the east. If you wander to the right above the shelter, it may be possible to get some views, but nothing outstanding.

From the shelter, retrace your route to the parking lot. Note that in the first 0.6 mile of the return trip, at the cement posts, you are able to take a short spur trail

Byrds Nest Summit and Byrds Nest Shelter No. 4

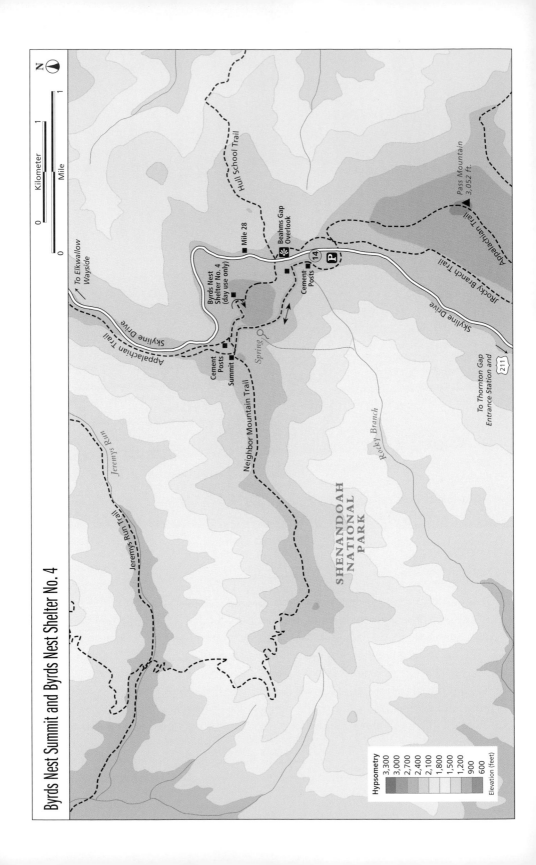

Hypsometry
- 3,300
- 3,000
- 2,700
- 2,400
- 2,100
- 1,800
- 1,500
- 1,200
- 900
- 600

Elevation (feet)

SHENANDOAH
NATIONAL
PARK

Pass Mountain
3,052 ft.

Appalachian Trail

Rocky Branch Trail

Skyline Drive

To Thornton Gap
Entrance Station and

211

Rocky Branch

Neighbor Mountain Trail

Jeremys Run Trail

Jeremys Run

Appalachian Trail

Skyline Drive

To Elkwallow
Wayside

Cement
Posts

Summit

Spring

Byrds Nest
Shelter No. 4
(day use only)

Cement
Posts

14

P

Mile 28

Beahms Gap
Overlook

Hull School Trail

N

0   Kilometer   1

0   Mile   1

down to Skyline Drive. If you do make this choice, be aware that you will come out north of where you left your vehicle at Beahms Gap.

If you are in the mood for only a very short walk in the forest—a loop walk of only 0.4 mile—try this: Access the trail at the cement post at the north end of the parking lot. Go 0.1 mile to another cement post at a T, which is the AT intersection. Go left (south) on the AT, following the blue blazes on the trees. Soon you'll ascend briefly and return to Skyline Drive, beside the trailhead parking lot.

Hikers on the trail to Byrds Nest.

Miles and Directions

0.0   Start at Beahms Gap parking area, Mile 28.5 on Skyline Drive. The trailhead is located at a cement post at the north end of the parking lot.

0.1   Cement post and junction with the Appalachian Trail. Turn north (right) onto the AT.

0.2   Spring on left; stay on AT.

0.8   Byrds Nest Summit. Four-way junction at cement post. Turn right onto the Neighbor Mountain Trail.

0.9   Another cement post; stay straight on Neighbor Mountain Trail.

1.3   Cement post; stay straight on Neighbor Mountain Trail.

1.4   Byrds Nest Shelter No. 4. Retrace your steps back to parking lot.

2.8   Arrive back at the trailhead and the Beahms Gap parking lot.

Central District

Skyline Mile 31.6 to 65.5

Some of the park's roughest and tallest peaks are in the Central District. These include Old Rag, the park's most formidable and spectacular mountain, and Hawksbill, the park's highest mountain (4,050 feet). With the exception of Old Rag, which requires special driving directions, access to the Central District is most easily made by taking US 33 from Stanardsville or Harrisonburg and entering Shenandoah National Park at Swift Run Gap. From the north, take US 211 from either Sperryville to the east or Luray to the west, and access the park at Thornton Gap.

Hazel Falls is naturally beautiful, but when laced with autumn leaves, it assumes an entirely new grandeur.

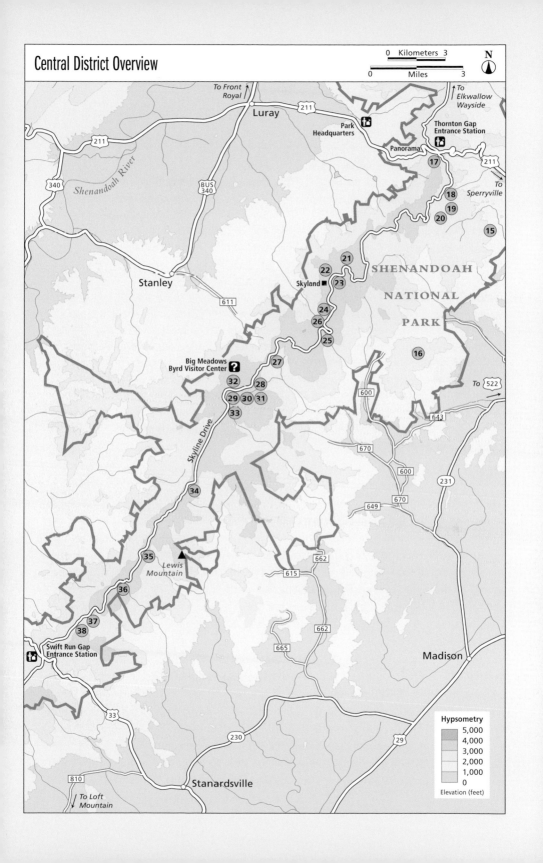

Central District Overview

0 Kilometers 3

0 Miles 3

N

To Front Royal

Luray

211

Park Headquarters

To Elkwallow Wayside

Thornton Gap Entrance Station

Panorama

211

17

To Sperryville

211

340

Shenandoah River

BUS 340

18

19

20

15

Stanley

611

21

22

Skyland ■

23

SHENANDOAH

NATIONAL

PARK

24

26

25

16

Big Meadows Byrd Visitor Center

27

To 522

32

28

29 30 31

33

600

643

670

600

231

649

670

Skyline Drive

34

35

Lewis Mountain

662

615

662

36

37

38

Swift Run Gap Entrance Station

665

Madison

33

230

29

810

To Loft Mountain

Stanardsville

Hypsometry

5,000
4,000
3,000
2,000
1,000
0

Elevation (feet)

15 Pine Hill Gap–Broad Hollow Loop

A hike along a trail often overgrown with much vegetation provides, toward the trail's end, glimpses of a bygone era.

Skyline Mile: 31.5. The trailhead is not on Skyline Drive. To reach it, leave the park at Thornton Gap and take US 211 to Sperryville.
Distance: 5.8-mile loop
Approx. hiking time: 3 to 8 hours
Difficulty: Moderate
Trail surface: Dirt and naturally occurring rock

Traffic: Light
Canine compatibility: Leashed dogs allowed
Maps: National Geographic Trails Illustrated Topographic Map 228; Map 10, Appalachian Trail and Other Trails in Shenandoah National Park, Central District (PATC, Inc.)

Finding the trailhead: From Mile 31.5 at Thornton Gap on Skyline Drive, take US 211 east to Sperryville. From Sperryville continue on US 211, picking up US 522 southbound. Go 0.8 mile; turn right onto SR 231 and go 3.3 miles. Just before the bridge over the Hazel River, take CR 681, a dirt and gravel road, west past CR 600 (CR 600 enters from the right after 1 mile). Continue on CR 681 for a total of 2.5 miles, where you encounter a cement post at the top of a left bend in the road immediately adjacent to a private road. Park well to the right of the private drive, in a pullout that can accommodate one or two cars. You'll return to this point along the Broad Hollow Trail, which this post designates. Hike CR 681 to the road's end, then climb a poorly maintained road that parallels the park boundary. GPS: N38 35.501974' / W78 16.497086'

The Hike

Trails in this part of Shenandoah are remote and difficult. On the other hand, these trails wander through some of the park's best examples of artifacts from a bygone era. On this particular trail, you'll encounter remains of old cabins. Remember that some sections of the trail are falling into disuse, and you might need to allocate more time than you would for other trails of a comparable distance. In some places, the vegetation is so thick that it almost blots out the sky overhead.

After parking your vehicle in a very restrictive space (two small cars maximum), follow the key points carefully. The trail follows CR 681 to its terminus, then follows an old road.

At mile 2.2 the Pine Hill Gap Trail joins with the Hazel Mountain Trail, which you will follow. At mile 2.5 the Hazel Mountain Trail intersects with the Hot Mountain–Short Mountain Trail from the west, and you continue on the Hazel Mountain Trail. At mile 3.5, turn right onto the Sams Ridge Trail, which soon crosses a small stream. Just 0.1 mile later, turn right onto the Broad Hollow Trail.

At mile 4.4 you encounter a cabin on your immediate left. Just 0.2 mile later cross a stream, which may in fact be part of the trail. Keep your eyes open for a roofless cabin, then two old cabins and several stone walls. At mile 5.2 the trail crosses a

Pine Hill Gap-Broad Hollow Loop

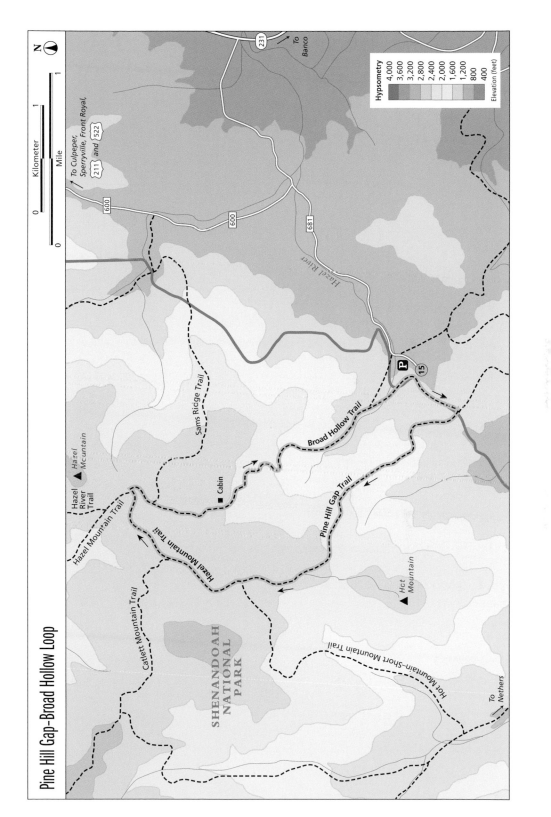

N

Kilometer
0   1

Mile
0   1

Hypsometry
- 4,000
- 3,600
- 3,200
- 2,800
- 2,400
- 2,000
- 1,600
- 1,200
- 800
- 400

Elevation (feet)

To Culpeper,
Sperryville, Front Royal,
211 and 522

600

600

681

231

To
Banco

Hazel River

Sams Ridge Trail

Hazel
Mountain

Hazel
River
Trail

Cabin

Hazel Mountain Trail

Catlett Mountain Trail

Hazel Mountain Trail

Broad Hollow Trail

Pine Hill Gap Trail

Hot Mountain

SHENANDOAH
NATIONAL
PARK

Hot Mountain–Short Mountain Trail

To
Nethers

P

15

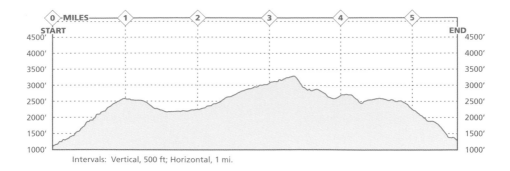

Intervals: Vertical, 500 ft; Horizontal, 1 mi.

stream, only to cross the same stream again and at mile 5.8 yet again. From the crossing climb the short bank to return to the trailhead and your vehicle.

Miles and Directions

0.0 Start at the cement post along CR 681.

0.5 Cement post and access to the Pine Hill Gap Trail. Climb steadily on the Pine Hill Gap Trail.

2.2 Cement post. Junction and join with the Hazel Mountain Trail. Continue straight, now on the Hazel Mountain Trail, still climbing.

2.5 Cement post marking access to the Hot Mountain–Short Mountain Trail to the west. Continue climbing on the Hazel Mountain Trail.

3.5 Turn right to access Sams Ridge Trail.

3.6 Cross small stream.

3.7 Turn right onto the Broad Hollow Trail and remain on this trail until hike's end.

4.4 Pass the cabin on the trail's immediate left.

4.6 Cross the stream, which for 15 yards or so is actually part of the trail, depending on the weather. (The stream is typically at its highest in spring.)

4.8 An old roofless cabin overgrown with vines and squeezed by maturing trees sits 30 feet to the trail's right.

5.0 Two old cabins and several stone walls are off the trail 50 yards.

5.2 Cross stream. Trail levels but continues slow descent.

5.4 Cross stream again, which is now on the right.

5.8 Cross stream, climb short bank, and arrive at the trailhead and your vehicle.

16 Old Rag

A climb to the top of one of the park's most famous peaks presents incredible views from the summit.

Skyline Mile: 31.5. The trailhead is not on Skyline Drive. To reach it, leave the park at Thornton Gap and take US 211 to Sperryville.
Distance: 8.8-mile loop
Difficulty: Strenuous
Traffic: Heavy (especially on weekends and holidays)

Canine compatibility: Dogs not allowed on Saddle Trail or Ridge Trail
Maps: National Geographic Trails Illustrated Topographic Map 228; Map 10, Appalachian Trail and Other Trails in Shenandoah National Park, Central District (PATC, Inc.)

Finding the trailhead: The most popular and easiest way to climb Old Rag is to access the trailhead from outside the park. We recommend using a good road map, such as the *Virginia Atlas and Gazetteer*. From Mile 31.5 at Thornton Gap on Skyline Drive, take US 211 8 miles east to Sperryville. Turn onto US 522 southbound. Go 0.8 mile, turn right onto SR 231, and go 8 miles. Turn right onto CR 601. In 0.3 mile turn right at a T intersection and continue on CR 601 until it becomes CR 707 some 0.8 mile later. In 1.7 miles the road becomes SR 600 (bearing left). Follow it for 0.5 mile to its terminus, represented by the designated Old Rag parking lot. From here you must walk 0.8 mile along a very rural road to the blue-blazed trailhead for the Ridge Trail.

From the south (Charlottesville) take US 29 about 35 miles north to Madison, Virginia. From Madison, take SR 231 north for 12.8 miles. Turn left onto SR 602. In 0.5 mile the road becomes CR 601. Continue on CR 601. In 0.8 mile it becomes CR 707, which becomes CR 600 1.7 miles later. Follow CR 600 for 0.5 mile to the parking area on the left. Park and walk 0.8 mile to the Ridge Trail. GPS: N38 34.2245' / W78 18.0196'

Restrictions and suggestions: Because of Old Rag's popularity and fragile resources, the park service suggests you consider climbing the peak on weekdays, particularly during the popular fall hiking season. This reduces crowding, improves wilderness character, and helps protect sensitive plants and soils from trampling.

If the parking lot is full, do not park on private property. Drive elsewhere for an alternative hike. The park also recommends that hiking groups carpool and not send out groups by the busload. The parking lot is 0.8 mile from the trailhead.

The National Park Service enforces strict parking regulations at the trailhead. Anyone over the age of 16 without a seven-day pass, a yearly pass, or a Golden Eagle or Golden Age pass must buy a permit for a small fee. Such permits are available from park personnel on busy weekends and holidays or by self-registration at the trailhead. If you plan to stay in the backcountry, obtain a free backcountry permit from one of the visitor centers or entrance stations.

The park prohibits camping at elevations of more than 2,800 feet on Old Rag, to protect fragile soils and plants. Camping is not permitted near Byrds Nest Shelter No. 1 and the Old Rag Shelter. Byrds Nest Shelter No. 1 and the Old Rag Shelter are for day use only. You can find good backcountry camping options near the intersection of Weakley Hollow Fire Road and Berry Hollow Fire Road.

Scrambling atop massive granite boulders adds character and challenge to a hike at Old Rag.

The Hike

At 3,268 feet, Old Rag is not the highest mountain in Shenandoah National Park (Hawksbill summit, at 4,050 feet, has that distinction), but it is without question the park's most challenging and exciting mountain to climb.

For one thing the rock is ancient almost beyond belief, meaning that although you can say "over a billion years old," such a time frame has little meaning. Naturalists try to add a sense of relativity by reducing such an expanse to human longevity or human history. They say that if the Blue Ridge Mountains represented an event that occurred twelve hours ago, then all the time that has elapsed since the birth of Christ would be less than a tenth of a second.

Using plate tectonic theory, geologists say rocks atop Old Rag began their formation when ancient continents collided to form a supercontinent called Rodinia. These collisions, which occurred over a billion years ago, created immense forces that acted on the massive plates on which these continents float, forcing them to buckle. The huge "Grenville Mountains" formed, and they equaled today's Rockies in size and in length, spanning a distance equal to traveling from Mexico to Canada. Concurrent with the orogeny, magma formed deep within the crust and crystallized to form granite. Over the eons, the rocks above the granite eroded away. The granite eventually made its way to the surface and is now exposed as today's Old Rag Mountain.

But the story is not complete. Rodinia subsequently rifted apart about 570 million years into separate continents. As the continents drifted apart from each other, the Iapetus Ocean formed in between. About 320 million years later, these massive tectonic plates were to meet again. This time they assumed a different configuration, one that many of today's high school students know as the giant continent Pangaea.

Simultaneously this action, known as the Allegheny orogeny, set into motion pressures that would force the rocks into a more familiar landscape. During the continental collision that formed Pangaea, the Appalachian Mountains were pushed upward and forced westward into present-day Virginia, and here they rested, waiting for the final chapter to expose Old Rag granite.

More time passed, perhaps 150 million years, and the geologic forces reversed themselves, causing Pangaea to break apart and the Atlantic Ocean to form.

Exposing Old Rag granite required still more time. Rain, snow, sleet, hail, freezing and thawing, driving winds: All combined to wear away at the rocks surrounding the granite of Old Rag. Eventually these forces succeeded, reducing the towering 10,000-foot-high mountains created during the Allegheny orogeny to the ones now seen in Shenandoah. The highest reaches just over 4,000 feet, meaning the elevation of the range was reduced by 6,000 feet.

Today, Old Rag granite manifests itself as massive boulders. When you near the summit you'll see these massive boulders, and you can confirm the rock type by the presence of large white crystals geologists call feldspar.

Greatly abbreviated, such is the story that will unfold as you climb, but from the trailhead (elevation 1,068 feet), there is little to hint that the trail will soon be winding among some of the earth's most ancient artifacts.

Begin the hike in a forest of maple, oak, and hickory. In 0.5 mile, cross a stream that varies seasonally from a trickle to a torrent. A short distance later the forest gives way to huge boulders, and here's where the hike ends and the crawl begins.

For about 1 mile or more, you must shinny over boulders using, in places, three-point stands. In several places it is helpful if taller people assist shorter people, helping them search for better handholds in the rocks. Some hikers will master some of the rudiments of Rock Climbing 101. Some, however, may have a genuine fear of heights, and one man we encountered decided to turn back. He was smart, for he knew his limits. Others have slipped and fallen, and some have broken bones. Yet others, such as Senator Byrd, made annual climbs up Old Rag in their late seventies!

Regardless, the going is slow and requires time to navigate the labyrinth of rocks. The route is well marked with blue blazes, and without them finding the way could be difficult. Pay attention to the blazes, and after reaching one, look for the next before proceeding.

Though the trail becomes more obvious after threading through the first maze, another soon follows. Fortunately, this one is much easier to negotiate, and shortly thereafter you reach the summit of Old Rag.

The top is marked by a sign. Turn right from the sign and go about 30 yards to get the full effect of the views. And look around for such manifestations of weathering as the

large rounded holes known as "opferkessels." They make interesting photographic subjects, and their creation begins when standing water lingers in slight depressions and can then hold fast to the needles of evergreen trees after they've dropped. If the action is repeated over a period of years, water then leaches out the organic acids in the needles. The acids, in turn, begin to eat away at the rock, and each time this happens the hole grows larger. In larger holes the acids linger longer and can obviously work longer. Following years of such action, acids will etch out a hand- to fist-size hole. When the action is concurrent, acids may etch out many such holes, imparting a pockmarked look to these ancient granitic boulders.

On the day of our most recent climb, we departed the trailhead at 9:30 a.m. and reached the summit about noon. From our vantage we had a complete 360-degree view. To the north and northwest we could see the route of Skyline Drive and the dozen peaks that the route accesses. To the west and southwest we could pick out the Old Rag

Opferkessels were created by the evaporation of standing water laced with the organic acids of leaves and pine needles. Over time, the acids etched out the holes that now cover rocks atop Old Rag.

overlook and Big Meadows, where we often camp. We could also see a little of our return route, which we would combine to make this 2,200-foot climb into a circular hike of over 8 miles. But more than anything, it was the timeless rocks at the base of our feet that would remain so indelibly etched in the landscapes of our minds.

From the summit, you have the option of either retracing your steps or following the longer but easier route back to your car. Time-wise it is probably a toss-up, but if you return by the same route, you must scramble down the boulders and, for most, this is more difficult than climbing up.

To return by the longer route, leave the summit of Old Rag and proceed 0.4 mile down to Byrds Nest Shelter No. 1. Another mile and you will reach the Old Rag Shelter. From there the trail continues downhill. At mile 5.7—about 0.4 mile past the shelter—turn right onto the Weakley Hollow Fire Road at the cement post marked OLD RAG PARKING. The fire road descends gradually, and eventually parallels Brokenback Run. Just before reaching the upper parking lot, the trail crosses three footbridges over the stream. As you reach the fourth footbridge, 0.1 mile beyond the other three, you're nearly at the emergency vehicle parking lot. From that lot, follow the paved road 0.8 mile to the parking area.

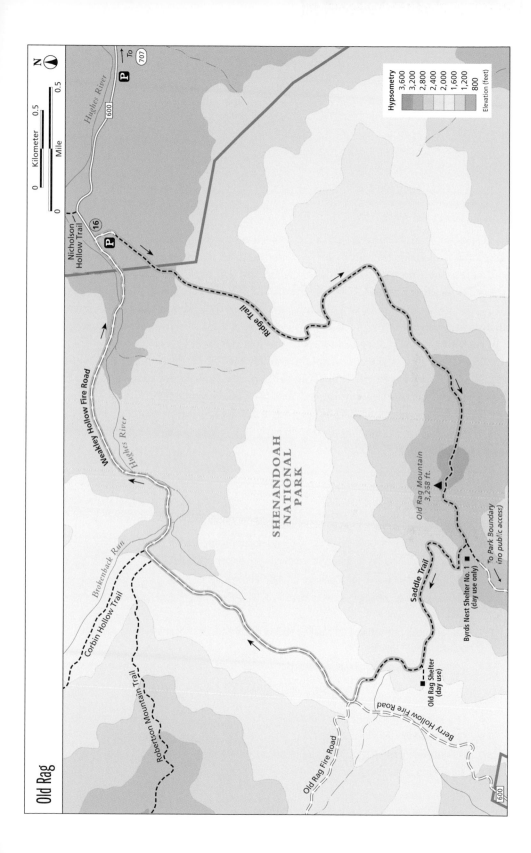

Old Rag

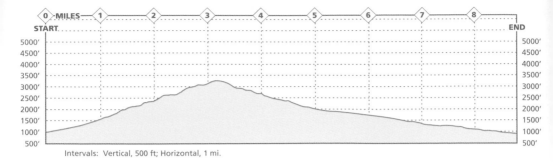

Intervals: Vertical, 500 ft; Horizontal, 1 mi.

Option: To embark on an Old Rag trek from Skyline Drive, for an out-and-back hike of approximately 14 miles, park on the east side of Skyline Drive at Mile 43.0 and access the Old Rag Fire Road. Stay on the fire road, going east-southeast for about 5 miles to the Old Rag Shelter. Along the way, you cross the Whiteoak Canyon Trail, the Limberlost Trail, and the Skyland Horse Trail. About 0.4 mile before the shelter, cross the intersection of Berry Hollow and Weakley Hollow Fire Roads. You can find good backcountry camping options just beyond this intersection.

From Old Rag Shelter, it's about 1.8 miles farther to the summit of Old Rag, reached by taking the Saddle Trail. From the summit, retrace your steps for a total hike distance of about 14 miles. Ideally, you'll want to make this a three-day trek.

There are yet other Old Rag hikes; study a good topographic map for all the varying trails to and from Old Rag.

Miles and Directions

0.0 Start at the Old Rag parking lot.

0.8 Trailhead (Ridge Trail).

2.3 Top of ridge—out of the trees and into the rocks.

3.8 Summit of Old Rag. Descend at cement post, following the Saddle Trail.

4.2 Byrds Nest Shelter No. 1. Turn right, continuing to follow the Saddle Trail.

5.3 Old Rag Shelter and spring. Continue on the Saddle Trail/fire road.

5.7 Double junction. Turn right onto the Weakley Hollow Fire Road at cement post marked OLD RAG PARKING.

6.7 Cement post. Stay straight on Weakley Hollow Fire Road. The Robertson Mountain Trail comes in from the left.

6.8 Cement post. Stay straight on Weakley Hollow Fire Road. The Corbin Hollow Trail comes in from the left.

6.9 Cross a metal footbridge.

7.8 Cross three consecutive wooden footbridges.

7.9 Cross a fourth wooden footbridge.

8.0 Park boundary and beginning of pavement on CR 600.

8.8 Arrive back at the parking lot and the end of the hike.

17 Marys Rock North

Appropriate for families, this hike offers natural history, geology, panoramic views, and folklore.

Skyline Mile: 31.6
Distance: 3.6 miles out and back
Approx. hiking time: 3 to 5 hours
Difficulty: Easy to moderate
Trail surface: Dirt and naturally occurring rock
Traffic: Moderate

Canine compatibility: Leashed dogs allowed
Maps: National Geographic Trails Illustrated Topographic Map 228; Map 10, Appalachian Trail and Other Trails in Shenandoah National Park, Central District (PATC, Inc.)

Finding the trailhead: The trail begins at the Panorama upper parking lot, Mile 31.6 on Skyline Drive. GPS: N38 39.549' / W78 19.295'

The Hike

If you have the luxury of time, pick a clear day for this hike and go early in the morning. Sunrise is a great time to enjoy the views and get some superb photos. (Save foggy days for hikes to waterfalls; fog adds to the aura of wetness.)

According to one version of park lore, a young woman named Mary Thornton once made this hike alone to the rocky summit. When she returned, she carried a bear cub under each arm. The park service certainly does not endorse such intimacy with wildlife today, but the story is a good one.

To begin the trek, head left (south) on the Appalachian Trail, which is marked with white blazes. Within 30 yards, the trail begins to climb. Twelve log steps help you upward. Within 100 yards, five more log steps do the same thing. The trail winds upward through a hardwood forest interspersed with mountain laurel and ferns. It follows the east side of the ridge.

Soon the trees are more widely spaced and views begin. The trail becomes very rocky and is fortified on your left with a man-made shelf of rocks. On the upward slope, the trees seem to be trying to restrain the force of gravity, preventing large boulders from tumbling down the hillside. The ascent is steady, with some switchbacks and few level areas.

After about a mile, you can see large rock monoliths on your right and a lovely panorama to the east. As you approach the summit, the trail swings back into the trees. On the uphill side

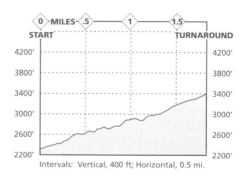

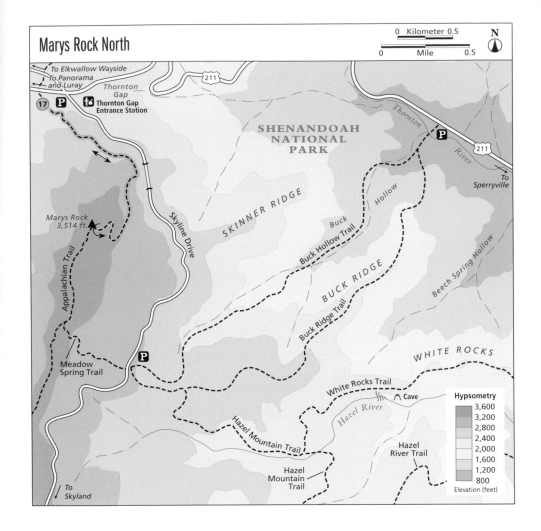

of the trail, thick stands of mountain laurel line the path. You may see a ruffed grouse take wing along this stretch.

Watch for the first cement post after 1.7 miles. Do not turn left onto the AT. Continue straight ahead, taking the spur trail to the top, which is 0.1 mile farther. Be sure to follow the blue blazes, not the white ones along the AT.

Marys Rock is composed of Pedlar granodiorite. The vista below is wonderful; you can see Thornton Gap. Plan to spend some time resting in the clearing or carefully climbing the rocks for different views. You may see peregrine falcons soaring on the wind drafts, as we did.

Now that you've climbed 1,210 feet to the top, you can enjoy the luxury of a downhill return. Backtrack, taking the AT north, but use caution: The steep, rocky descent can be more hazardous than the uphill trek, especially when wet.

An overlook near Marys Rock trailhead offers a tantalizing hint of what the hike has in store.

Miles and Directions

0.0 Start at Mile 31.6 on Skyline Drive at Panorama upper parking lot.

0.1 Junction with the Appalachian Trail. Turn left.

1.0 Large rock monoliths on right.

1.7 Cement post. Go straight on spur trail. Do not turn left on the AT.

1.8 Summit of Marys Rock. Turnaround point.

3.6 Arrive back at the trailhead and upper parking lot at Panorama.

18 Marys Rock South

Shorter and somewhat less rigorous than Marys Rock North, this trail passes the remains of an old PATC hiker cabin and provides intimate views of oak, hickory, and maple forest.

Skyline Mile: 33.5
Distance: 2.6 miles out and back
Approx. hiking time: 3 to 5 hours
Difficulty: Moderate
Trail surface: Dirt and naturally occurring rock
Traffic: Moderate

Canine compatibility: Leashed dogs allowed
Maps: National Geographic Trails Illustrated Topographic Map 228; Map 10, Appalachian Trail and Other Trails in Shenandoah National Park, Central District (PATC Inc.)

Finding the trailhead: The trail begins at the Meadow Spring trailhead at Mile 33.5. Park in the Meadow Spring lot on the east side of the road. Marys Rock Trail is on the west side of the road, about 30 feet south of the parking lot. GPS: N38 38.281' / W78 18.853'

Mary's Rock Tunnel runs close to the Marys Rock trailhead.

A rustic log bench provides a resting spot for those hiking Marys Rock South.

The Hike

Yet another trail leads to Marys Rock. This route gains less in elevation (830 feet instead of 1,210 feet) and is 0.8 mile shorter than Marys Rock North.

Meadow Spring Trail begins to ascend immediately, then levels only to climb again. After about 0.4 mile you'll see a huge stone chimney—all that remains of a PATC hiker cabin. Originally built in the early 1930s, the cabin was torn down in 1939, then rebuilt, only to burn to the ground on Thanksgiving Day of 1946 under mysterious circumstances.

From the cabin the trail ascends. A log bench provides a nice spot to sit, recoup, and admire the forest of oak, hickory, and maple.

At 0.6 mile you encounter a cement post. Turn right here and pick up the AT. The trail ascends, then descends several hundred feet, at which point you come to another post marking another 0.6 mile. Here you meet the trail you would have followed if you had begun this hike from Panorama. Turn left onto the spur trail that ascends to Marys Rock summit, reaching the top at 1.3 miles. Return as you came.

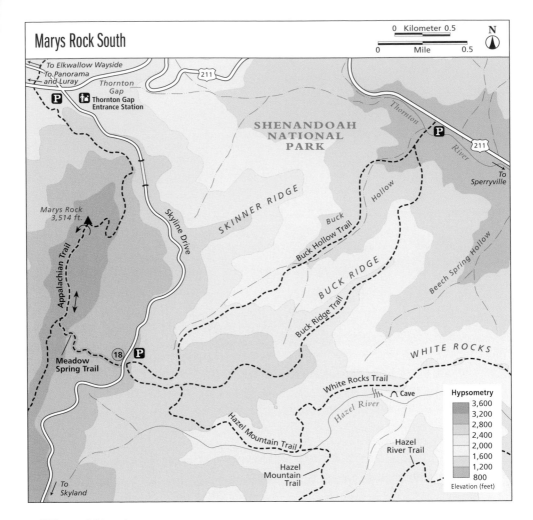

Miles and Directions

0.0 Meadow Spring parking lot. Cross Skyline Drive to the west side to access Meadow Spring trailhead.

0.6 Cement post at junction with AT; turn right.

1.2 T junction. Turn left, following the blue-blazed spur trail.

1.3 Marys Rock summit. Turn around and retrace your steps back to the trailhead.

2.6 Arrive back at the Meadow Spring trailhead. Your car is across the drive.

19 Buck Hollow–Buck Ridge Trail Loop

This invigorating loop hike along a rushing stream descends through a hollow, then climbs Buck Ridge. The trail leads to a rarely visited, wild section of the park.

Skyline Mile: 33.5
Distance: 5.6-mile loop
Approx. hiking time: 3 to 6 hours
Difficulty: Moderately strenuous
Trail surface: Dirt and naturally occurring rock
Traffic: Light

Canine compatibility: Leashed dogs allowed
Maps: National Geographic Trails Illustrated Topographic Map 228; Map 10, Appalachian Trail and Other Trails in Shenandoah National Park, Central District (PATC, Inc.)

Finding the trailhead: The trail begins at Mile 33.5 on Skyline Drive, at the south end of the Meadow Spring parking area. Stay left on the Buck Hollow Trail and descend. GPS: N38 38.295' / W78 18.824'

The Hike

Within 0.1 mile the Buck Hollow Trail approaches a stream, which comes in from the right. The stream is only a small trickle, but within 0.7 mile its volume increases, and then at 1 mile from the trailhead it cascades over a series of rock tiers. The trail remains steep and continues its descent into Buck Hollow.

At 2.8 miles from the trailhead, the Buck Hollow Trail joins the Buck Ridge Trail. The Buck Ridge Trail goes right at a metal tag on a cement post. The Hazel Mountain Trail is 2.3 miles away and Skyline Drive is 2.8 miles away.

From the junction, the Buck Ridge Trail begins a gradual descent that is deceiving. Within 0.1 mile the trail begins an ascent of sixty-some log steps. Though it seems forever, the trail tops out at the stairs in about 0.1 mile, a brutally steep section.

In early July, and along this particular exposure, the laurel will have all gone to seed, but what a sight this is in late spring. Blueberry and huckleberry bushes also abound, and bears feed on them in late summer and early fall. Also along the trail are an abundance of Indian pipes, a saprophyte that is pure white when it first emerges.

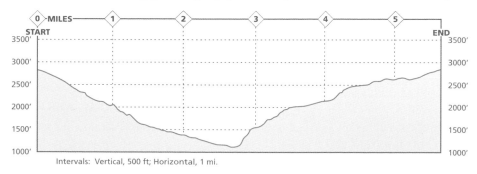

Intervals: Vertical, 500 ft; Horizontal, 1 mi.

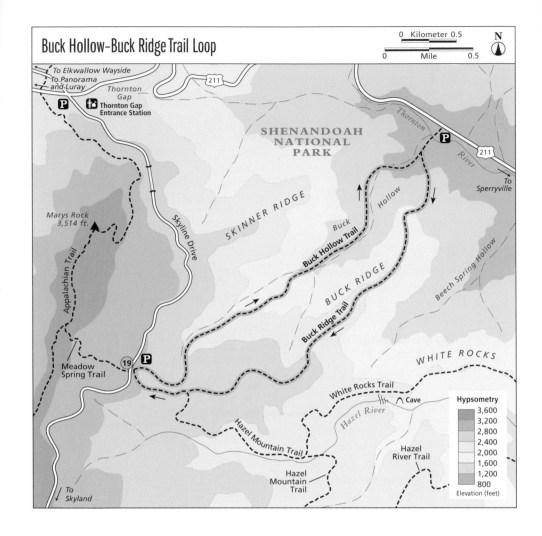

Buck Hollow–Buck Ridge Trail Loop

0   Kilometer   0.5

0   Mile   0.5

N

To Elkwallow Wayside
To Panorama
and Luray

Thornton
Gap

🅿️

Thornton Gap
Entrance Station

211

SHENANDOAH
NATIONAL
PARK

Thornton

🅿️

211

River

To
Sperryville

SKINNER RIDGE

Hollow

Buck

Buck Hollow Trail

Marys Rock
3,514 ft.

Appalachian Trail

Skyline Drive

BUCK RIDGE

Buck Ridge Trail

Beech Spring Hollow

Meadow
Spring Trail

19

🅿️

WHITE ROCKS

White Rocks Trail

Cave

Hazel River

Hypsometry

	3,600
	3,200
	2,800
	2,400
	2,000
	1,600
	1,200
	800

Elevation (feet)

Hazel Mountain Trail

Hazel
River Trail

Hazel
Mountain
Trail

To
Skyland

Toward the end of the route, still along Buck Ridge, the trail approaches a boulder field. Most of the rocks are lichen covered. With time, these elementary plants play a vital role in the creation of soils.

Again, the trail cuts sharply into the ridge, then ascends. Several tenths of a mile later the trail levels, but only briefly. It begins a gradual ascent, where it follows a rounded yet exposed ridge. A bit farther, the ridge merges with other hills. To the right climbs Skinner Ridge; to the left stands Hazel Mountain. Woods flanking the trail offer excellent wildlife habitat. We've heard a woodpecker and seen several white-tailed deer here.

At mile 5.1 you reach a trail junction with the Hazel Mountain Trail. Turn right on the Hazel Mountain Trail and return to the parking lot, completing your journey in 0.5 mile for a total of 5.6 miles.

Miles and Directions

0.0 Start at Mile 33.5 on Skyline Drive, at the south end of the Meadow Spring parking area.

0.7 Trail swings right. Cross stream on rocks.

1.8 Trail swings right, crosses small stream, then swings hard left and crosses a wider part of the stream. Avoid old road.

2.7 Cross main Buck Hollow stream.

2.8 Cement post; trail junction. Take hard right onto the Buck Ridge Trail. Cross stream and begin ascending steeply.

3.9 Views of Thornton Gap.

5.1 The Hazel Mountain Trail comes in on the left. Bear right on the Hazel Mountain Trail.

5.6 Arrive at the end of the loop and the parking lot.

The Shenandoah landscape changes with the seasons, making it worthwhile to visit numerous times throughout the year.

20 Hazel Falls and Cave

A four- to five-hour hike provides views of a small but spectacular falls, with the added feature of a lovely cave.

Skyline Mile: 33.5
Distance: 5.4 miles out and back
Approx. hiking time: 4 to 5 hours
Difficulty: Relatively easy except for the last 0.2 mile, which is very steep
Trail surface: Dirt and naturally occurring rock
Traffic: Moderate

Canine compatibility: Leashed dogs allowed
Maps: National Geographic Trails Illustrated Topographic Map 228; park handout map; Map 10, Appalachian Trail and Other Trails in Shenandoah National Park, Central District (PATC, Inc.)

Finding the trailhead: The trail begins at Mile 33.5 on Skyline Drive at the south end of the Meadow Spring parking area. Stay right on the Hazel Mountain Trail and descend. GPS: N38 38.295' / W78 18.824'

The Hike

Though not a high drop, Hazel Falls is impressive as it snakes down a mountainside, pausing long enough to create several tranquil pools. In the fall, when leaves variegated with reds, yellows, and oranges dot these pools, the falls have an added charm. Looking upstream, several caves flank the run to the right, and because of their size, the mind can have fun conjuring up the different uses people and various species of wildlife have invariably made of them through the years.

The trail to Hazel Falls and Cave begins at a large park service interpretive sign, located a few yards from the trailhead, which recounts the recent history of fire in the area. According to the sign, the Big Run Fire of 1986 burned 4,475 acres, while the Calvary Rocks Fire burned 1,431 acres in 1998. The sign further points out

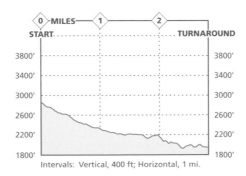

Intervals: Vertical, 400 ft; Horizontal, 1 mi.

that the largest fire in Shenandoah began in the Pinnacles Picnic Area on October 29, 2000. Another fire was discovered on Old Rag Mountain the next day. By the time the fires were contained, more than 24,000 acres had burned. The sign is worth studying, as you will see some of the devastating effects of several of the fires as you hike toward Hazel Falls. In fact, fires killed so much timber that in sections, trail crews dropped many hazardous snags to protect hikers on days when high winds often topple snags. You'll see the remaining stumps and downed snags, for there are many.

The trail is relatively flat and a generally easy hike. At mile 1.6 pick up the White Rock Trail on the left and follow it north. At mile 2.5 you'll reach the only difficult part of the hike. Though steep, the last 0.2 mile is straight down, but the short distance means your suffering will be

Hikers along this route can look forward to enjoying a rest at beautiful Hazel Falls.

brief—both down and up. But despite the brevity, don't underestimate the down portion. Sometimes those with "football knees" have more trouble going down than they do going up—even if they're otherwise in tremendous shape. Well-placed flat rocks facilitate the descent—and ascent—to and from the falls.

Enjoy the first small pool, then proceed up and along the right side of the stream. Within about 30 yards you'll come to one of the area's caves. The other cave is located high among the rocks and will require some scrambling and some searching. This cave is much larger and can be most easily accessed from the pool you first reached following that 0.2-mile descent.

The return to the trailhead is generally uphill, so factor in more time than what you needed for your trip down. Because of the area's general beauty and the amount of time you'll probably spend at the various pools and caves, you may need a total of about five hours to do this hike, particularly if you're a photographer.

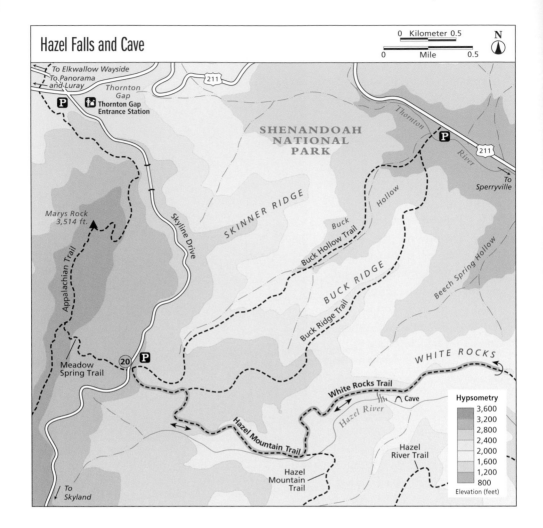

Hazel Falls and Cave

Miles and Directions

0.0   Meadow Spring parking lot; access the Hazel Mountain Trail on right.

0.5   The Buck Ridge Trail comes in from the left. Stay right (east) on Hazel Mountain Trail.

1.6   The White Rocks Trail comes in from left. Take this trail.

2.5   Signpost indicating that the cave and falls are 0.2 mile downhill; make a sharp right.

2.7   Falls and, about 100 yards upstream on the right, a cave. Other caves are in the area but require some looking. Retrace your steps to the trailhead.

5.4   Arrive back at the trailhead and the Meadow Spring parking lot.

21 Corbin Cabin Cutoff–Nicholson Hollow–Appalachian Trail Loop

This 4.2-mile hike provides glimpses of the bygone era of the mountain people.

Skyline Mile: 37.9
Distance: 4.2-mile loop
Approx. hiking time: 5 to 6 hours
Difficulty: Moderately strenuous
Trail surface: Dirt and naturally occurring rock
Traffic: Moderate

Canine compatibility: Leashed dogs allowed
Maps: National Geographic Trails Illustrated Topographic Map 228; Map 10, Appalachian Trail and Other Trails in Shenandoah National Park, Central District (PATC, Inc.)

Finding the trailhead: Park at Mile 37.9 on the west side of Skyline Drive. The trailhead is at a cement post (cross Skyline Drive at the north end of the parking lot). Access the Corbin Cabin Cutoff Trail here and travel south. GPS: N38 36.933' / W78 21.034'

The Hike

This loop trail descends on the Corbin Cabin Cutoff Trail and ascends via the Nicholson Hollow Trail and, on the other side of Skyline Drive, ends by way of the Appalachian Trail. The trail passes "Freestate" Hollow and an abandoned cabin.

Corbin Cabin and other artifacts from mountain families provide a legacy of a bygone era. Put in other words, hiking the trail provides a glimpse of what life may have been like for the men, women, and families who lived in the hollows.

George Corbin lived and farmed near the head of the Hughes River, raised his family, and, like many others, left the area when Congress created Shenandoah National Park. Oral history recalls that Corbin borrowed $500 to remodel the cabin and to add a metal roof. Today, the place must look very much like the home Corbin originally built in 1910, when he was twenty-one. The small, cozy place is separated into two sections, one for cooking and lounging, the other for sleeping, and it can be rented from the Potomac Appalachian Trail Club (see Appendix A: For More Information).

Corbin Cabin perches on a bank of the Hughes River. On the other bank, about 100 yards to the west, another cabin apparently served as the home of John T. Nicholson, an in-law of Corbin. That cabin, however, is slowly melting into the forest of pine, oak, and maple.

Other artifacts of a bygone era also exist, most of which you'll discover if you take the time. If you're interested in the area's history, take a look around—this is not an area to rush through.

Appropriately, the hike begins by descending a trail built by the mountain people who once inhabited the area. Begin at the trailhead on the south side of Skyline

In October 2000 a mysterious fire consumed nearby structures, but the concerted efforts of firefighters saved the George Corbin Cabin, located in the upper end of Nicholson Hollow. This cabin is on the National Register of Historic Places.

Drive and drop gradually for about 25 yards to a cement post that identifies the 1.4-mile hike to the Corbin Cabin.

As the trail continues to drop, you are flanked on either side by lush stands of mountain laurel. The trail is steep and rocky. After about 0.5 mile, it turns to the right in a southeasterly direction. To your east is a small, dry streambed. Shortly thereafter, the trail levels and begins to climb gradually.

About 0.9 mile you encounter the first clear remnants of early human activity. Jumbles of rocks flank the right side of the trail, and to the left (downhill) are the ruins of the John R. Nicholson Cabin. The flowing stream below it has a nice pool.

Continue on the trail to the Corbin Cabin. Just before rock hopping across the Hughes River, you may see another cabin that once belonged to Albert and Mamie Nicholson. It is hidden in the trees to the right of the trail. This one is fairly intact, allowing you to get an idea of how it was constructed.

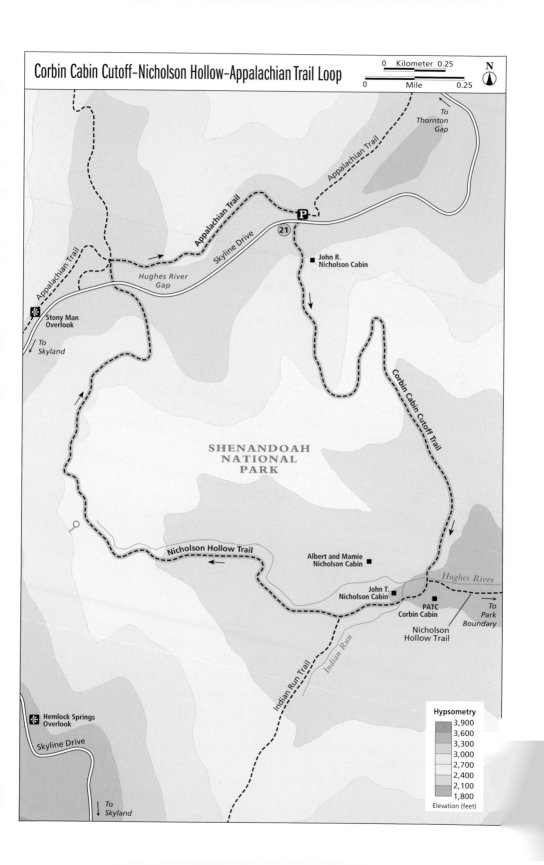

Corbin Cabin Cutoff–Nicholson Hollow–Appalachian Trail Loop

0   Kilometer 0.25

0   Mile   0.25

N

To Thornton Gap

Appalachian Trail

Appalachian Trail

P

21

Skyline Drive

John R. Nicholson Cabin

Appalachian Trail

Hughes River Gap

Stony Man Overlook

To Skyland

Corbin Cabin Cutoff Trail

SHENANDOAH NATIONAL PARK

Nicholson Hollow Trail

Albert and Mamie Nicholson Cabin

Hughes River

John T. Nicholson Cabin

PATC Corbin Cabin

To Park Boundary

Nicholson Hollow Trail

Indian Run Trail

Indian Run

Hemlock Springs Overlook

Skyline Drive

To Skyland

Hypsometry

	3,900
	3,600
	3,300
	3,000
	2,700
	2,400
	2,100
	1,800

Elevation (feet)

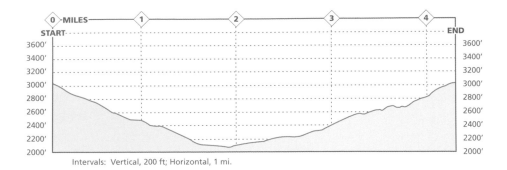

Intervals: Vertical, 200 ft; Horizontal, 1 mi.

The Corbin Cabin is in front of you as you cross the river. The Potomac Appalachian Trail Club (PATC) renovated it in 1954 and now rents it to hikers. The spot is idyllic, and you may want to have a picnic in the yard if no one is currently renting.

At this point, you must make a choice. Do you retrace your steps, for a hike of 2.9 miles? Or do you return via the somewhat steep Nicholson Hollow Trail and add another 1.4 miles to your route?

If you choose to continue on the loop hike, return to the cement post below the Corbin Cabin and take the old mountain road that leads west (left). This is the Nicholson Hollow Trail, which ascends (steeply in places) to Skyline Drive. The first part of the trail is extremely rough and rocky as it crosses Indian Run (often dry) and climbs through the forest. More than a mile from the cabin, you'll encounter a walled-in spring on the left side of the trail, but it is usually dry.

The upper portion of the Nicholson Hollow Trail is a fairly straight climb to Skyline Drive. The path is flanked by mountain laurel and lots of oak.

Upon reaching the drive, turn left and walk south for about 75 yards. Cross the drive to your right at an opening in the trees and continue straight ahead to access the AT at a cement post. Turn northeast (right) onto the AT. Follow it as it winds up and down to the parking area, thus completing this scenic loop.

Miles and Directions

0.0   Start at Mile 37.9 on west side of Skyline Drive.

0.5   The Corbin Cabin Cutoff Trail goes left, then right, to parallel a streambed.

0.9   Stone wall on right. John R. Nicholson Cabin ruins downhill to left.

1.4   John T. Nicholson cabin in woods to right of trail. Hughes River crossing. Cement post below Corbin Cabin. Head west on Nicholson Hollow Trail.

1.5   Junction with the Indian Run Trail. Keep straight on Nicholson Hollow Trail.

1.8   Indian Run stream crossing (often dry).

2.9   Enclosed spring on left.

3.8   Skyline Drive. Turn south onto the drive; cross drive to cement post. Turn northeast onto the Appalachian Trail.

4.2   Follow the AT to arrive back at the trailhead and your vehicle.

22 Stony Man Trail

This interpretive trail climbs to the peak of Stony Man mountain.

Skyline Mile: 41.7
Distance: 1.4-mile lariat
Approx. hiking time: 1 to 3 hours
Difficulty: Easy
Trail surface: Dirt and naturally occurring rock
Traffic: Moderate to heavy

Canine compatibility: Dogs not allowed
Maps: National Geographic Trails Illustrated Topographic Map 228; Map 10, Appalachian Trail and Other Trails in Shenandoah National Park, Central District (PATC, Inc.)

Finding the trailhead: The trailhead is at the north entrance of Skyland—a complex that includes a lodge, restaurant, and riding stable—at Mile 41.7. Park just inside at the Stony Man Trail lot. At the cement post, access the Appalachian Trail north. GPS: N38 35.6113' / W78 22.5402'

The Hike

At 4,011 feet, Stony Man is the park's second-highest mountain after Hawksbill. The park provides a brochure for this interpretive hike, which includes twenty stops. Pets are not allowed on this trail.

From the Stony Man parking area inside Skyland, access the Appalachian Trail at the cement post. Follow the trail north (right) for 0.4 mile. Here, the AT reaches its highest point in Shenandoah. At this point, the Stony Man Trail continues straight while the AT goes right. Follow the Stony Man Trail. In another 0.1 mile the Stony Man Trail splits. Either fork will take you to the summit, because the two trails actually meet to form a loop.

At the summit, take time, particularly in the spring, to search the sky for falcons. Over the years, the National Park Service has sponsored a peregrine reintroduction program intended to restore the nation's

Turkey tail fungus grows on this decomposing mass of wood.

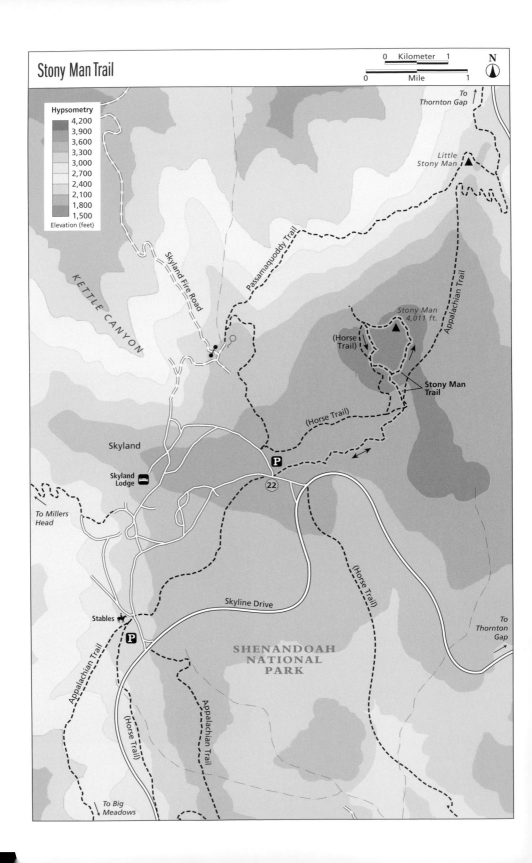

Stony Man Trail

Hypsometry

4,200
3,900
3,600
3,300
3,000
2,700
2,400
2,100
1,800
1,500

Elevation (feet)

KETTLE CANYON

Skyland Fire Road

Passamaquoddy Trail

Stony Man
4,011 ft.

(Horse Trail)

Stony Man Trail

(Horse Trail)

Skyland

Skyland Lodge

To Millers Head

22

Appalachian Trail

Little Stony Man

To Thornton Gap

Skyline Drive

(Horse Trail)

To Thornton Gap

SHENANDOAH NATIONAL PARK

Stables

Appalachian Trail

(Horse Trail)

Appalachian Trail

To Big Meadows

0   Kilometer   1

0   Mile   1

N

fastest-diving bird to the wild. This program, also embraced by the state of Virginia, took place from 1989 to 1993 and from 2000 to 2005 in Shenandoah.

To complete the hike, continue around the loop and back to the AT. You're on familiar ground; return the way you came.

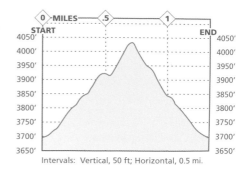

Intervals: Vertical, 50 ft; Horizontal, 0.5 mi.

Miles and Directions

0.0 Start at Mile 41.7, north entrance of Skyland, just inside Stony Man Trail lot.

0.4 Junction at cement post with the Stony Man Trail. Go straight on the blue-blazed Stony Man Trail.

0.5 Fork in trail. Stay right.

0.7 Summit of Stony Man, cement post, and junction. Right or left trails form loop to viewpoint.

1.0 Cement post and junction with the Appalachian Trail. Head south on the AT.

1.4 Arrive back at the trailhead and the Stony Man parking lot.

23 Millers Head

A short hike starting from the Skyland complex leads to an observation platform with delightful views.

Skyline Mile: 42.5
Distance: 1.6 miles out and back
Approx. hiking time: 1 to 2 hours
Difficulty: Easy
Trail surface: Dirt and naturally occurring rock
Traffic: Moderate

Canine compatibility: Leashed dogs allowed
Maps: National Geographic Trails Illustrated Topographic Map 228; Map 10, Appalachian Trail and Other Trails in Shenandoah National Park, Central District (PATC, Inc.)

Finding the trailhead: From the north, turn right off Skyline Drive at Mile 42.5, the south entrance into the Skyland complex, where many folks stay during their visit. Pass the stables on your left. The road forks; follow the left fork. Soon you'll encounter a gravel road; turn in and park. Walk about 75 yards up the paved road (to the top of Bushytop mountain) to a cement post indicating the MILLERS HEAD TRAIL. Turn left (west) onto the trail. GPS: N38 35.463' / W78 23.039'

The Hike

You can begin your hike in one of two ways. You can walk up the gravel road from your car for 0.2 mile to the Millers Head Trail on the left, or you can walk up the paved road to the cement post. Either way, you'll reach Bushytop Mountain. There you see some large microwave dishes, part of the Skyland communication system.

Once on the Millers Head Trail, head downhill via a series of switchbacks. About 0.3 mile before the observation platform, you encounter a cement post. Keep going down the trail to the platform. The best views are from the Millers Head observation platform, at an elevation of about 3,460 feet. You'll have full views to the west of the Page Valley, the town of Luray, Massanutten Mountain, Stony Man, Hawksbill, and Marys Rock. Below the platform is a hang glider launch site.

Staghorn sumac is edible and will appear almost velvety when it is ready for consumption. The taste is tart and some say a bit lemony.

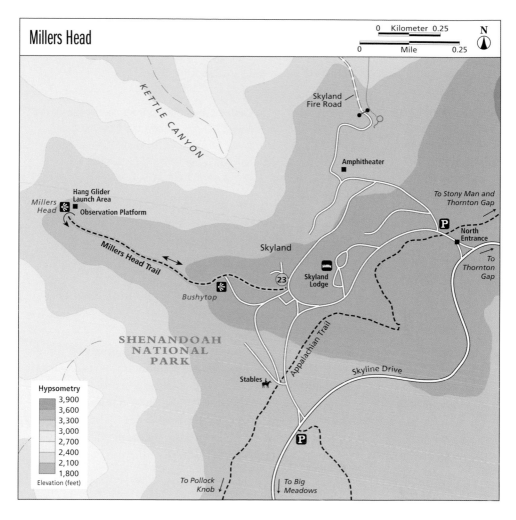

Millers Head

Kilometer 0.25 — Mile 0.25

N

KETTLE CANYON

Skyland Fire Road

Amphitheater

Hang Glider Launch Area

Millers Head

Observation Platform

Millers Head Trail

Skyland

To Stony Man and Thornton Gap

P

North Entrance

To Thornton Gap

23

Skyland Lodge

Bushytop

Appalachian Trail

SHENANDOAH NATIONAL PARK

Skyline Drive

Stables

Hypsometry

Elevation (feet)
3,900
3,600
3,300
3,000
2,700
2,400
2,100
1,800

P

To Pollock Knob

To Big Meadows

Miles and Directions

0.0 Start near Skyline Drive at Mile 42.5.

0.2 Summit of Bushytop. View of Kettle Canyon Skytop to the right. Begin descent on the Millers Head Trail.

0.5 Cement post. Head downhill to observation platform.

0.8 Observation platform on Millers Head. Retrace your steps.

1.6 Arrive back at trailhead.

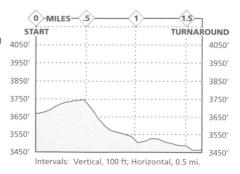

Intervals: Vertical, 100 ft; Horizontal, 0.5 mi.

24 Limberlost

This short walk is along a crushed greenstone surface.

Skyline Mile: 43.0
Distance: 1.3-mile loop
Approx. hiking time: 1 to 2 hours
Difficulty: Easy
Trail surface: Crushed greenstone
Traffic: Moderate to heavy, depending on time of year

Canine compatibility: Dogs not allowed
Maps: National Geographic Trails Illustrated Topographic Map 228; Map 10, Appalachian Trail and Other Trails in Shenandoah National Park, Central District (PATC, Inc.)

Finding the trailhead: The trail begins at Mile 43.0 on Skyline Drive. Turn east off the drive at the Limberlost Trail sign. Park at the upper Old Rag Fire Road in a paved lot. GPS: N38 34.801304' / W78 22.875556'

The Hike

The Limberlost Trail, once lined by ancient hemlocks, can provide inspiration for all. The nearly level path is lined with mountain laurel. Until recently, it was also rimmed by the hemlock trees, some said to be 400 years old. Sadly, the exotic insect pest known as the woolly adelgid, which sucks the stored food from hemlock needles, wreaked havoc on Limberlost's hemlocks. Now all are gone—dead—having either fallen or been cut down for safety. The trees will lie in place, gradually decaying into the soil. A different plant life-form will begin to arise now that the sun can reach the forest floor.

The oak trees in Limberlost have also suffered greatly due to gypsy moth invasions. However, wildflowers bloom in spring and summer; white pine, birch, and maple trees still flourish in this beautiful place. Limberlost is truly "the story of a changing forest."

The Limberlost Forest also preserves some of the park's oldest and largest red spruce trees. This species is a remnant from the last ice age, and one such tree is believed to be more than 250 years old. This patriarch stands alone by a small stream that you will encounter along the walk.

Addie Pollock laid the groundwork for preserving the Limberlost Forest. In 1920 she bought one hundred of the largest trees in the area for $1,000. Her husband, George, who established Skyland, named the remnant forest after the Gene Stratton Porter novel *Girl of the Limberlost*.

Because this has been designated an Outstanding Natural Area, no bicycles, pets, or camping is allowed along the trail in the Limberlost. The reconstructed trail was officially dedicated in the summer of 1997.

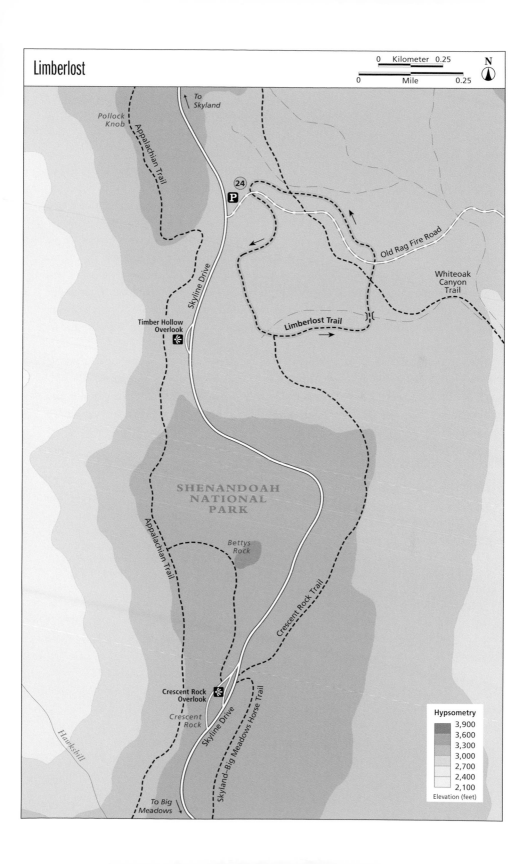

Limberlost

0　Kilometer　0.25

0　Mile　0.25

N

Pollock Knob

Appalachian Trail

To Skyland

24

P

Skyline Drive

Old Rag Fire Road

Whiteoak Canyon Trail

Timber Hollow Overlook

Limberlost Trail

SHENANDOAH NATIONAL PARK

Bettys Rock

Appalachian Trail

Crescent Rock Trail

Hawksbill

Crescent Rock Overlook

Crescent Rock

Skyland–Big Meadows Horse Trail

Skyline Drive

To Big Meadows

Hypsometry

3,900
3,600
3,300
3,000
2,700
2,400
2,100

Elevation (feet)

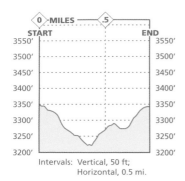

Intervals: Vertical, 50 ft;
Horizontal, 0.5 mi.

After parking, read the information on the kiosk and the cement post. Note that other trails radiate from and cross the hard-packed crushed greenstone Limberlost Trail. The path is described in a counterclockwise direction, starting to the right (south) from the trailhead.

As you meander through what was once an old meadow, notice the abundance of wood benches for resting and observing. There is a bench about every 400 feet. Cross a boardwalk over a wet, swampy area. After 0.4 mile, you encounter a cement post indicating that at this point the Crescent Rock Trail enters the Limberlost Trail from Skyline Drive. The Limberlost Trail proceeds straight ahead and offers yet another lesson in the devastating power of nature. In the fall of 1996, Tropical Storm Fran swept through the area, uprooting many mature trees and causing extensive trail erosion. The latter was repaired in 1997 after several months of work. More recent storms have also caused damage.

At 0.7 mile you cross a large wooden bridge. Beyond that, a cement post points the way to the Whiteoak Canyon Trail access.

Near the trail's end, another cement post shows the Whiteoak Canyon Trail going left and right. Stay on the crushed greenstone trail with the Limberlost markers to the trail's end.

Miles and Directions

0.0 Start at the Old Rag Fire Road near Mile 43.0 on Skyline Drive.

0.4 Cement post showing the Crescent Rock Trail going south. Stay on the wooden boardwalk of the Limberlost Trail.

0.7 Cross wooden bridge.

1.0 Cross other trails such as the Whiteoak Canyon Trail, Old Rag Fire Road, Whiteoak Canyon Trail (a second time), and Skyland–Big Meadows Horse Trail. Stay on the Limberlost Trail.

1.3 Arrive back at the trailhead and parking lot. Loop completed.

25 Cedar Run–Whiteoak Canyon Loop

A very strenuous loop hike through two gorges passes nine beautiful waterfalls in Cedar Run and Whiteoak Canyon.

Skyline Mile: 45.6
Distance: 8.8-mile loop
Approx. hiking time: 6 to 9 hours
Difficulty: Strenuous
Trail surface: Dirt and naturally occurring rock
Traffic: Light on Cedar Run, heavy in Whiteoak Canyon, especially on weekends

Canine compatibility: Leashed dogs allowed
Maps: National Geographic Trails Illustrated Topographic Map 228; Map 10, Appalachian Trail and Other Trails in Shenandoah National Park, Central District (PATC, Inc.)

Finding the trailhead: The hike begins at Mile 45.6 on Skyline Drive at the Hawksbill Gap parking area. Park on the east side of the road if you can—the trail begins at the cement post. There is additional parking on the west side. GPS: N38 33.370963' / W78 23.197997'

The Hike

According to signs at the trailhead, the 6.3-mile descent and return ascent along the Whiteoak Canyon Trail can be made in six hours. That is certainly true, particularly for someone in good shape. However, because the trail takes you to an area of such great natural beauty, it would be far better, and probably necessary, to plan to make this a full-day hike. Pack a picnic lunch, swimsuit, and camera, for the trail puts you within easy access of two beautiful waterfalls, relatively easy access of four more, and not-so-easy access of three others, for a total of nine falls.

For this incredibly beautiful yet strenuous hike, you need lots of endurance. The trail takes you straight down an extremely rocky, rough path; it winds through the wilderness and leads through areas of great beauty. Because of the area's precipitous nature, this is one of the few places in the park that was never inhabited. Be sure to carry plenty of water.

The first trail, Cedar Run, is also a place where accidents could easily happen. We both fell on slick rocks. A note, too, about trail maintenance: It is as well cleared as possible and could not be much better given the nature of the terrain. Hike the entire loop only if you have at least six hours. On the descents, it seems each step must be planned, and the ascents are steep enough to force a slow pace. However, if you're up to it, the rewards are among the park's best.

Begin the hike on the Cedar Run Trail, at the cement post on the east side of Skyline Drive at the Hawksbill Gap parking area (Mile 45.6). Remain on the Cedar Run Trail and avoid turning onto two other trails that diverge from this trail within the first 100 feet. Simply follow the cement posts that indicate you're on the Cedar Run Trail.

Ascending White Oak Canyon can be arduous.

A steep descent begins immediately as this rough, rocky trail passes through the woods and courses beneath a canopy of oak trees. Soon a dry streambed can be seen to the right, and it isn't long before the flow begins, gently coursing over rocks and into small pools. The peace, beauty, and solitude of Cedar Run are a delight. We saw a black bear cub scamper across the trail and into the woods here. Hiking at a slow pace is a necessity since slick rocks of varying sizes are potentially dangerous and demand calculated steps. By going slowly you'll have better glimpses of the surroundings.

At about 1.1 miles you encounter the first view of lovely falls and pools. For the next 0.6 mile, the beautiful vista continues with a series of falls and pools, giving an understanding to the word "run." It's easy as well to comprehend why this is one of the few areas of the park that was never inhabited or farmed by the mountain folk.

Hikers find shelter from rain in rocks along Cedar Run.

At 1.5 miles the trail crosses Cedar Run on rocks and climbs the opposite bank. Soon it winds back to parallel the stream again. Then the water courses down a steep descent and settles into a gorgeous pool at the base of Half Mile Cliffs. Take time out to soak your feet or dunk yourself. There are no rock faces to climb here, and a more idyllic setting is hard to imagine.

The rocky trail continues, now high above the stream but still with steep declines. It finally drops to meet the stream at 2.6 miles. Look across the stream to locate the blue blazes on the other side, for this is the crossing point. If you walk as far as the orange blazes on rocks and trees, you'll be on private property. The stream crossing is easy, but beware of the slick rocks.

At 2.8 miles you encounter a cement post. Stay to the left. In order to access the Whiteoak Canyon Trail, which is 0.8 mile farther, the trail splits and becomes the Cedar Run Link Trail. For this next 0.8 mile, the path becomes a delight to sore feet and ankles. No more rocks, just a nice, wide, soft path with gentle ups and downs. The spur leads to a stream crossing (now Whiteoak Run) at about mile 3.6. As you cross, you see a cement post directly in front of you. Take the left trail, which is the Whiteoak Canyon Trail. Skyline Drive is 4.8 miles ahead.

The trail now ascends Whiteoak Canyon. The ascent is quite steep, with lots of rocks to scramble around. Great views of waterfalls and pools begin: These are closer to the trail than those along the Cedar Run Trail, and they make great picnic and

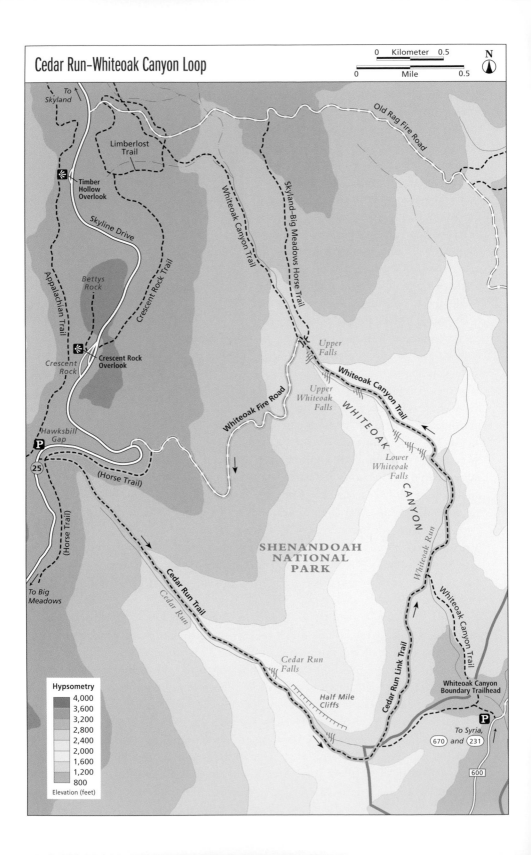

Cedar Run–Whiteoak Canyon Loop

0   Kilometer   0.5

0   Mile   0.5

N

To Skyland

Old Rag Fire Road

Limberlost Trail

Timber Hollow Overlook

Whiteoak Canyon Trail

Skyland–Big Meadows Horse Trail

Skyline Drive

Crescent Rock Trail

Bettys Rock

Appalachian Trail

Upper Falls

Whiteoak Canyon Trail

Crescent Rock

Crescent Rock Overlook

Whiteoak Fire Road

Upper Whiteoak Falls

WHITEOAK

Lower Whiteoak Falls

Hawksbill Gap

P

CANYON

25

(Horse Trail)

Whiteoak Run

SHENANDOAH NATIONAL PARK

(Horse Trail)

Cedar Run Trail

Whiteoak Canyon Trail

To Big Meadows

Cedar Run

Cedar Run Link Trail

Cedar Run Falls

Whiteoak Canyon Boundary Trailhead

Half Mile Cliffs

P

To Syria, 670 and 231

600

Hypsometry

	Elevation
	4,000
	3,600
	3,200
	2,800
	2,400
	2,000
	1,600
	1,200
	800

Elevation (feet)

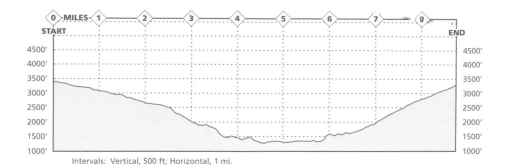

Intervals: Vertical, 500 ft; Horizontal, 1 mi.

resting spots. They also provide great photographic opportunities, particularly on overcast days. Ideally, you should use a tripod.

After following this path straight up for about 2.5 miles, you encounter a cement post. This is the last waterfall along the route outlined here—and obviously the first for those proceeding from the top. The route swings right, still climbing. About 0.2 mile later, walk out on the rocks to the left for an awesome view of the falls and the pool below. A nearby sign indicates that camping is prohibited from this point back down to the junction with the spur trail, since the area is designated as an Outstanding Natural Area.

Several trails converge after the viewpoint. Stay left, then right, following the blue blazes uphill to the footbridge on the left. Cross the bridge to the cement post and go left onto the connector path, which parallels the stream for a short distance. The trail swings left onto a wide old road and horse trail—the Whiteoak Fire Road—at about mile 6.6.

The ascent on the fire road is steady and gradual. Finally, at mile 8.3 you encounter a cement post. Turn left and walk a long 0.5 mile on a yellow-blazed horse trail. At the very last cement post, within sight of the road, swing right to the trailhead to complete the loop and return to your vehicle.

Miles and Directions

0.0 Start at the cement post in the parking area of Hawksbill Gap.

1.5 Cross Cedar Run and climb the bank.

2.6 Second stream crossing on left. Watch for and follow blue blazes. Do not continue straight on the old road as it enters private property.

2.8 Cement post at split in trail. Go left onto the Cedar Run Link Trail.

3.6 Cross Whiteoak Run to the cement post. Go left, now on the Whiteoak Canyon Trail.

6.1 Cement post at base of first falls. Trail swings to the right.

6.3 Walk out on rocks to the left for beautiful views of falls and pool.

6.6 Cement post. Trail becomes Whiteoak Fire Road. Go left, then right, following blue blazes to the footbridge.

8.3 Cement post. Turn left. It's a long 0.5 mile to your vehicle.

8.8 At last, the trail bears right at another cement post and continues to the trailhead, completing the loop at Hawksbill Gap.

26 Hawksbill Summit

A loop hike to the summit of the park's highest mountain offers spectacular views.

Skyline Mile: 45.6
Distance: 2.8-mile loop
Approx. hiking time: 2 to 3 hours
Difficulty: Moderate
Trail surface: Dirt with naturally occurring rocks

Traffic: Moderate to heavy
Canine compatibility: Leashed dogs allowed
Maps: National Geographic Trails Illustrated Topographic Map 228; Map 10, Appalachian Trail and Other Trails in Shenandoah National Park, Central District (PATC, Inc.)

Finding the trailhead: Park at the Hawksbill Gap parking area at Mile 45.6 on Skyline Drive. The trailhead is at the north end of the lot. GPS: N38 33.369' / W78 23.214'

The Hike

At 4,051 feet, Hawksbill is the park's highest peak. It's also a good place to see birds. In fact, much of Virginia's endangered peregrine falcon history has been recorded at Hawksbill and on several other surrounding park mountains. Since 1989, biologists have raised and released thirty-seven young falcons from Hawksbill and Franklin Cliffs. In July 1994, 1996, and 1997, biologists confirmed a pair of peregrines had successfully nested in the park. With luck, you may see peregrines from atop Hawksbill.

Several trails lead to the peak, and because the view from the peak is so commanding, the somewhat steep climb is well worth the effort even if you don't see peregrines. Because the loop hike to the summit travels partly along the Appalachian Trail, the trek has added allure. Near the summit the trail passes through an area designated an Outstanding Natural Area, which is precisely what the name implies. All along the way, mountain laurel flanks either side of the trail, adding blends of incredible color.

Byrds Nest Shelter No. 2 is located at the summit of Hawksbill. The three-sided structure was built with funds provided by Sen. Harry F. Byrd Sr. and is one of four such shelters in the park. No water is available at the site, and camping is not permitted on or near the summit.

The trail begins at the north end of the Hawksbill Gap parking lot at Mile 45.6 on Skyline Drive. A level spur trail about 100 yards long leads to the

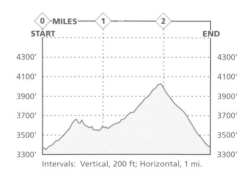

Intervals: Vertical, 200 ft; Horizontal, 1 mi.

At 4,051 feet Hawksbill summit is the park's highest point, commanding some impressive views.

Appalachian Trail, which is marked with white blazes. Turn south (left) onto the AT and begin climbing. The trail is rocky and, as always, good hiking boots are recommended.

Within 0.4 mile the trail approaches a rock slide. After another 25 yards, it passes a second talus slope, and you will have a view of mountains and valleys spilling off to the west. Half a mile from the trailhead, the trail approaches a rock-strewn outcropping, suggestive once again of the erosion of the park's mountains. Lichens cover the rocks, and here and there trees struggle for a foothold in soils formed relatively recently.

Toward the summit, foxtail blooms in great abundance. Columbine also rears its head, as does a species of geranium. Several rock outcrops tilt upward, revealing layers that look like a stack of pancakes. The area is one of outstanding natural splendor.

About a mile along the trail, you come to a cement post noting the mileage along the AT and the distance to the Rock Spring Cabin. The post points toward Hawksbill and back toward Fishers Gap. Make a hard left onto the Salamander Trail at this point and continue climbing. The summit is only 0.9 mile away. Within 0.25 mile of the junction, the rocks covering the trail become more exposed, probably the result of tremendous spring runoff. Near the top, the trail joins a fire road. Keep climbing to

Hawksbill Summit

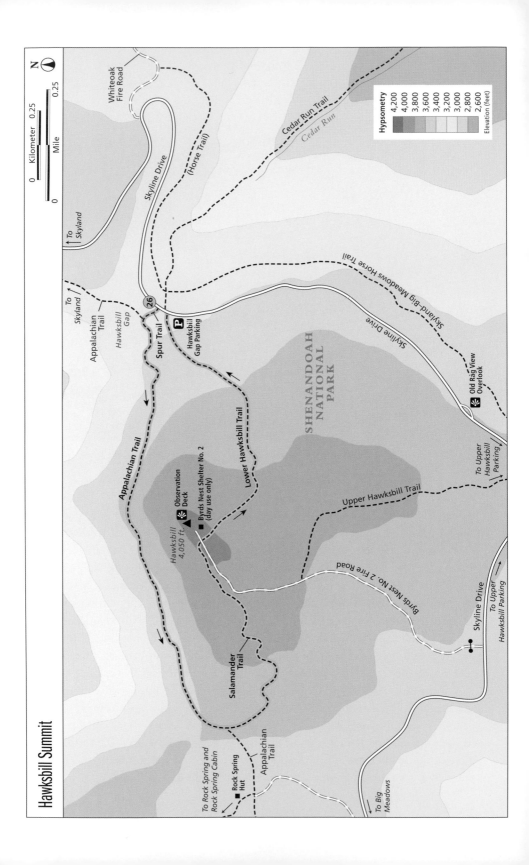

N

Kilometer
0   0.25
Mile
0   0.25

To Skyland

Whiteoak
Fire Road

Skyline Drive

(Horse Trail)

Cedar Run Trail

Cedar Run

Hypsometry
4,200
4,000
3,800
3,600
3,400
3,200
3,000
2,800
2,600
Elevation (feet)

To Skyland

Appalachian
Trail

Hawksbill
Gap

Spur Trail

26

P
Hawksbill
Gap Parking

Skyland–Big Meadows Horse Trail

SHENANDOAH
NATIONAL
PARK

Skyline Drive

Old Rag View
Overlook

Appalachian Trail

Observation
Deck

Byrds Nest Shelter No. 2
(day use only)

Lower Hawksbill Trail

Hawksbill
4,050 ft.

Upper Hawksbill Trail

To Upper
Hawksbill
Parking

Salamander
Trail

Byrds Nest No. 2 Fire Road

Skyline Drive

To Upper
Hawksbill Parking

To Rock Spring and
Rock Spring Cabin

Rock Spring
Hut

Appalachian
Trail

To Big
Meadows

the summit, not far away. There, you find Byrds Nest Shelter No. 2. No water is available at the site, and camping is not permitted on or near the summit.

The shelter is surrounded by red spruce, balsam fir, and mountain ash. Continue the last few yards to the observation platform, and you are standing on the highest point in the park.

The view from the top of Hawksbill is commanding and panoramic. Mountains roll off in all directions, blending gradually into yet more mountains in the hazy distance. Within the cement overlook, the park service has placed a huge compass, which helps those with maps to orient themselves. Stony Man, with its jagged features, is to the north, while Brown Mountain spreads neatly to the east. To the south is Graves Mountain. Just below, Skyline Drive threads through the hardwood forest. The town of Luray lies to the northwest.

To return to Hawksbill Gap from the summit, retrace your steps to the shelter and take the fire road to its left (south). This leads very shortly to a cement post. Turn left onto the Lower Hawksbill Trail and follow it for 0.7 mile to the parking lot. The descent is steep and the going a bit slow for some.

Although it seems that returning to Hawksbill Gap involves fairly easy route finding, the series of trails that ascend—and descend—can be confusing. Make sure you follow the metal bands on the cement posts that take you back to Hawksbill Gap or you'll have to hike an additional mile along Skyline Drive.

Option: To make a shorter out-and-back hike of 1.9 miles, access the Lower Hawksbill Trail near the center of the parking lot at Hawksbill Gap. The trail begins in the woods and ascends steeply for about 0.7 mile to a cement post near the summit. Turn right and go another 0.1 mile, passing Byrds Nest Shelter No. 2 and reaching the observation deck at the summit. Retrace your steps.

Miles and Directions

0.0 Start at Hawksbill Gap parking area at Mile 45.6 on Skyline Drive.

0.5 First of three talus slopes; some views.

1.0 Cement post. Make hard left onto the Salamander Trail.

1.9 Hawksbill summit and observation deck.

2.1 Cement post below and left of the shelter. Turn left onto the Lower Hawksbill Trail.

2.8 Arrive back at the parking lot at Hawksbill Gap. End of loop hike.

27 Rose River

The trail provides access to a number of pools and cascades, including Rose River Falls.

Skyline Mile: 49.4
Distance: 4-mile loop
Difficulty: Moderate
Traffic: Moderate

Canine compatibility: Leashed dogs only
Maps: National Geographic Trails Illustrated Topographic Map 228; Map 10, Appalachian Trail and Other Trails in Shenandoah National Park, Central District (PATC, Inc.)

Finding the trailhead: Park at Mile 49.4, at the Fishers Gap Overlook parking lot on the west side of Skyline Drive. Walk to the north end and cross the drive to the east. Go down the fire road to a cement post. Turn left onto the Rose River Loop Trail (blazed yellow at first, then veer right later at the blue blaze). GPS: N38 32.009254' / W78 25.252717'

The Hike

Rose River Falls is a delightful series of large cascades that drop gently over a distance of several hundred yards. After each rush, the creek seems to regroup at a quiet pool, then hurry forward once again. You can follow the trail down to the falls and retrace your steps, but it is much more rewarding to make this a loop hike, dropping down to the falls, then continuing out and back along the Hogcamp Branch, eventually returning to the Fishers Gap Overlook parking lot via the wide and heavily used Rose River Fire Road.

Begin by descending on the Rose River Fire Road. Within 100 feet you see a cement post with the familiar aluminum strip noting distances. From the post to Rose River Falls, it's 1.2 miles—as the sign notes. Turn left onto the yellow-blazed Skyland–Big Meadows Horse Trail and follow it for 0.6 mile to another cement post. The horse trail goes left (north). Stay right on the blue-blazed Rose River Loop Trail.

Within another 0.5 mile the trail approaches the Rose River and begins to parallel it. The Rose River is immediately attractive. It presents itself as a delightful stream of short cascades, natural flutes and small pools, and steep but abbreviated banks. The trail veers away from the falls, then quickly returns to parallel the river. Again it presents itself as a series of small pools and brief drops.

All too soon the trail leaves the Rose River and assumes a more southerly course. At 1.9 miles, a cement block lies mysteriously in the trail. Rooted in the cement are metal rods with nuts. Perhaps it had something to do with the old copper mine site, uphill on the right.

At 2.1 miles from the trailhead, the trail approaches the Hogcamp Branch and, in about 100 feet, crosses the creek on a bridge. The trail climbs, still paralleling Hogcamp Branch, which also contains its share of pools and runs. At 2.9 miles the trail

Rose River

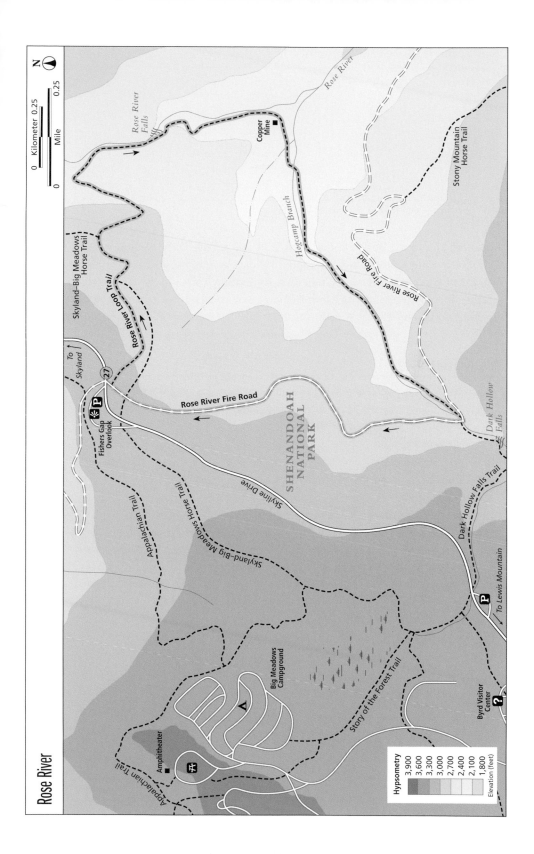

Rose River Falls

Copper Mine

Rose River

Hogcamp Branch

Rose River Fire Road

Stony Mountain Horse Trail

Skyland–Big Meadows Horse Trail

Rose River Loop Trail

Fishers Gap Overlook

To Skyland

27

Rose River Fire Road

Appalachian Trail

Skyland–Big Meadows Horse Trail

Skyline Drive

SHENANDOAH NATIONAL PARK

Dark Hollow Falls

Dark Hollow Falls Trail

To Lewis Mountain

Appalachian Trail

Amphitheater

Big Meadows Campground

Story of the Forest Trail

Byrd Visitor Center

N

0   Kilometer   0.25

0   0.25
        Mile

Hypsometry

3,900
3,600
3,300
3,000
2,700
2,400
2,100
1,800
Elevation (feet)

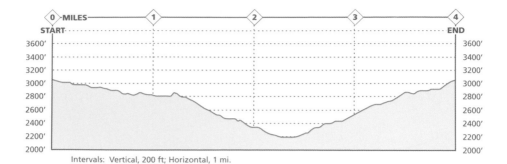

Intervals: Vertical, 200 ft; Horizontal, 1 mi.

links with the lower Dark Hollow Falls Trail and to the Dark Hollow parking lot; the falls are only a short climb away (0.3 mile). The trail crosses the nearby bridge, which also provides access to the trail up Dark Hollow Falls. On the north side of the bridge—the north side of Hogcamp Branch—you'll encounter another cement post directing you to turn right (north) onto the Rose River Fire Road, which leads to the parking area at the Fishers Gap Overlook, thus completing the loop hike.

Miles and Directions

0.0 Start at the cement post near Fishers Gap Overlook parking lot at Mile 49.4.

0.6 Cement post. Stay straight on the blue-blazed Rose River Loop Trail. The Skyland–Big Meadows Horse Trail heads off to the left (north).

1.0 Trail turns sharply to the right.

1.2 Top of Rose River Falls.

1.7 Trail bears right, ascending Hogcamp Branch.

1.8 Old copper mine on right.

1.9 Cross Hogcamp Branch on bridge, staying on trail. Do not turn left.

2.9 Cement post and junction with the Rose River Fire Road. Turn right, cross Hogcamp Branch, and stay to right on the fire road. (You can also turn left for a 0.6-mile out-and-back trip to Dark Hollow Falls.)

4.0 Cross Skyline Drive to arrive back at the trailhead and the Fishers Gap Overlook parking area, ending the loop hike.

28 Dark Hollow Falls

A short out-and-back hike leads to one of the park's most popular and easily accessible falls.

Skyline Mile: 50.7
Distance: 1.4 miles out and back
Approx. hiking time: 2 to 3 hours
Difficulty: Moderately strenuous going in; strenuous coming out
Trail surface: Dirt with naturally occurring rocks

Traffic: Heavy; highest use in the park
Canine compatibility: Dogs not allowed
Maps: National Geographic Trails Illustrated Topographic Map 228; Map 10, Appalachian Trail and Other Trails in Shenandoah National Park, Central District (PATC, Inc.)

Finding the trailhead: The trail begins at Mile 50.7 on Skyline Drive. GPS: N38 32.627' / W78 23.597'

The Hike

The trail descends from the parking lot and follows Hogcamp Branch. At 0.6 mile you encounter an overlook of 70-foot Dark Hollow Falls. Along the trail, you encounter rails that shouldn't require a statement of intent but apparently do, because invariably some fail to realize that not only are the fences intended to prevent further erosion but also to save life and limb. This is one place with a history of injury. Please remain on the trail! Rocks can be wet and very slippery.

Continue for another 0.1 mile to the base of Dark Hollow Falls. If you enjoy the spectacle, be aware that you're in good company. According to a resident naturalist, this scene was once appreciated by Thomas Jefferson.

The falls are obviously appealing, especially if you consider their source. Hogcamp Branch drains the Big Meadow Swamp, which can be

Waters at Dark Hollow Falls drop nearly 70 feet in a series of cascades and were once admired by Thomas Jefferson.

Dark Hollow Falls

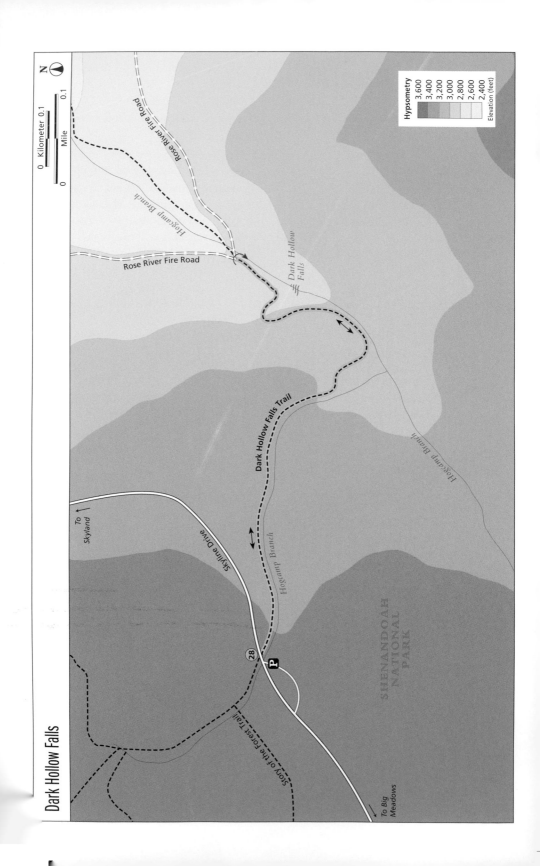

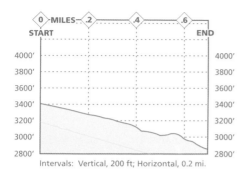

Intervals: Vertical, 200 ft; Horizontal, 0.2 mi.

relatively dry during some of the summer. Nevertheless, Hogcamp manages to gather enough water in its progression toward Dark Hollow Falls to create a lovely falls.

You can descend farther to enjoy yet other falls created by Hogcamp Branch, or you can return to the trailhead. From the base of Dark Hollow Falls, you will climb 0.7 mile and about 440 feet in elevation to your starting point. The descent to the falls is the easy part of the hike.

Miles and Directions

0.0 Start at the parking lot, Mile 50.7 on Skyline Drive

0.6 Overlook of Dark Hollow Falls.

0.7 Base of Dark Hollow Falls. Retrace your steps.

1.4 Arrive back at the trailhead.

Stairs help hikers make their ascent and descent along the trail to Dark Hollow Falls.

An easy, one- to two-hour interpretive, round-trip hike tours a trail showing plant succession in the surrounding Blue Ridge forest.

Skyline Mile: 51.0
Distance: 1.8-mile loop
Approx. hiking time: 1 to 2 hours
Difficulty: Easy
Trail surface: Dirt with naturally occurring rocks

Traffic: Moderate to heavy
Canine compatibility: Dogs not allowed
Maps: National Geographic Trails Illustrated Topographic Map 228; Map 10, Appalachian Trail and Other Trails in Shenandoah National Park, Central District (PATC, Inc.)

Finding the trailhead: The trail begins at Mile 51.0, across Skyline Drive from the Harry F. Byrd Sr. Visitor Center. Stay on the paved path to the right. GPS: N38 31.128' / W78 26.146'

Wildlife is often seen along the Story of the Forest Trail.

Story of the Forest Trail

Big Meadows Lodge Complex

Amphitheater

Appalachian Trail

Skyland-Big Meadows Horse Trail

To Skyland

Lewis Spring Falls Trail

Blackrock
3,721 ft.

Blackrock
Trail

Big Meadows
Campground

Story of the Forest Trail

Skyline Drive

SHENANDOAH
NATIONAL
PARK

Appalachian Trail

Water
Treatment
Plant

Lewis
Spring
Falls

29

Hogcamp Branch

Byrd
Visitor Center

BIG
MEADOWS

Tanner
Ridge
Overlook

Rapidan Fire Road

Skyland-Big Meadows Horse Trail

To Lewis
Mountain

Hypsometry	
	3,900
	3,600
	3,300
	3,000
	2,700
	2,400
	2,100
Elevation (feet)	

The Hike

This delightful, informative walk is a self-guided tour to the wonders of a Blue Ridge forest. This is a hike for everyone, especially children, as they'll probably get good views of wildlife.

At the trailhead, bear right (the maintenance area is to the left). You are on a wide trail, suitable for all ages. The trail is gravel, then forest floor, then paved.

The first part of this hike is 0.8 mile long and well marked. After that section, turn left and head south via the paved biking/walking path, which leads back to the visitor center, adding another mile to your route.

According to a park naturalist, the marks on this tree were most likely made by a bear clawing off the bark to expose the cambium layer, a much sought after food item.

Miles and Directions

0.0 Start at Mile 51.0, across Skyline Drive from the Harry F. Byrd Sr. Visitor Center.

0.2 Bridge over Hogcamp Branch. Reach a junction shortly and stay left on Story of the Forest Trail.

0.4 Junction with horse trail. Proceed straight.

0.8 Proceed straight to the Big Meadows Campground. Turn left to access the paved bike path back to the visitor center.

1.8 Arrive back at the trailhead.

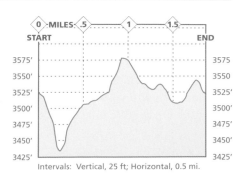

30 Big Meadows

Follow paths through a landscape probably created by Native Americans and maintained as such because of long use by the mountain people and by the park service.

Skyline Mile: 51.0
Distance: Walk the maze of trails until you tire
Approx. hiking time: Take an hour, take all day; quit when you are tired
Difficulty: Easy
Trail surface: Dirt
Traffic: Heavy

Canine compatibility: Leashed dogs allowed
Maps: National Geographic Trails Illustrated Topographic Map 228; Map 10, Appalachian Trail and Other Trails in Shenandoah National Park, Central District (PATC, Inc.)
Special considerations: Bikes allowed

Finding the trailhead: The trail begins at Mile 51.0, across Skyline Drive from the Harry F. Byrd Sr. Visitor Center at Big Meadows. GPS: N38 30.984' / W78 26.403'

The Hike

As you hike, remember that Big Meadows has a known geologic history of close to 40,000 years, during which time the climate varied from tropical to that of northern Canada. Archaeologists know that American Indians first hunted and camped in the meadow nearly 8,000 years ago, when the climate was colder. These early hunters may have used fire to keep the area open, but there is no scientific evidence to verify this.

In the late eighteenth century, homesteaders moved into the area and took advantage of the clearing the Native Americans had created to farm and graze their livestock. Today, just beyond the meadow, you can still find the foundations and root cellars of these mountain people's homes.

Subsequent to the park's establishment, Big Meadows has served many purposes. In 1933 it became the setting for a large Civilian Conservation Corps camp. On July 3, 1936, the meadow was the site of the park's dedication, with

Monarch caterpillars sometimes choose a grassy idyll like Big Meadows as the grand backdrop for their transformation.

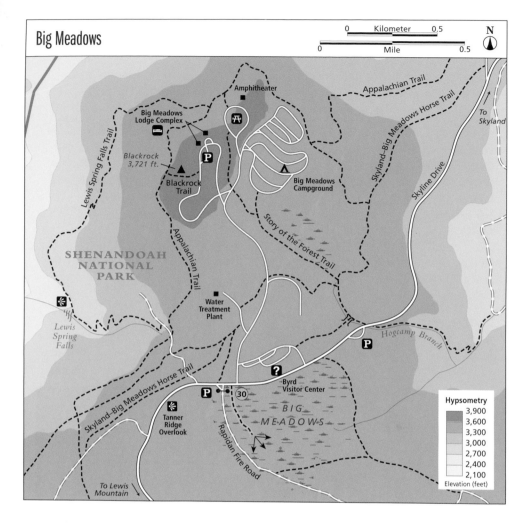

Big Meadows

President Franklin D. Roosevelt presiding. During World War II, over 2,000 soldiers with the US Army Corps of Engineers camped in the meadow.

To thwart intrusions from the surrounding forest and maintain the meadow in its historical condition, park rangers have used a variety of techniques, including mowing, spraying, and controlled burning.

The meadow offers sanctuary for a variety of wildlife, including deer, some of which are quite tame. If they approach you, please don't feed them because the microflora in their stomachs can't process human food. Hand-feeding also decreases their fear of humans and thus their chance of survival during hunting season should they wander out of the park.

So don't feed the deer!

There is no official trail through Big Meadows, though there is a series of trails, some of which have been created by decades of use by game animals. Others, of

Much like park managers do today, Native Americans may have used controlled burns to create grassy settings like Big Meadows.

course, have been enhanced by people. All paths are quite easy to see and wander on. Ranger-led tours depart frequently from the visitor center.

One trail does course throughout the meadow and, because of continuous use, is better defined than most of the others. This path begins at the parking area east of Skyline Drive, directly across from the filling station at the turnoff into Big Meadows. The trail is on the left, just beyond the chain that crosses the Rapidan Fire Road. You are pretty much on your own here; the distance across the meadow is less than a mile, and you can wander at will.

You're likely to find an abundance of wildlife in the meadow, including deer. Study the different types of grasses. Look at the herbs and the incredible variety of wildflowers. See the milkweed and asters? Notice the blueberries and the shrub with the dogwood-like leaves; it is the panicled dogwood, which is rare and in need of protection.

As you continue your walk, look for the various species of trees, such as the black locust, that grow along the edge of the meadow. Edges are important to wildlife because they provide a transition from areas that offer food to areas that offer protection. Park managers have used fire to prevent the encroachment of black locust and maintain these edges. Shenandoah is fortunate to have such a prairielike habitat. This is the only sustained meadow in the park, and it currently encompasses about 134 acres.

When you tire, simply wander back to your vehicle. If you're lucky, you'll be more keenly aware of the rich biological diversity that is inherent in Shenandoah National Park.

31 Lewis Spring Falls Trail

A loop trail through the hardwood forest descends to 81-foot Lewis Spring Falls and climbs out again.

Skyline Mile: 51.2
Distance: 3.3-mile loop
Approx. hiking time: 3 to 5 hours
Difficulty: Moderate
Trail surface: Dirt and naturally occurring rock
Traffic: Light to moderate

Canine compatibility: Leashed dogs allowed
Maps: National Geographic Trails Illustrated Topographic Map 228; Map 10, Appalachian Trail and Other Trails in Shenandoah National Park, Central District (PATC, Inc.)

Finding the trailhead: Exit Skyline Drive at Mile 51.2, at the Big Meadows complex. Leave from the amphitheater located across the road from the Big Meadows Campground, 0.7 mile from the visitor center. GPS: N38 31.871' / W78 26.422'

The Hike

At 81 feet in height, Lewis Spring Falls is the fourth-highest falls in the park. It's a beautiful, gentle falls, cascading from two creeks and then descending to a false bottom, where it spills once again. The falls often branch, depending on the time of year. You have a commanding view of the falls from an overlook constructed by young men working in Civilian Conservation Corps camps in the 1930s, which offers a safe and contained view.

To begin, access the amphitheater behind the picnic area. Below the amphitheater, at the cement post, pick up the blue blazes of the Lewis Falls Trail, which branches to the right off the Appalachian Trail. (If you were to stay on the AT, Milam Gap is 2.6 miles south; Fishers Gap is 1.6 miles north.)

This well-maintained trail descends immediately and continues to do so for about 1 mile. The rocky trail requires sturdy hiking boots. Watch yourself on the rocks—even dry ones can be slippery. Notice the many fallen trees, evidence of the power of ice and wind storms.

The path is flanked on both sides by hardwood trees and low-growth bushes. You will descend into a hollow with some granite outcroppings. Stay alert for wildlife. Deer abound, and on our hike we ran into one of the forest's spotted skunks. Though the animal lifted its tail, it also lowered it as we backed off, so we carried no bad smell back to our tent.

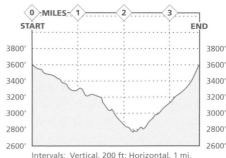

Intervals: Vertical, 200 ft; Horizontal, 1 mi.

Big Meadow Campground is centrally located to a number of hikes, such as Dark Hollow and Lewis Spring Falls. Deer are often seen in the area.

When the trail finally levels, you can hear the falls. Another brief ascent brings you to a nice overlook with views to the western mountains. Turn left, to the southeast, and follow the blue blazes to the observation point. Cross a small stream and parallel an iron railing. Don't attempt to climb down to the falls. People have suffered serious, even fatal, falls trying this.

From the overlook, backtrack north for about 50 feet and pick up the blue blazes going east. The trail maintains an uphill grade, sure and steady. It parallels a creek on your right, and then switchbacks away from the stream.

After climbing for 0.6 mile, you reach a cement marker. Go east for 70 yards on the Lewis Spring Fire Road, then turn north (left) onto the AT. Follow the white blazes on the trees. From this point (you're still chugging uphill), the Big Meadows Lodge is another 1.4 miles. The campground is 0.5 mile beyond that.

Be sure to carry water on this hike. There are several signs cautioning you not to drink the water along the way. Some is contaminated, say the signs, and requires vigorous boiling. One common contaminant is giardia, a waterborne parasite that can cause severe diarrhea, cramps, and fatigue. The parasite can survive in very cold

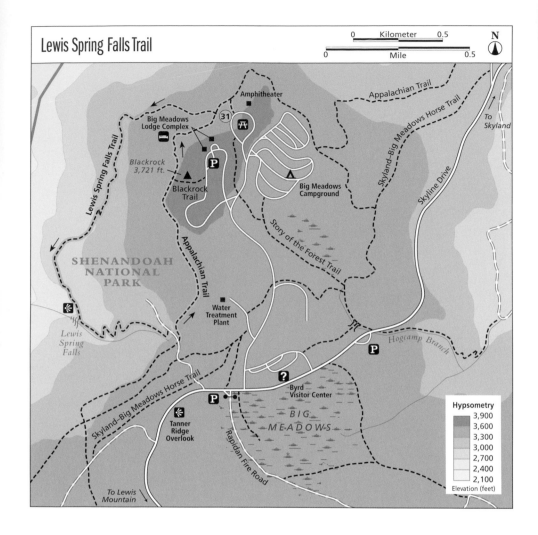

Lewis Spring Falls Trail

water and is spread by the droppings of dogs, horses, cattle, elk, rabbits, and other small mammals, as well as humans.

Option: For families with children under the age of 9 or 10, the hike to Lewis Spring Falls described above may be too strenuous. A somewhat shorter, easier alternative descends a wide, gravel service road that is just south of the Big Meadows complex. This hike is 2.5 miles round-trip and has an elevation gain and loss of about 800 feet. If you're hiking with young children, it may take longer. Be sure to carry sufficient water. You pass yellow-blazed horse trails to the left and right and come to a junction with the Appalachian Trail at 0.3 mile. Just past the junction, take the blue-blazed Lewis Falls Trail on your left. Follow that for 0.6 mile to another junction. Take the spur trail to your left, which leads to a nice overlook near the top of the falls. Retrace your steps from this point, going mostly uphill.

Water pours forth at Lewis Spring Falls, the fourth-highest falls in Shenandoah National Park.

Miles and Directions

0.0   Start at the amphitheater located across the road from the Big Meadows Campground.

0.1   Amphitheater and junction with AT. Take the Lewis Falls Trail behind the amphitheater (blue blazes) and begin descent.

1.0   View to west. Turn south to overlook.

1.3   Observation point overlooking falls is 250 feet ahead. Backtrack to main trail.

1.9   Cement post. Go east 70 yards to access the Appalachian Trail. Follow AT back to amphitheater.

3.3   Arrive back at the trailhead.

32 Blackrock

A very short and easy walk leads to a rocky viewpoint offering good views.

Skyline Mile: 51.2
Distance: 0.4 mile out and back
Approx. hiking time: 30 minutes
Difficulty: Easy
Trail surface: Dirt and naturally occurring rock
Traffic: Moderate to heavy

Canine compatibility: Leashed dogs allowed
Maps: National Geographic Trails Illustrated Topographic Map 228; Map 10, Appalachian Trail and Other Trails in Shenandoah National Park, Central District (PATC, Inc.)

Finding the trailhead: From Skyline Drive, turn north into the Big Meadows complex and proceed 0.9 mile to the dining hall at the Big Meadows Lodge. The trailhead is at the far end of the lodge parking lot, beyond the dining hall. GPS: N38 31.649648' / W78 26.489715'

Through the eons erosion has transformed huge quartzite rocks into a talus slope.

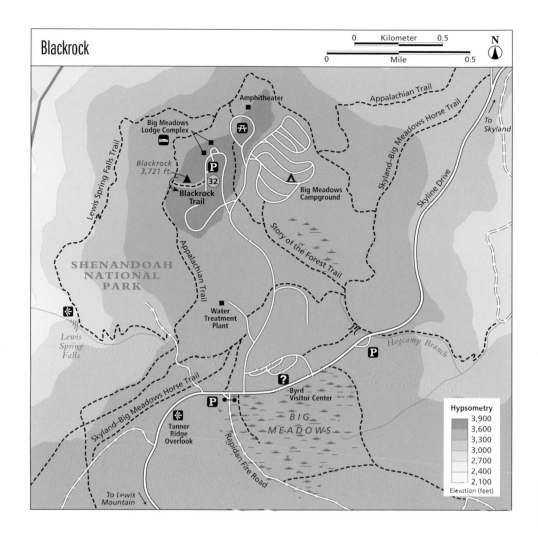

Blackrock

The Hike

The trail is well marked with a sign in the parking lot. Begin a leisurely ascent to the viewpoint (3,721 feet). On clear days, you have excellent views to the left and right. Use caution: The rocks here are quite slick. This is a nice stroll, especially in the evening when town lights below are lit.

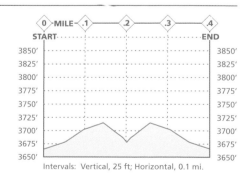

Intervals: Vertical, 25 ft; Horizontal, 0.1 mi.

33 Rapidan Camp–Laurel Prong–Hazeltop Loop

A moderately difficult hike leads to a falls, to the retreat of a former US president, and returns along one of the park's higher and more geologically interesting peaks.

Skyline Mile: 53.0
Distance: 7.4-mile loop (4.2-mile out-and-back option)
Approx. hiking time: 4 to 8 hours
Difficulty: Strenuous
Trail surface: Dirt and naturally occurring rock

Traffic: Light
Canine compatibility: Leashed dogs allowed
Maps: National Geographic Trails Illustrated Topographic Map 228; Map 10, Appalachian Trail and Other Trails in Shenandoah National Park, Central District (PATC, Inc.)

Finding the trailhead: The trail begins at Milam Gap, at Mile 53.0 on Skyline Drive. GPS: N38 29.883' / W78 26.743'

The Hike

Of the original thirteen structures that once formed Rapidan Camp, only three remain today: the Brown House (which has been fully restored, inside and out), the Creel Cabin, and the Prime Minister's Cabin. The setting is attractive—and certainly as beautiful today as it was when former president Herbert Hoover retreated to Shenandoah. Hoover was searching for three features: (1) His retreat had to be within 100 miles of Washington, DC; (2) the retreat had to be located on a trout stream; and (3) it had to be at least 2,500 feet above sea level. Because of the camp's significance, the US Department of the Interior designated the area a National Historic Landmark in 1988. Rapidan Camp is closed to backcountry camping.

The trail begins from the south side of the Milam Gap parking lot, located just a little north of Mile 53.0. To reach the trailhead walk across Skyline Drive to the side opposite the parking lot and decide whether you wish to make this a loop hike or a 4.2-mile out-and-back hike down the Mill Prong Trail to Rapidan Camp and back. We elected to make the 7.4-mile loop hike, traveling first to Rapidan Camp and then

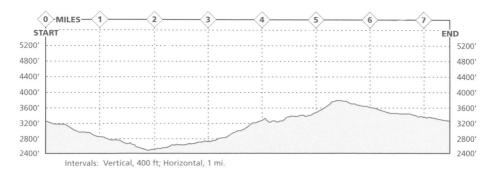

Intervals: Vertical, 400 ft; Horizontal, 1 mi.

President Hoover relaxed at his Rapidan Camp and often fished for brook trout in Mill Prong.

back along the Laurel Prong Trail, linking with the Appalachian Trail. Others have reversed the loop.

Begin on the Mill Prong Trail, which gradually descends and soon begins to follow Mill Prong. Shortly thereafter a sign explains that this is a catch-and-release creek. The sign reads: ALL FISH MUST BE HANDLED CAREFULLY AND RETURNED IMMEDIATELY TO THE STREAM. ONLY ARTIFICIAL FLIES OR LURES WITH A SINGLE HOOK ARE PERMITTED.

At about 1.9 miles, you will pass a junction with the Rapidan Fire Road. Stay straight on the Mill Prong Trail. The trail continues downhill, quickly reaching Rapidan Camp at the 2.1-mile mark. Once you reach the camp, explore the surroundings. In addition to the various structures, two streams converge near the camp—Laurel Prong and Mill Prong—both of which combine to create the Rapidan River. The river is full of deep pools that still contain the trout that enticed President Hoover. Retrace your steps from here for the 4.2-mile out-and-back hike.

To make this a loop hike, take the Laurel Prong Trail, which departs near the Rapidan Camp parking lot. Within 100 yards you encounter a maintenance road, which goes uphill to the right. Ignore the spur road and follow the trail marked with a yellow slash.

The Rapidan River gurgles among rocks near President Hoover's onetime retreat.

In 0.4 mile the trail meets the Fork Mountain Trail. Take the right fork to stay on the Laurel Prong Trail. Within 0.1 mile the trail will cross four or five streams (depending on the time of year), after which it continues its gradual ascent. In about 1 mile the trail intersects with a trail marked by a cement post and the typical metal plate. On one side of the post the inscriptions point the way to the Cat Knob Trail and the Jones Mountain Trail, a distance of about 0.5 mile. Take the right fork to the AT, about 1 mile uphill.

Just before accessing the AT, the Laurel Prong Trail becomes fairly steep and rocky. When the Laurel Prong Trail meets the AT, your route proceeds in a northerly direction on the AT. The climb continues to Hazeltop (3,812 feet) and then begins a thoroughly delightful descent. The trail is wide, well maintained, and generally free of rocks.

Option 1: To reach Big Rock Falls, take the Mill Prong Trail for a 3.4-mile out-and-back hike. Though not one of the park's more spectacular falls, Big Rock Falls is deserving of a visit. It cascades down a long slope and then settles into a quiet little pool. The hike is relatively easy and provides a nice family excursion. The trail departs from Milam Gap.

Option 2: To hike from Milam Gap to Hazeltop (the third-highest point in the park) and back, the park service recommends following the last segment of the loop described above, for a 4.2-mile out-and-back hike.

Miles and Directions

0.0   Start at Mile 53.0 on Skyline Drive, Milam Gap.

1.7   Big Rock Falls.

1.9   Junction with the Rapidan Fire Road. Continue on the Mill Prong Trail.

2.1   Rapidan Camp. Pick up the Laurel Prong Trail.

2.5   Junction with the Fork Mountain Trail. Turn right on the Laurel Prong Trail.

4.8   The Appalachian Trail; turn right (north) on the AT.

5.3   Hazeltop summit.

7.4   Arrive back at the trailhead at Milam Gap, completing the circuit.

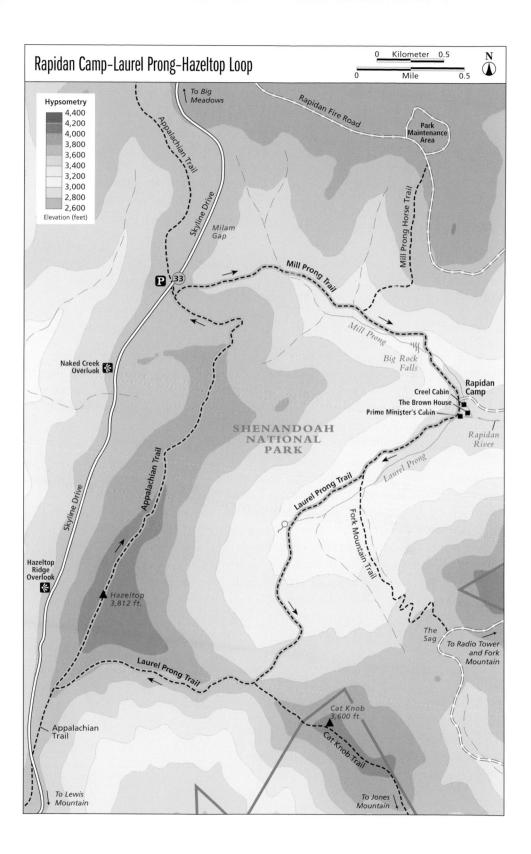

Rapidan Camp–Laurel Prong–Hazeltop Loop

Hypsometry

	Elevation (feet)
	4,400
	4,200
	4,000
	3,800
	3,600
	3,400
	3,200
	3,000
	2,800
	2,600

0   Kilometer   0.5
0   Mile   0.5

N

To Big Meadows

Rapidan Fire Road

Park Maintenance Area

Appalachian Trail

Skyline Drive

Milam Gap

Mill Prong Trail

Mill Prong Horse Trail

P 33

Mill Prong

Big Rock Falls

Naked Creek Overlook

Creel Cabin
The Brown House
Prime Minister's Cabin

Rapidan Camp

Rapidan River

SHENANDOAH NATIONAL PARK

Appalachian Trail

Laurel Prong Trail

Laurel Prong

Fork Mountain Trail

Skyline Drive

Hazeltop Ridge Overlook

Hazeltop 3,812 ft.

The Sag

To Radio Tower and Fork Mountain

Laurel Prong Trail

Appalachian Trail

Cat Knob 3,600 ft.

Cat Knob Trail

To Lewis Mountain

To Jones Mountain

34 Bearfence Mountain

This short hike features a 360-degree view and a real rock scramble toward the summit.

Skyline Mile: 56.4
Distance: 1.2-mile lariat
Approx. hiking time: 1 to 2 hours
Difficulty: Moderate
Trail surface: Dirt and naturally occurring rock
Traffic: Moderate to heavy

Canine compatibility: Dogs not allowed
Maps: National Geographic Trails Illustrated Topographic Map 228; Map 10, Appalachian Trail and Other Trails in Shenandoah National Park, Central District (PATC, Inc.)

Finding the trailhead: Park at the Bearfence Mountain parking lot on the west side of Skyline Drive at Mile 56.4. Cross the drive to the east side to a cement post, and take the Bearfence Mountain Trail going southeast. Follow the blue blazes. GPS: N38 27.143' / W78 28.018'

The Hike

Bearfence Mountain (3,620 feet) is one of several summits in the park that command a complete panoramic view. Once you have reached the top, you are able to see Massanutten Mountain and the Shenandoah Valley to the west and Laurel Gap, Fork Mountain, and Bluff Mountain to the east. In the short hike from the parking lot to the summit, you pass through the sandstone of the Swift Run Formation, capped by Catoctin basalt.

Hiking to the summit requires some degree of coordination. Though expertise in rock climbing is not necessary, you need some dexterity to maneuver through jumbled rocks. In some cases, you may find yourself scooting along on your bottom. To ensure good traction and to diminish the possibility of bruised feet, we recommend that you wear good hiking boots, although they won't help much if the rocks are wet or covered with snow. In summer park officials have seen rattlesnakes in the area, so watch where you place your feet and hands. Park handouts indicate this is not a trail for small children, especially those who must be carried.

The hike to Bearfence begins at Mile 56.4 on the east side of Skyline Drive, across the road from the Bearfence Mountain parking lot. Almost immediately after leaving the parking lot, you begin to climb. In several places you will see trees (felled by many severe storms since 1996) whose giant, exposed roots provide mute testimony to the humbling power of nature.

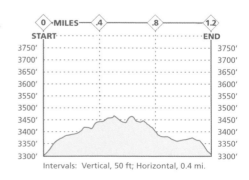

Intervals: Vertical, 50 ft; Horizontal, 0.4 mi.

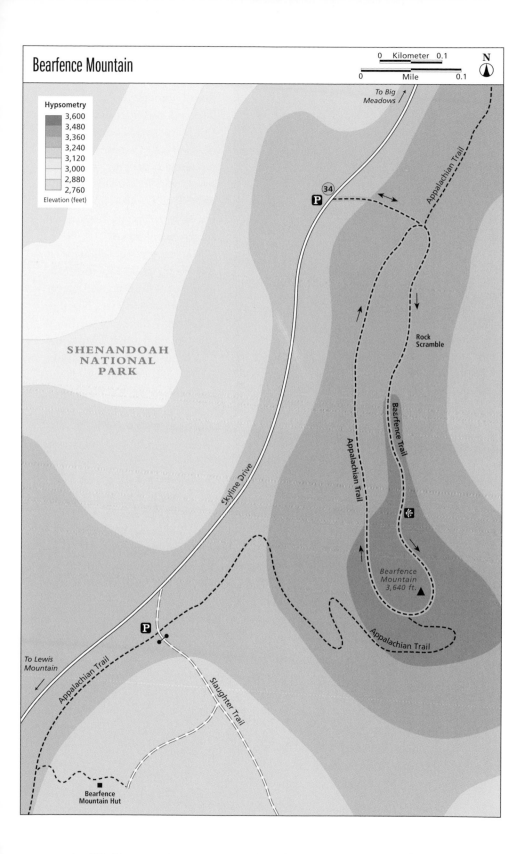

Lichen-covered basaltic boulders perch atop Bearfence Mountain's summit.

Within 300 yards of the parking lot, the trail begins to thread through huge boulders. This rock was originally volcanic lava, but with millions of years of compression it has metamorphosed into the gray green rock you see before you today. Appropriately, it is called greenstone, but only recent fractures reveal the green coloration.

If you are out of shape, it may seem as if the torturous maze of boulders will never end, but in reality you begin to break into the open within a few hundred yards. You know you've reached the summit when you can peer down on everything. Looking east, you can see mountains ranging from Hazeltop to Kirtley Mountain. Looking west, you can see Skyline Drive, the Shenandoah Valley, and Devils Tanyard. You are standing 3,620 feet above sea level, and the view is magnificent.

From the summit of Bearfence Mountain, you can retrace your steps to the trailhead for a total hike of 0.8 mile, or you can continue on toward the Appalachian Trail, which you reach very shortly. At the cement post, take the AT north for about 0.7 mile back to the parking lot, for a trek of 1.2 miles.

Miles and Directions

0.0 Start at the Bearfence Mountain parking lot on the west side of Skyline, Skyline Drive mile 56.4.

200 yards Cross the Appalachian Trail. Remain on the Bearfence Trail.

0.4 Bearfence Mountain summit.

0.5 AT junction. Turn right onto the AT and descend.

1.1 Turn left onto the main Bearfence Trail.

1.2 Arrive back at the trailhead. Return to the parking lot.

35 Lewis Mountain Trail

Leading directly from the Lewis Mountain Campground, this hike makes a pleasant short stroll for adults and a small adventure for children.

Skyline Mile: 57.5
Distance: 1 mile out and back
Approx. hiking time: 1 hour
Difficulty: Easy
Trail surface: Dirt and naturally occurring rock
Traffic: Moderate

Canine compatibility: Leashed dogs allowed
Maps: National Geographic Trails Illustrated Topographic Map 228; Map 10, Appalachian Trail and Other Trails in Shenandoah National Park, Central District (PATC, Inc.)

Finding the trailhead: The trail begins in the Lewis Mountain Campground (Mile 57.5 on Skyline Drive), at campsite 16. GPS: N38 26.086' / W78 28.658'

The Hike

If you're not camping at Lewis Mountain, you may park either at the picnic area or at the camp store, then walk the short distance through the campground to campsite 16, where the trail begins. Follow the blue blazes.

What a great hike this is for imaginative kids! Children can conjure images of trolls and bears as they hike up the path, overgrown on all sides with mosses and ferns.

This hike is not too big on scenery, though, even at the summit, as trees have grown enough to block the views. However, it's a fun stroll that ascends very gently to the top of Lewis Mountain, on land once owned by John Lewis, a surveyor for George Washington.

From the summit backtrack to campsite 16. For a longer trek, you can hike south on the Appalachian Trail to the Pocosin Trail.

A colorful monarch caterpillar investigating some milkweed.

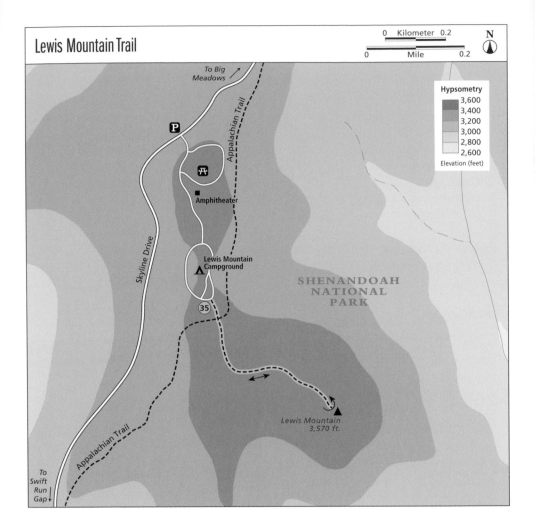

Lewis Mountain Trail

Hypsometry
- 3,600
- 3,400
- 3,200
- 3,000
- 2,800
- 2,600

Elevation (feet)

To Big Meadows

Appalachian Trail

Amphitheater

Lewis Mountain Campground

Skyline Drive

35

SHENANDOAH NATIONAL PARK

Appalachian Trail

Lewis Mountain 3,570 ft.

To Swift Run Gap

Miles and Directions

0.0 Start at campsite 16, Lewis Mountain Campground.

0.1 Junction with the Appalachian Trail. Do not access it. Stay left on the Lewis Mountain Trail.

0.5 Tree-covered summit. Trail ends. Backtrack from here.

1.0 Arrive back at the trailhead at campsite 16.

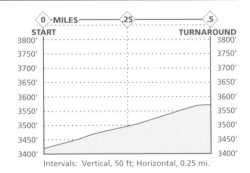

Intervals: Vertical, 50 ft; Horizontal, 0.25 mi.

36 Pocosin Trail

An inspiring venture along an easy trail provides insights into Shenandoah's history and wildlife.

Skyline Mile: 59.5
Distance: 2.2 miles out and back
Approx. hiking time: 2 to 4 hours
Difficulty: Easy
Trail surface: Dirt and naturally occurring rock
Traffic: Light

Canine compatibility: Leashed dogs allowed
Maps: National Geographic Trails Illustrated Topographic Map 228; Map 10, Appalachian Trail and Other Trails in Shenandoah National Park, Central District (PATC, Inc.)

Finding the trailhead: Locate the trailhead by driving first to Mile 59.5 on Skyline Drive. Turn left onto the Pocosin Fire Road, on the east side of the drive. Park near the yellow chain, about 50 yards down the yellow-blazed Pocosin Fire Road. Pass the chain and follow the fire road. GPS: N38 24.790195' / W78 29.30793'

The Hike

Begin your hike by walking down the fire road, which proceeds in an easterly direction and crosses the Appalachian Trail in 0.1 mile. In 0.2 mile the road approaches the Pocosin Cabin, one in a chain of cabins that serve hikers using the AT. The cabins are managed by the Potomac Appalachian Trail Club (PATC) and are available for rent. To visit the cabin (if unoccupied), turn right onto the side path.

Continue along the fire road, which begins a slight descent. Throughout the spring and summer—and sometimes into the fall—wildflowers flank the trail. Look for columbine in the late spring and for milkweed in the summer. The latter is associated with disturbed sites.

Soon the trail levels, and after about 1 mile you encounter a cement post, indicating the Pocosin Horse Trail (yellow blazes). Turn right onto the Pocosin Horse Trail and look immediately to the left at what seems to be an old mountain cabin. This is actually part of the ruins of an Episcopal mission established around 1904. Near the ruined cabin is all that remains of the old church: its stone steps.

Though the forest is swallowing the artifacts of the period, a number of features from the mission days remain. Old stone stairs and crumbling mission walls are among them.

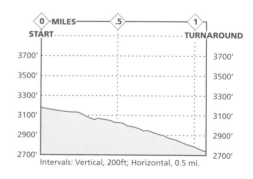

Intervals: Vertical, 200ft; Horizontal, 0.5 mi.

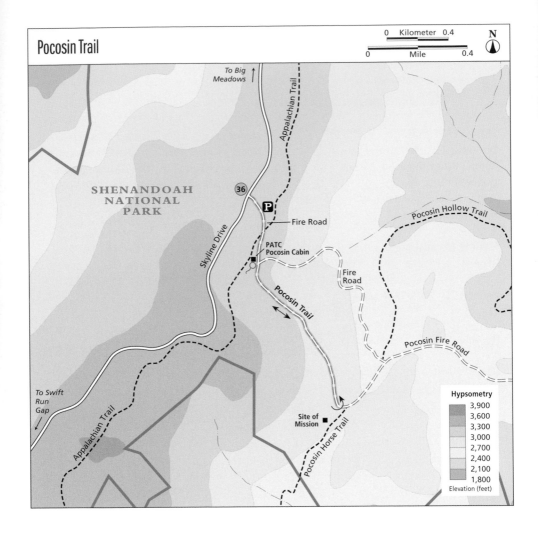

To Big
Meadows

Appalachian Trail

SHENANDOAH
NATIONAL
PARK

36

Skyline Drive

Fire Road

PATC
Pocosin Cabin

Pocosin Hollow Trail

Fire
Road

Pocosin Trail

Pocosin Fire Road

To Swift
Run
Gap

Appalachian Trail

Site of
Mission

Pocosin Horse Trail

Hypsometry
3,900
3,600
3,300
3,000
2,700
2,400
2,100
1,800
Elevation (feet)

0   Kilometer   0.4

0   Mile   0.4

N

Hiking the several spur trails that take you to the old mission provides a rewarding excursion, but remember that old timbers and dilapidated rock walls attract snakes, so watch where you're going and where you put your hands. Once you've finished exploring, retrace your steps.

Option 1: If you're full of energy and wish to explore farther, continue on the Pocosin Horse Trail, cross a stream, and make a gentle ascent. Watch for snakes in this area, as it is often overgrown. About 1.3 miles from the mission site, a marker indicates a right turn on the main trail. Go left for about 0.1 mile to visit the South River Cemetery, still in use. The park boundary is only 0.1 mile away. Retrace your steps to the parking lot for a hike of about 5 miles out and back.

Option 2: The Pocosin Mission can also be accessed from the Lewis Mountain Campground at Mile 57.5 on Skyline Drive. Although this route adds another 3.4

The Pocosin Cabin is a fascinating stop for hikers..

miles, it is a delightful trek that follows the Appalachian Trail, and on a cool day the extra distance will hardly be noticed. Access this alternative route from campsite 16 of the Lewis Mountain Campground. About 70 feet along the trail to Lewis Mountain, you will encounter the Appalachian Trail. Follow the AT south (right) for 1.7 miles to the Pocosin Cabin. Proceed along the Pocosin Fire Road (as described above) to the mission. Return along the same route—back to the AT going north—which will return you to the campground for a total of 5.6 miles out and back.

Miles and Directions

- **0.0** Start 50 yards down the yellow-blazed Pocosin Fire Road.
- **0.1** Cement post. Stay on the fire road as it crosses the Appalachian Trail.
- **0.2** Cement post. Stay on the fire road. PATC Pocosin Cabin (locked) to right.
- **1.0** Cement post. Junction with the Pocosin Horse Trail and Pocosin Hollow Trail to the left. Turn right onto the Pocosin Horse Trail and follow the yellow blazes.
- **1.1** Ruins of the mission on the right. Retrace your steps.
- **2.2** Return to the parking lot.

37 Saddleback Mountain

This circuit hike passes an Appalachian Trail maintenance hut, threads through a forest that is growing back after decades of farming, and concludes by passing through tangles of large trees toppled by Tropical Storm Fran in September 1996.

Skyline Mile: 62.8
Distance: 3.8-mile lariat
Approx. hiking time: 2 to 3 hours
Difficulty: Easy to moderate
Trail surface: Dirt and naturally occurring rock
Traffic: Light

Canine compatibility: Leashed dogs allowed
Maps: National Geographic Trails Illustrated Topographic Map 228; Map 10, Appalachian Trail and Other Trails in Shenandoah National Park, Central District (PATC, Inc.)

Finding the trailhead: The trail begins at the South River Picnic Area, at Mile 62.8 on Skyline Drive. Go to the lower loop of the picnic area, to the kiosk at the trailhead for South River Falls. Follow the blue blazes downhill. GPS: N38 22.758' / W78 31.276'

The Hike

For those interested in an easy hike that includes the Appalachian Trail in over three-fourths of the trail's length—and for those interested in witnessing the aftermath of violent storms—this trail is for you.

In itself, Saddleback Mountain is rather insignificant, for it offers no real views in the spring, summer, or fall. As a result, it's appropriate that the trail simply circles the mountain and returns you to your starting point. The route is somewhat unremarkable, and it's difficult to tell just where Saddleback Mountain is in relation to the hike, but it is a pleasant walk through the woods. The trail makes no spectacular climbs, but near the end, along the AT, it passes through an area of immense blowdown. For about 0.1 mile the trail threads through an area where blowdown once thoroughly covered the trail. The trail crew has cleaned up the litter, leaving, of course, trees in the

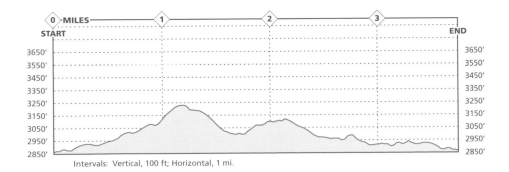

Intervals: Vertical, 100 ft; Horizontal, 1 mi.

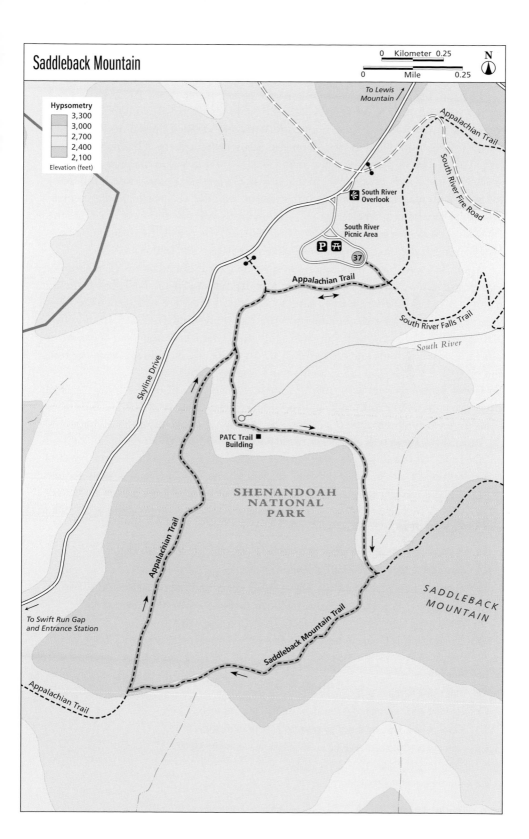

Saddleback Mountain

0 Kilometer 0.25

0 Mile 0.25

N

Hypsometry
3,300
3,000
2,700
2,400
2,100
Elevation (feet)

To Lewis Mountain

Appalachian Trail

South River Fire Road

South River Overlook

South River Picnic Area

P

37

Appalachian Trail

South River Falls Trail

South River

Skyline Drive

PATC Trail Building

SHENANDOAH NATIONAL PARK

Appalachian Trail

SADDLEBACK MOUNTAIN

To Swift Run Gap and Entrance Station

Saddleback Mountain Trail

Appalachian Trail

woods as they were when they fell. This will give you a good idea of how damaging 70-mile-per-hour winds can be.

The trail begins off the lower loop of the South River Picnic Area, at the kiosk for the trail to South River Falls. Follow the trail's blue blazes downhill for 0.1 mile to a cement post, where there is a junction with the AT. Turn right onto the AT and follow it for another 0.2 mile to a T junction. Turn left; now the AT is part of an old service road. The trail begins to get overgrown, but not nearly as much as farther on.

A canopy of trees obscures the sky, and you can see much new growth following the abandonment of an old settlement. At about 0.5 mile, you reach another cement post. Bear left onto a very overgrown old service road. For the next 0.3 mile, this fairly level portion remains overgrown. Use caution; when wet, the path can be slick. You'll soon see the blue blazes of the Saddleback Mountain Trail on the trees.

About 0.8 mile from your start, you encounter what once was an AT shelter but now is a PATC maintenance hut. There is a fire pit and picnic table, but camping is not allowed. To the left, a fairly large spring sits at the edge of a somewhat open meadow. Continue past the building (on the right) and straight ahead on the blue-blazed trail. A slight ascent begins here, and the terrain becomes even more overgrown. Carpets of ferns line the trail. You begin to see the blowdown along the trail, and the scene increases in drama as the trail winds gently upward.

Cross a tiny creek at about mile 1.8, then reach a cement post at mile 1.9. Turn right onto the AT (north) and, still ascending, follow the white blazes through a tremendous blowdown; note the extremely shallow root systems of these huge trees.

At mile 3.3 you reach another cement post. Stay on the AT by going left (still on an old road). In 0.2 mile you encounter another cement post. Go to the right, still following the AT north. Near the end, you encounter one last cement post. Follow the blue blazes straight up the hill to the starting point and completion of the hike.

Miles and Directions

0.0 Start at the kiosk at South River Falls located in lower loop of the picnic area.

0.1 Turn right at the cement post. Follow the Appalachian Trail (white blazes).

0.3 Cement post at T junction. Go left, still on the AT, which is now part of an old road.

0.5 Cement post. Bear left, no longer on the AT but on the service road that leads to the Saddleback Mountain Trail (blue blazes).

0.8 Spring on the left—hard to see. South River PATC maintenance building. No camping. Walk straight, with building on your right.

1.0 Begin ascending.

1.8 Tiny creek, which may be almost dry.

1.9 Cement post. Junction with the AT. Go north (right). Ascend.

3.3 Cement post. Stay on the AT by going left, still on old road.

3.5 Cement post. Go right, closing the loop and still following the AT.

3.7 Cement post. Follow blue blazes uphill.

3.8 Arrive back at the trailhead.

38 South River Falls

An enjoyable hike leads to the park's third-largest waterfall.

Skyline Mile: 62.8
Distance: 4.4 miles out and back
Approx. hiking time: 3 to 6 hours
Difficulty: Moderate
Trail surface: Dirt and naturally occurring rock
Traffic: Light

Canine compatibility: Leashed dogs allowed
Maps: National Geographic Trails Illustrated Topographic Map 228; Map 11, Appalachian Trail and Other Trails in Shenandoah National Park, South District (PATC, Inc.)

Finding the trailhead: The trail begins at the South River Picnic Area, at Mile 62.8 on Skyline Drive. GPS: N38 22.758' / W78 31.276'

The Hike

At 83 feet, South River Falls is the park's third-largest falls. A refreshing pool at its base would be invigorating on a hot summer day—all the better to prepare you for the challenging hike back to the trailhead.

The trailhead to South River Falls is to the right of the drinking fountain in the picnic grounds at Mile 62.8 on Skyline Drive. The trail descends gradually for 0.1 mile to a junction with the Appalachian Trail. A cement post orients you to the surrounding features. Milam Gap and Swift Run Gap are 11.5 miles and 3 miles to the southwest, respectively.

Continue your hike on the South River Falls Trail from the post. You begin a series of gradual switchbacks as you descend the trail. In places the trail is rocky, but it is wide and, for the most part, smooth until it approaches the first of several creeks that combine to create the South River. In the past, hikers have attempted to save time by

South River Falls is the park's third largest and can at times be truly spectacular.

The trail to the falls is wide and mainly smooth until it approaches the first of several creeks that combine to create the South River.

cutting across the trail, creating erosion. As a result, the park stipulates via several signs that hikers remain on the trail.

At 0.75 mile you encounter another creek entering from the left. It's difficult to see because it runs beneath the rocks, but it certainly is audible. Just past the creek lie a number of trees downed by the strong winds of the 1996 Tropical Storm Fran. Other creeks continue to flow from the left into the South River, which parallels the trail as it continues its descent.

At about 1 mile the trail plunges dramatically downward into a great hollow. It is difficult to see the falls until you approach a natural overlook, located 1.3 miles from the trailhead. Don't get too close to the edge. A few yards farther along the trail, cement walls provide a more protected spot from which to view the falls below you.

At this point, you may turn around and retrace your steps, making this a 2.6-mile out-and-back hike. If you have the time and energy, continue to the base of the falls for a journey of 4.4 miles.

If you continue, the trail will join an old road that comes in from the left in 0.2 mile. It leads to the South River Fire Road. However, continue along the widening South

South River Falls

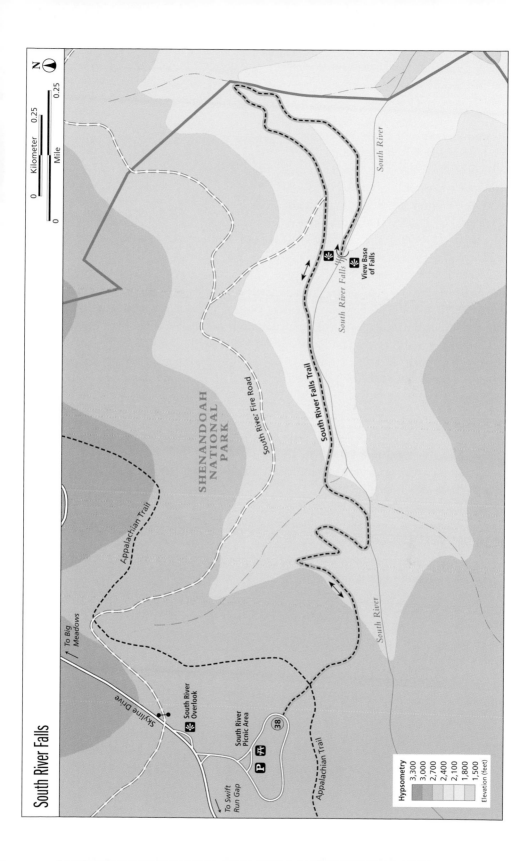

Hypsometry

- 3,300
- 3,000
- 2,700
- 2,400
- 2,100
- 1,800
- 1,500

Elevation (feet)

SHENANDOAH NATIONAL PARK

South River Fire Road

South River Falls Trail

Appalachian Trail

South River Falls

View Base of Falls

South River

South River

Skyline Drive

To Big Meadows

South River Overlook

South River Picnic Area

To Swift Run Gap

Appalachian Trail

38

N

0   0.25   Kilometer

0   0.25   Mile

River Falls Trail, which was once used by inhabitants traveling from one hollow to another. This wider trail descends for 0.6 mile and then swings back toward the base of the falls and a cement post encircled by an aluminum band. The post states that it is 0.3 mile to the end of the road and the park's boundary with the Virginia Wildlife Management Area. It also advises you of the existence

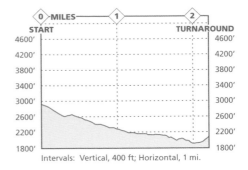

Intervals: Vertical, 400 ft; Horizontal, 1 mi.

of a short spur trail to the waterfall's base about 0.1 mile away. Take the narrow spur trail. You may have to scurry over downed trees.

Return as you came.

Option: For a 4.7-mile hike, retrace your steps from the falls. In 0.7 mile you come to the trail junction where a cement post offers an alternative route back to the South River parking lot by turning right onto the old road. Go 0.4 mile to the yellow-blazed South River Fire Road and turn left. Go 0.8 mile to the Appalachian Trail (white blazes) and turn south (left). Go 0.5 mile to a cement post at a four-way junction; turn right onto the South River Falls Trail. It's now 0.1 mile back to the parking lot.

Miles and Directions

0.0 Start at the South River Picnic Area.

0.1 Cross the Appalachian Trail and continue descent on the South River Falls Trail.

1.3 Overlook for South River Falls.

1.5 Junction with old road.

2.1 Path from trail to spur trail.

2.2 Spur trail ends at the overlook of the base of South River Falls. Retrace your steps from here.

4.4 Arrive back at the trailhead.

South District

Skyline Mile 65.5 to 105.4

The South District offers an abundance of panoramic views and interesting place names, such as Hightop, Rockytop, and Rocky Mount. The South District also has its share of spectacular falls and several designated wilderness areas.

Access to this portion of the park is relatively easy. The South District begins at Swift Run Gap in the north and ends just north of Waynesboro. US 33 runs through Swift Run Gap on the northern edge of this section, between Stanardsville and Harrisonburg.

Sassafras is one of the park's more common species of trees.

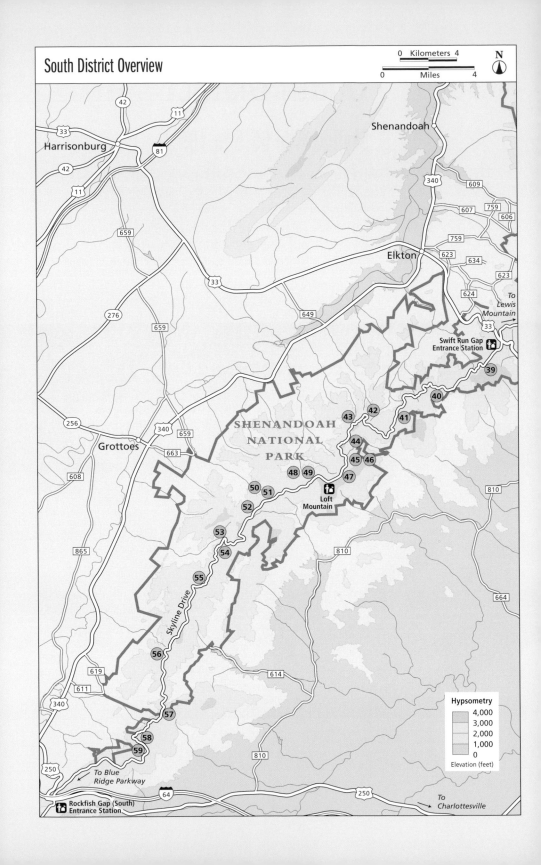

0   Kilometers   4

0   Miles   4

N

Shenandoah

Harrisonburg

Elkton

To
Lewis
Mountain

Swift Run Gap
Entrance Station

Grottoes

SHENANDOAH
NATIONAL
PARK

Loft
Mountain

Skyline Drive

To Blue
Ridge Parkway

Rockfish Gap (South)
Entrance Station

To
Charlottesville

Hypsometry

4,000
3,000
2,000
1,000
0
Elevation (feet)

39 Hightop Mountain Lariat

This is a moderately easy climb to the summit of the highest point in the park's South District. It includes magnificent westerly views.

Skyline Mile: 69.9

Distance: 3.6-mile lariat; 4 miles with spur trail to Hightop Hut

Approx. hiking time: 3 to 4 hours

Difficulty: Moderate

Trail surface: Dirt and naturally occurring rock

Traffic: Light

Canine compatibility: Leashed dogs allowed

Maps: National Geographic Trails Illustrated Topographic Map 228; Map 11, Appalachian Trail and Other Trails in Shenandoah National Park, South District (PATC, Inc.)

Finding the trailhead: Park at Smith Roach Gap, at Mile 69.9 on the east side of Skyline Drive. At a cement post in the parking lot, access the Smith Roach Gap Fire Road for about 10 yards to another cement post indicating the Appalachian Trail junction. Turn north (left) onto the AT; follow the white blazes. GPS: N38 19.698' / W78 34.449'

The Hike

Hightop Mountain is the highest peak in the park's South District. It is possible that John Lederer, the noted German explorer, reached the area in 1669. The hike begins at the Smith Roach Gap parking lot (2,620 feet).

Because the trail ascends so gradually, the entire trip should take about three hours. The lot can accommodate only a small number of vehicles, so if it is full (unlikely), choose an alternative hike. Begin your hike at the fire road and follow it for about 10 yards, at which point it intersects the Appalachian Trail. Go north (left), following the familiar white blazes.

The trail begins in a hardwood forest and switches back and forth as it begins a gradual ascent. The trail is not rocky and continues as an easy to moderate hike for the first mile. Flanking the trail is an old field that once was used by local inhabitants who farmed the area about sixty years ago—time enough for pioneer vegetation to take hold but not long enough for the resurgence of a mature forest. Still about a mile from the trailhead, the trail begins to level, and at 1.2 miles you will encounter a cement post. The summit is 0.6 mile farther. Continue straight on the AT, crossing the fire road.

In 0.1 mile you might want to follow the spur trail to the Hightop Hut. The hut sleeps about eleven hikers, who

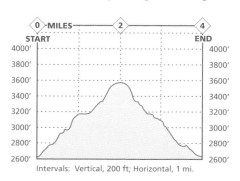

Intervals: Vertical, 200 ft; Horizontal, 1 mi.

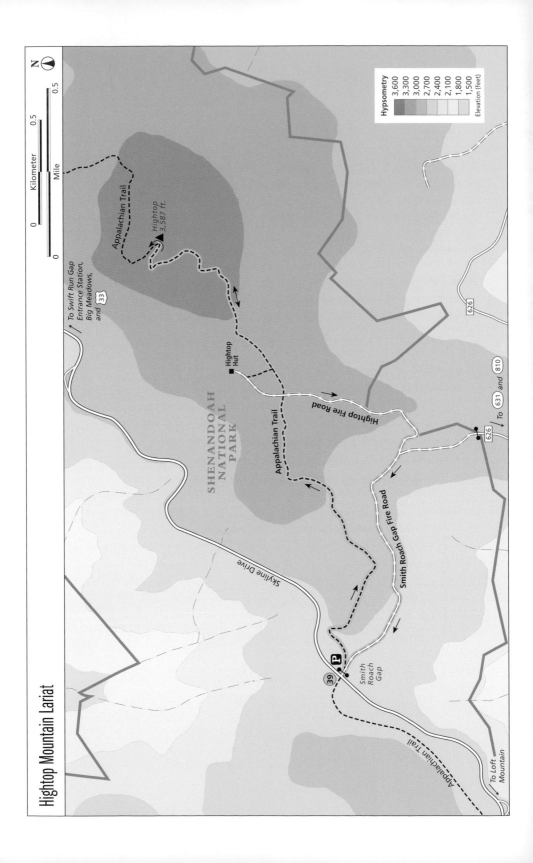

Hightop Mountain Lariat

N

Hypsometry

3,600
3,300
3,000
2,700
2,400
2,100
1,800
1,500

Elevation (feet)

Kilometer
0   0.5
0   0.5
Mile

To Swift Run Gap
Entrance Station,
Big Meadows,
and 33

Appalachian Trail

Hightop
3,587 ft.

Hightop
Hut

SHENANDOAH
NATIONAL
PARK

Appalachian Trail

Hightop Fire Road

Skyline Drive

Smith Roach Gap Fire Road

626

To 631 and 810

626

To 631 and
810

P

39

Smith
Roach Gap

Appalachian Trail

To Loft
Mountain

Hickory trees commonly produce vivid fall colors.

need permits for two nights or more. (If the hut is full, you can sleep in a "designated campsite" under the stars nearby.) The Potomac Appalachian Trail Club (PATC) provides a log book, and it is inspiring as well as amusing to read the entries made by AT hikers. Many make mention of the overabundance of aggressive mice. It would seem that almost all AT hikers take an alias for the trek, with signatures in the book including names such as "Tadpole," "Earthsurfer," "Purple Haze," "Grin-and-Bear-It," "Rusted Boot," and so on.

Backtrack from the hut to the AT north, and continue the climb to the summit of Hightop. The peak is designated by a cement post, but you must continue for about 25 yards to an overlook on the left that provides sweeping views to the west, southwest, and northwest, as well as a jumble of boulders that are in themselves worthy of inspection. Near the summit, alder bushes form a canopy over the trail.

On a clear day, you can see Skyline Drive below you, a little to the south of west. Looking west, you can see the Massanutten Mountain range, once considered

Fall color as seen from Skyline Drive

as the site for establishment of a national park. Because the overlook is slightly downhill from the summit, views to the east are obscured by vegetation. Take time to study the boulders; it took billions of years to get them where they are.

Your descent can retrace your route, or it can follow Hightop Fire Road to the old Smith Roach Gap Fire Road. In either case, you must descend, retracing your steps along the AT for 0.6 mile. For the sake of variety, we suggest you follow Hightop Fire Road, which goes left at the cement post near the AT hut (blue blazes). It will add another 0.2 mile to the return trip but no elevation gain. Assuming you follow this route, go left on the fire road and travel 0.6 mile.

Option: If you'd like a slightly shorter trip up to the Hightop summit, park on the west side of Skyline Drive at Mile 66.7. Cross the drive to the east side and follow the Appalachian Trail south to the summit, which is approximately 1.4 miles away.

Retrace your steps from the summit for an out-and-back hike of 2.8 miles.

Miles and Directions

0.0　From the cement post in the parking lot, access the Smith Roach Gap Fire Road for about 10 yards to another cement post indicating the Appalachian Trail junction and nearby trailhead.

1.2　Cement post. Trail goes to left on the Appalachian Trail to the PATC Hightop Hut.

1.8　Hightop summit. For panoramic view, turn left at the double white blaze just beyond the cement post. Retrace your steps on the AT going south.

2.4　Cement post. Junction with the Hightop Fire Road. Turn left onto the road.

3.0　Cement post on left. Bear right onto the Smith Roach Gap Fire Road toward Skyline Drive.

4.0　Arrive back at the trailhead and parking lot. Mileage includes visit to hut.

40 Powell Gap

This is a leg stretcher on the Appalachian Trail that leads to a rock overlook offering excellent views of Powell Gap Hollow and the mountains and farmlands to the east.

Skyline Mile: 70.0
Distance: 1 mile out and back
Approx. hiking time: 1 hour
Difficulty: Moderate
Trail surface: Dirt and naturally occurring rock
Traffic: Light

Canine compatibility: Leashed dogs allowed
Maps: National Geographic Trails Illustrated Topographic Map 228; Map 11, Appalachian Trail and Other Trails in Shenandoah National Park, South District (PATC, Inc.)

Finding the trailhead: The trail begins at Mile 70.0 on Skyline Drive at the sign for Powell Gap. Park along the east side of the road near the small meadowlike area. GPS: N38 19.267' / W78 35.524'

One of the authors' favorite short hikes, the route at Powell Gap follows the Appalachian Trail.

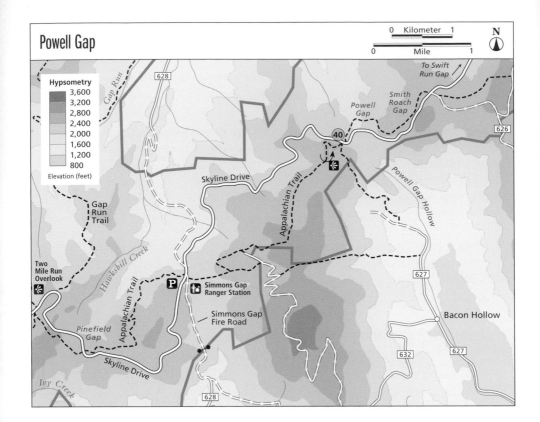

The Hike

Access the trail by walking to the cement post adjacent to the Powell Gap sign. This hike follows the Appalachian Trail south. It immediately begins to climb, gradually but steadily, and peaks at a short spur trail that provides an overlook to the east. After soaking in the countryside and, if you're lucky, some sun, return to your vehicle.

On a late fall or early winter day, this hike could lead to some spectacular views. This is one of our favorite short hikes.

Miles and Directions

0.0 Start at Mile 70.0 on Skyline Drive at the sign for Powell Gap.

0.5 Rock ledge with great views on your left. Retrace steps.

1.0 Arrive at trail's end and your vehicle.

Mountain folks piled rocks at this spot in Powell Gap, presumably to clear space for farming. ▶

41 Simmons Gap

A short stroll on a historic road passes the site of an Episcopal mission.

Skyline Mile: 73.2
Distance: 1.6 miles out and back
Approx. hiking time: 1 to 2 hours
Difficulty: Easy
Trail surface: Dirt and naturally occurring rock
Traffic: Light

Canine compatibility: Leashed dogs allowed
Maps: National Geographic Trails Illustrated Topographic Map 228; Map 11, Appalachian Trail and Other Trails in Shenandoah National Park, South District (PATC, Inc.)

Finding the trailhead: The trail begins at Skyline Drive (Mile 73.2) at the sign for the Simmons Gap Ranger Station. From the south, park on the left (west) side of the road. Cross Skyline Drive and walk down the paved road to the dirt fire road on the right. Begin at the cement post by the yellow chain barring the fire road. GPS: N38 18.008' / W78 37.350'

The Hike

The Simmons Gap Fire Road descends gently, is marked by yellow blazes, and soon parallels a small creek on the right. This stroll follows an old road once used by mountain people traveling from the east and west valleys to access an Episcopal mission. Later, valley folks used the road for park access. Little remains of this once active area other than an old stone wall.

Today, the park service maintains the road as a fire road. Apple trees dot the area, providing mute testimony of a once flourishing agricultural community. A multitude of trees and bushes grace the old road. Near the bottom the trail crosses the creek. A few yards later the trail reaches the park boundary, and you must retrace your route.

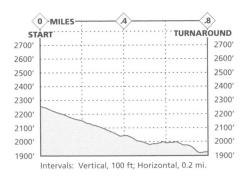

Intervals: Vertical, 100 ft; Horizontal, 0.2 mi.

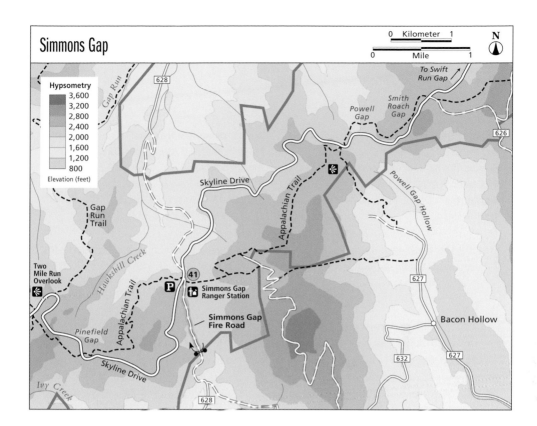

Miles and Directions

0.0 Start at Skyline Drive (Mile 73.2) at the sign for the Simmons Gap Ranger Station.

0.8 Area of old Episcopal mission and park boundary (well marked). Retrace route.

1.6 Arrive at the trailhead and the end of the hike.

42 Rocky Mount–Gap Run Lariat

This is one of the park's most difficult wilderness hikes, but one that also provides spectacular views.

Skyline Mile: 76.2
Distance: 9.8-mile lariat
Approx. hiking time: 5 hours to all day
Difficulty: Strenuous
Trail surface: Dirt and naturally occurring rock
Traffic: Light

Canine compatibility: Leashed dogs allowed
Maps: National Geographic Trails Illustrated Topographic Map 228; Map 11, Appalachian Trail and Other Trails in Shenandoah National Park, South District (PATC, Inc.)

Finding the trailhead: The hike begins at Mile 76.2 on Skyline Drive, at a cement post that reads rocky mount, just north of Two Mile Run Overlook on the drive. GPS: N38 17.949' / W78 38.825'

The Hike

Do not embark on this hike unless you are in excellent shape! However, if you are in good shape, this hike may be just the one for you, particularly if you like remote country that provides a number of spectacular views. At various points along the trail, the abundance of rocks adds to the challenge but also increases the drama and beauty of the area. In addition, the trail proceeds in a roller coaster–like fashion so that you've ascended many more total feet than the actual 1,600-foot difference between the hike's extreme high and low points. For example, the elevation at the trailhead is 2,800 feet, while the low point is at 1,200. Rocky Mount's elevation is 2,741 feet, and to reach it you descend, climb, descend, climb, and descend again before climbing back to the trailhead.

Park at Two Mile Run Overlook (Mile 76.4) and walk north along Skyline Drive to the trailhead (Mile 76.2), which will be on your left. The Rocky Mount Trail crosses back and forth over a ridge, climbs gradually, and descends to its intersection at mile 2.2 with the Gap Run Trail. What goes down must go up, and whether you proceed counterclockwise or clockwise along what, from here, forms a loop, is up to

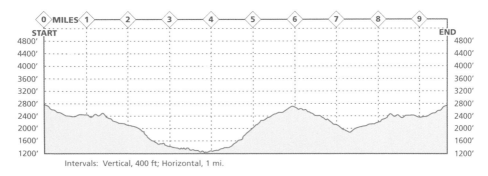

Intervals: Vertical, 400 ft; Horizontal, 1 mi.

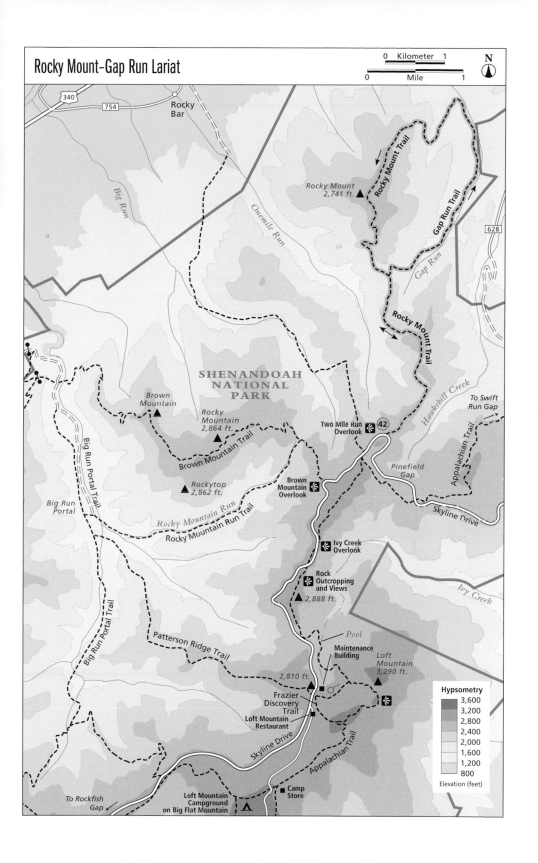

Rocky Mount-Gap Run Lariat

0 Kilometer 1
0 Mile 1

N

340
754
Rocky
Bar

Big Run

Onemile Run

Rocky Mount Trail

Rocky Mount
2,741 ft.

Gap Run Trail

628

Gap Run

Rocky Mount Trail

SHENANDOAH
NATIONAL
PARK

Hawksbill Creek

To Swift
Run Gap

Brown
Mountain

Rocky
Mountain
2,864 ft.

Two Mile Run
Overlook 42

Appalachian Trail

Brown Mountain Trail

Pinefield
Gap

Rockytop
2,862 ft.

Brown
Mountain
Overlook

Big Run Portal Trail

Big Run
Portal

Rocky Mountain Run

Rocky Mountain Run Trail

Skyline Drive

Ivy Creek
Overlook

Rock
Outcropping
and Views
2,888 ft.

Ivy Creek

Pool

Patterson Ridge Trail

Maintenance
Building

Loft
Mountain
3,290 ft.

2,810 ft.

Big Run Portal Trail

Frazier
Discovery
Trail

Loft Mountain
Restaurant

Appalachian Trail

Skyline Drive

Hypsometry
3,600
3,200
2,800
2,400
2,000
1,600
1,200
800
Elevation (feet)

To Rockfish
Gap

Loft Mountain
Campground
on Big Flat Mountain

Camp
Store

Acorns are a favorite food of many park inhabitants, including squirrels and jays.

you. On the day we hiked, the temperature was cool and we wanted to remain in the sun, so we proceeded counterclockwise (the trail is described in this direction). On another day, you might want to proceed clockwise to avoid the sun's intensity.

The Gap Run Trail descends rather abruptly, dropping several hundred feet almost immediately. The descent becomes a little less intense as it encounters Gap Run, which it crosses about 4 miles from the trailhead. At 4.4 miles from the trailhead, the trail rejoins the Rocky Mount Trail. The trail climbs and does so very abruptly, ascending from a low of 1,200 feet at Gap Run to a high of 2,741 feet at Rocky Mount, 6.4 miles from your starting point.

The trail descends from Rocky Mount, dropping—but then climbing—to where, eventually, the Rocky Mount Trail culminates at an elevation of 2,000 feet as it intersects the Gap Run Trail. Along the way, take time to enjoy views of Two Mile Ridge, just beyond Two Mile Run, also in the distance.

Shortly thereafter, the trail begins to climb, intersecting at mile 7.6 with the Gap Run Trail. You're on familiar ground, and so you know you have 2.2 miles more of climbing yet to accomplish to complete the 9.8-mile lariat.

Miles and Directions

0.0 Start at the cement post reading rocky mount, near Mile 76.2 on Skyline Drive.

2.2 Intersection at cement post of the Rocky Mount Trail with the Gap Run Trail. Turn right onto the Gap Run Trail and begin a steep descent (or stay left on the Rocky Mount Trail if hiking the loop clockwise).

4.4 Northern junction of the Rocky Mount and Gap Run Trails.

6.4 Rocky Mount.

7.6 Southern intersection of the Gap Run and Rocky Mount Trails. Continue right following the Rocky Mount Trail.

9.8 Arrive back at the trailhead.

43 Brown Mountain–Rocky Mountain Run Lariat

Enjoy a hike across two mountain peaks, dropping down to cross the park's largest stream.

Skyline Mile: 76.9
Distance: 10.1-mile lariat
Approx. hiking time: 8 to 11 hours
Difficulty: Strenuous
Trail surface: Dirt and naturally occurring rock
Traffic: Light

Canine compatibility: Leashed dogs allowed
Maps: National Geographic Trails Illustrated Topographical Map 228; Map 11, Appalachian Trail and Other Trails in Shenandoah National Park, South District (PATC, Inc.)

Finding the trailhead: Park at the Brown Mountain Overlook, just north of Mile 76.9 on Skyline Drive. Look for the cement post marking the Brown Mountain Trail (blue blazes). Access the trail in the opening in the stone wall at the Brown Mountain Overlook. Descend. GPS: N38 17.561' / W78 39.484'

The Hike

Hikes through this portion of the park not only offer extraordinary views but also provide glimpses into the park's geological past. Along Brown Mountain, sandstone is embedded with 500-million-year-old fossil wormholes. Fire engulfed the area below Brown Mountain in 1986, and today's hikers have the opportunity to observe firsthand just how quickly nature can regenerate itself. Carry plenty of water, especially in summer.

The trail begins in a relatively open and dry site in the midst of a field of raspberries and begins to descend almost immediately. Within 0.7 mile you encounter the first cement post. Aluminum bands herald the return of the Rocky Mountain Run Trail from the left, but you remain on the Brown Mountain Trail, going right. Shortly thereafter the trail switchbacks several times as it begins to climb, soon reaching a knob. At about mile 1.6 you reach the trail's first exposure, which offers views of Rockytop Ridge and Patterson Ridge. Between them is Big Run Portal, where, in the mid-1980s, a hiker ignited a fire while preheating a camp stove on a dry and windy day. The fire eventually burned 4,500 acres.

The trail drops and switches back and forth, at times becoming exceedingly rocky. Vines encroach along the trail's flanks. Where the trail is rocky and flanked with vines, its very appearance suggests snakes. Just a few tenths of a mile later, the vegetation changes composition. In August ripe blackberries weigh heavily on branches and stems. It's hard to imagine better bear country and, as we hiked, we found that at least one such omnivore had left its calling card.

About 3 miles along, the trail traverses the right side of the ridge and cuts hard into the side of the mountain, creating a small rock cliff. Trail maintenance here is good but not excellent.

At about mile 3.8 the trail encounters a talus slope that spans almost 75 yards. The trail soon switches out of the rocks and into a clearing, which offers a great view of Rockytop—not far away as the crow flies. A rock promontory provides the view, which also looks down on Big Run Portal. The trail continues its general downward course and, in a stretch where rocks dominate, may be difficult to find. Look for the familiar blue blaze before moving ahead, one of which is on the rocks at foot level.

The trail continues its drops, switching no fewer than six times. As you progress, you'll see charred stumps, mute testimony of the fire that raged through here. Next to the path, however, is much new growth, which serves to recall the resiliency of nature. Just before reaching the low point of the loop portion of the hike (which you can see as you progress downward), the rocks across the valley containing Big Run Portal appear as palisades. They are prominent and form the base of Rockytop Mountain.

At 5.3 miles, just as you reach the low point of the Brown Mountain loop, you encounter the junction with the Big Run Portal Trail. Go left. In another 25 feet, you encounter another cement post. This points back toward the Brown Mountain Trail and ahead to the Rocky Mountain Run Trail, 1.4 miles away. The trail is level, more or less, as it crosses Big Run Portal and several feeder streams. Campsites abound. We encountered several backpackers who had been attracted by the opportunity to fish.

At a distance of about 6.7 miles from your point of origin, you again cross Big Run Portal. Although the stream has diminished in size, it is still substantial. Large boulders have cleaved the stream, creating two beautiful pools and providing an ideal picnic site and several good holes for fishing. Nearby, a cement post officially marks your mileage. Turn left at the cement post and take the Rocky Mountain Run Trail, which soon begins to climb. If you had proceeded in the other direction (don't), you'd encounter the Patterson Ridge Trail in 0.2 mile.

As the Rocky Mountain Run Trail climbs, you cross a feeder stream several times, which in late summer may run beneath the ground and be only a trickle. Often, however, enough water remains to form substantial pools. About 7.5 miles from your

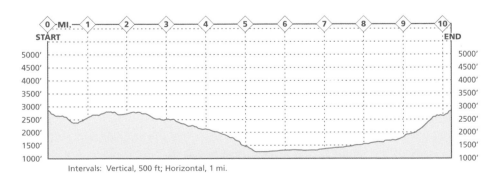

Intervals: Vertical, 500 ft; Horizontal, 1 mi.

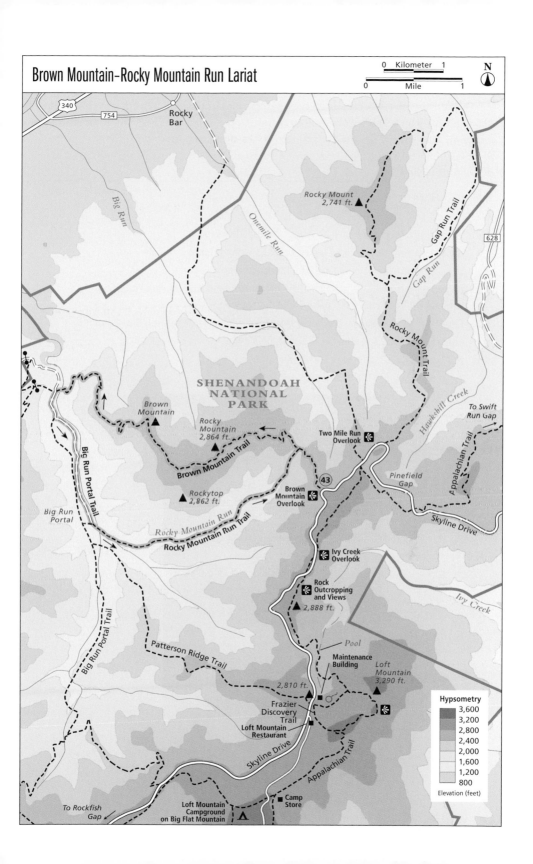

Brown Mountain-Rocky Mountain Run Lariat

0 Kilometer 1

0 Mile 1

N

340

754

Rocky
Bar

Big Run

Onemile Run

Gap Run Trail

628

Rocky Mount
2,741 ft.

Gap Run

Rocky Mount Trail

Hawksbill Creek

To Swift
Run Gap

Appalachian Trail

SHENANDOAH
NATIONAL
PARK

Brown
Mountain

Rocky
Mountain
2,864 ft.

Brown Mountain Trail

Two Mile Run
Overlook

43

Pinefield
Gap

Big Run Portal Trail

Rockytop
2,862 ft.

Brown
Mountain
Overlook

Skyline Drive

Big Run
Portal

Rocky Mountain Run

Rocky Mountain Run Trail

Ivy Creek
Overlook

Rock
Outcropping
and Views

2,888 ft.

Ivy Creek

Big Run Portal Trail

Patterson Ridge Trail

Pool

Maintenance
Building

Loft
Mountain
3,290 ft.

2,810 ft.

Frazier
Discovery
Trail

Loft Mountain
Restaurant

Skyline Drive

Appalachian Trail

Hypsometry

	3,600
	3,200
	2,800
	2,400
	2,000
	1,600
	1,200
	800

Elevation (feet)

To Rockfish
Gap

Loft Mountain
Campground
on Big Flat Mountain

Camp
Store

point of origin, you see the power of the wind. Off to the left dozens of toppled trees intertwine over the creek, the result of the strong winds of 1996.

At about mile 8.4, a 3-foot-high rock signals a switchback. The trail switches back and forth until you reach a cement post at mile 9.4, closing the loop. You're on familiar ground here, and your point of origin is 0.7 mile away.

Miles and Directions

0.0   Start at the cement post marking the Brown Mountain Trail.

0.7   Cement post. Remain on the Brown Mountain Trail.

1.6   Views of Rockytop and Patterson Ridges. Trail becomes rocky.

2.2   Rocky Mountain peak on right. Views. Begin to ascend Brown Mountain.

3.1   Descend from Brown Mountain. Views. Steep descent.

5.3   Cement post marking the junction of the Brown Mountain and Big Run Portal Trails. Turn left onto Big Run Portal Trail. Follow yellow blazes.

6.7   Cement post. Turn left onto the Rocky Mountain Run Trail (blue blazes). Steep ascent.

9.4   Cement post. Turn right onto the Brown Mountain Trail.

10.1   Arrive back at the trailhead at Mile 76.9.

Milkweed and aphids, often seen while hiking trails in Big Meadow.

44 Ivy Creek

This one-way hike contains some moderate and a few strenuous segments and concludes at the Loft Mountain Campground.

Skyline Mile: 77.5
Distance: 4.8 miles one way; shuttle required
Approx. hiking time: 3 to 6 hours
Difficulty: Moderate to strenuous
Trail surface: Dirt and naturally occurring rock
Traffic: Moderate

Canine compatibility: Leashed dogs allowed
Maps: National Geographic Trails Illustrated Topographic Map 228; Map 11, Appalachian Trail and Other Trails in Shenandoah National Park, South District (PATC, Inc.)

Finding the trailhead: The trailhead is at the Ivy Creek Overlook, on Skyline Drive at Mile 77.5. Access the Appalachian Trail southbound from the south end of the parking lot at the cement post (white blazes). GPS: N38 17.055' / W78 39.523'

The Hike

Let's say members of your group are tired of hiking and that they hanker to spend the day in camp, relaxing. Nevertheless, someone would be willing to drive a short distance and help with your logistical dilemma. What that means to you, the hiker, is that someone can make a fifteen-minute drive and you can walk back to the campground on your own schedule—or they could meet you at the store/dining area on Skyline Drive at Mile 79.5. If that's your situation, consider either of the longer hikes described below. If that's not the case, read this section anyway, since you can still make the delightful out-and-back alternative hike summarized at the end of this narration. The Miles and Directions below delineate the distances for one-way hikers who want to conclude at the campground. Regardless, all will pass a variety of the park's delights—some (the logistically unencumbered) more than others.

The hike begins from the south side of the Ivy Creek Overlook and immediately provides you with access to the Appalachian Trail. The trail begins with a slight descent amid sassafras, laurel, oak, and pine. The trail begins to ascend, then makes several switchbacks, passing by several large boulders. The trail continues its climb, providing beautiful views to the east of Loft Mountain. In late summer the trail is flanked by mint, goldenrod, and yellow daisies. In the winter the trail is open and spacious and provides unending views.

At 0.7 mile the trail reaches an opening and offers views of Skyline Drive below. Continuing, the trail drops and is flanked by blueberries—a species the bears love, as one terrified couple reminded us.

As the trail continues its descent, you can hear the gurgle of Ivy Creek, which soon appears from the left. At 1.4 miles from the point of origin, you cross the creek (but not before lingering at this delightful spot with a pool) and begin a 0.75-mile

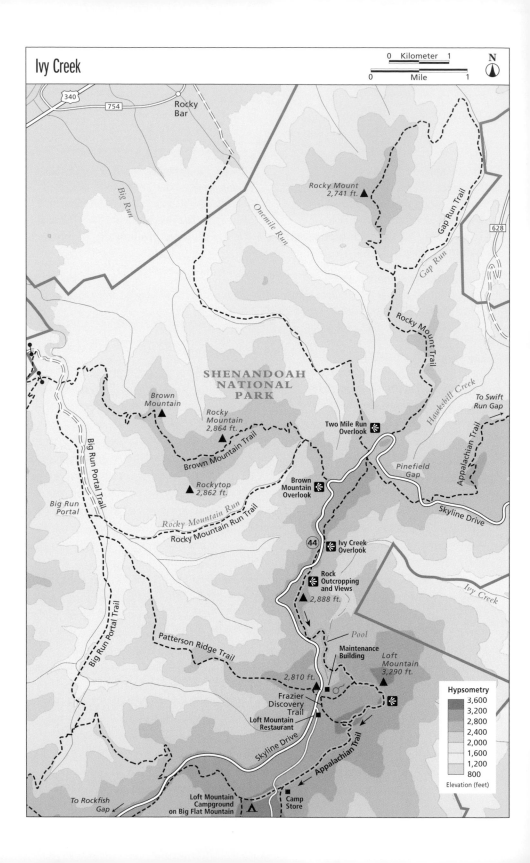

Ivy Creek

340
754

Rocky
Bar

Big Run

Onemile Run

Rocky Mount
2,741 ft.

Gap Run Trail

628

Gap Run

Rocky Mount Trail

SHENANDOAH
NATIONAL
PARK

Hawksbill Creek

To Swift
Run Gap

Brown
Mountain

Rocky
Mountain
2,864 ft.

Brown Mountain Trail

Two Mile Run
Overlook

Appalachian Trail

Pinefield
Gap

Rockytop
2,862 ft.

Brown
Mountain
Overlook

Big Run
Portal

Big Run Portal Trail

Rocky Mountain Run

Rocky Mountain Run Trail

44   Ivy Creek
Overlook

Skyline Drive

Ivy Creek

Rock
Outcropping
and Views
2,888 ft.

Pool

Patterson Ridge Trail

Big Run Portal Trail

Maintenance
Building

Loft
Mountain
3,290 ft.

2,810 ft.

Frazier
Discovery
Trail
Loft Mountain
Restaurant

Hypsometry
3,600
3,200
2,800
2,400
2,000
1,600
1,200
800
Elevation (feet)

Skyline Drive

Appalachian Trail

To Rockfish
Gap

Loft Mountain
Campground
on Big Flat Mountain

Camp
Store

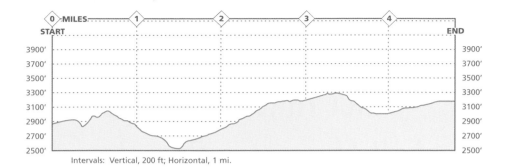

Intervals: Vertical, 200 ft; Horizontal, 1 mi.

climb. Along the way the trail parallels the creek—the only place in the park where the AT parallels a stream for any considerable distance. Enjoy!

At mile 2.2 the AT meets an access trail descending to Skyline Drive, as noted by a cement post. Turn left on the AT and continue the climb up Loft Mountain, which periodically offers views of the surrounding countryside.

At mile 3.2 the AT reaches a cement post and the summit of Loft Mountain. The right-hand fork at the summit drops down to the Frazier Discovery Trail. Continue left along the AT, which descends and then, once again, begins to climb and continues to do so. At 4.5 miles the trail passes the Loft Mountain camp store, then 0.3 mile later the trail concludes at the campground.

Option 1: Perhaps the nicest portion of the Frazier Discovery Trail is the portion that drops downhill from Loft Mountain, for that part of the trail passes by one of the park's more spectacular overhangs. From mile 3.2 on the Ivy Creek hike, proceed down the Frazier Discovery Trail, which takes you back to Skyline Drive. The Loft Mountain camp store is 0.9 mile up the road, across from the wayside, and the campground is 0.3 mile farther.

Option 2: For those who cannot resolve the problem of shuttle logistics, this hike provides the only alternative—an out-and-back hike from the Ivy Creek Overlook. Proceed as outlined above to mile 1.4, the Ivy Creek Pool. Then retrace your route, climbing back uphill to the overlook for a round-trip total of 2.8 miles.

Miles and Directions

0.0 Start at Ivy Creek Overlook near Skyline Drive at Mile 77.5.

0.7 Rock outcropping and views to the west, on right-hand side of trail.

1.4 Ivy Creek and pool.

2.2 Ivy Creek Spring and maintenance building. Stay left on the AT headed south.

3.2 Cement post. The right-hand fork proceeds down the Frazier Discovery Trail. Continue straight on the AT south.

4.5 The AT passes the camp store.

4.8 The AT passes the Loft Mountain Campground. Arrive at the end of the shuttle hike in the campground.

Loft Mountain and Other Hikes from the Loft Mountain Complex

Skyline Mile 79.5

The Loft Mountain Complex offers many amenities to travelers, the best of which are the area's relatively short hiking trails. For ease of reading, we've detailed several of the hikes you might make from the complex and mile 79.5 of Skyline Drive.

From the Loft Mountain Wayside on Skyline Drive, take the road east. Within 1 mile you'll see the camp store and the amphitheater. The Loft Mountain Campground is 0.3 mile farther, and is not on Loft Mountain at all but rather on Big Flat Mountain. Camping is on a first-come, first-served basis, with spaces for trailers, RVs, and tents. Walk-in sites are available for tents only. The bathrooms offer flush toilets and cold water. The campground makes a good base if you're hiking trails within a reasonable driving or walking radius.

Loft Mountain is the most southern of the park's complexes, and this area was severely damaged by the tropical storm of 1996. The park service has worked hard to restore the place, and has succeeded. However, you can find ample evidence of damage in the form of blowdown by hiking back-country trails in the vicinity. The trails are cleared, though, and in good condition. However, due to the large number of dead trees yet standing, this is one area where you need to assess the forest canopy before camping or picnicking.

Apple orchards are left over from the days when farmers tilled the land. This one stands near Loft Mountain Campground. See Hike 45.

45 Loft Mountain Loop

A fun family hike leads to the northeast summit of Loft Mountain; views are offered at several places.

Skyline Mile: 79.5
Distance: 2.7-mile loop
Approx. hiking time: 3 to 5 hours
Difficulty: Easy
Trail surface: Dirt and naturally occurring rock
Traffic: Light to moderate

Canine compatibility: Leashed dogs allowed except on Frazier Discovery Trail
Maps: National Geographic Trails Illustrated Topographic Map 228; Map 11, Appalachian Trail and Other Trails in Shenandoah National Park, South District (PATC, Inc.)

Finding the trailhead: Park at Mile 79.5 on Skyline Drive, at the Loft Mountain Wayside parking lot. Walk north on Skyline Drive (past the Patterson Ridge Trail on the left) for 150 yards to a dirt road on the right. Follow this road. GPS: N38 15.858' / W78 39.575'

An AT marker as seen along Loft Mountain Trail.

No one camped at Loft Mountain Campground should miss the easy hike that circles the mountain.

The Hike

This is a very enjoyable hike and one that is suitable for a fun family outing.

From the Loft Mountain Wayside parking lot, walk north on Skyline Drive for about 150 yards to a dirt road on the right. Along the way you pass the trailhead for the Patterson Ridge Trail (a one-way trail) on the left. Turn onto the dirt road, walk about 60 yards, and go right again on the dirt road. Soon you'll come to the Ivy Creek PATC maintenance building and Ivy Creek Spring. The Appalachian Trail junction is about 200 yards ahead. Upon reaching the AT, turn right and ascend through the hardwood forest.

As you approach the top, the trees become more widely spaced and blackberry bushes abound. After about 1 mile the trail levels out on the ridgetop. Soon there is an overlook to the left of the trail, with rock outcroppings. Here you'll find lovely 180-degree views to the east of the Piedmont (on clear days); to the left is Flat Top Mountain, and to the right is Fox Mountain with three peaks, a hollow, then two more peaks. The valley below offers pastoral settings, and you can watch clouds and storms roll in. Fields of yarrow (a medicinal plant) and more berry bushes also populate the ridgetop.

At the next cement post you have several options. To complete the loop we turned right onto the Frazier Discovery Trail, encountering another great viewpoint

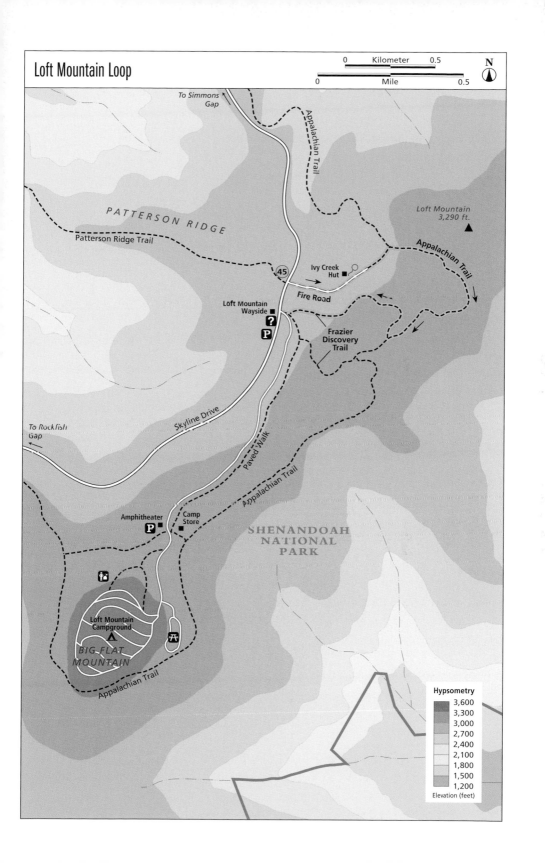

Loft Mountain Loop

0   Kilometer   0.5

0   Mile   0.5

N

To Simmons Gap

Appalachian Trail

PATTERSON RIDGE

Patterson Ridge Trail

Loft Mountain 3,290 ft.

Appalachian Trail

45

Ivy Creek Hut

Fire Road

Loft Mountain Wayside

?

P

Frazier Discovery Trail

To Rockfish Gap

Skyline Drive

Paved Walk

Appalachian Trail

Amphitheater

P

Camp Store

SHENANDOAH NATIONAL PARK

Loft Mountain Campground

Λ

BIG FLAT MOUNTAIN

Appalachian Trail

Hypsometry

	3,600
	3,300
	3,000
	2,700
	2,400
	2,100
	1,800
	1,500
	1,200

Elevation (feet)

on the right. Follow the Frazier Discovery Trail down to Skyline Drive and the wayside parking lot.

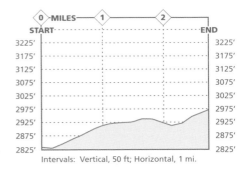

Intervals: Vertical, 50 ft; Horizontal, 1 mi.

Alternatively, from the cement post at mile 1.4, continue straight on the AT and access the other fork of the Frazier Discovery Trail, thus returning to your starting point. For a third option, continue straight on the AT for another 1.3 miles to the Loft Mountain Campground (if you haven't left your vehicle at the wayside parking lot).

Miles and Directions

0.0 Located about 150 yards along a dirt road near Mile 79.5 on Skyline Drive.

60 yards Cement post. Turn right on dirt road. Ascend.

0.4 Cement post. Ivy Creek PATC maintenance building and spring. Follow blue blazes uphill. Cross small creek.

0.6 Cement post. Junction with the Appalachian Trail. Turn right and follow white blazes uphill.

1.0 Trail levels on ridgetop.

1.1 Overlook on left looking northeast to the summit of Loft Mountain. Ascend once again briefly, then cross the saddle to the southwest summit of Loft Mountain.

1.4 Cement post. You have three options: (1) Turn right to return to the wayside via the Frazier Discovery Trail fork. This is the route described here. (2) Stay straight on the AT to access the other fork of the Frazier Discovery Trail and return to the Loft Mountain Wayside. (3) Stay straight on the AT to the Loft Mountain Campground, 1.3 miles farther.

1.5 Side trail to right, leading to overlook.

2.7 Arrive back at Skyline Drive and Loft Mountain Wayside parking lot.

46 Frazier Discovery Trail

This 1.3-mile loop introduces hikers to discoveries along the trail.

Skyline Mile: 79.5
Distance: 1.3-mile loop
Approx. hiking time: 2 hours
Difficulty: Moderate
Trail surface: Dirt and naturally occurring rock
Traffic: Light to moderate

Canine compatibility: Dogs not allowed
Maps: National Geographic Trails Illustrated Topographic Map 228; Map 11, Appalachian Trail and Other Trails in Shenandoah National Park, South District (PATC, Inc.)

Finding the trailhead: The trail begins at Mile 79.5 on the east side of Skyline Drive, on the northern end of the Loft Mountain Wayside parking lot. Look for a cement post marking the Frazier Discovery Trail. Access the right-hand fork of the trail (traveling counterclockwise). GPS: N38 15.772' / W78 39.631'

Greenstone lava flanks the Frazier Discovery Trail, easily accessible from the Loft Mountain Campground.

The Hike

The Frazier Discovery Trail is a 1.3-mile loop. The trail begins on the east side of Skyline Drive, immediately to the left of the spur road that departs the drive and begins its climb to the Loft Mountain Campground. The trail is blue blazed. You may purchase a guide at the trailhead or at the information center located across Skyline Drive from Loft Mountain Restaurant.

The Frazier Discovery Trail begins its climb quickly: In other words, you get out of your car and begin climbing immediately (if you choose to take the loop counterclockwise as described here). There's nothing gradual about the climb. But be of good cheer: The climb, though steep, isn't too long. Just watch yourself at first if you are not used to climbing. Take time to rest and absorb the sounds of nature, which are many. On our hike, we were immediately confronted by a catbird that voiced its disapproval of our presence.

In about 0.5 mile a cement post identifies your location, pointing to the Loft Mountain Campground (1.2 miles away), and directs you along your way. Take the Appalachian Trail north (left) and continue up (you're almost to the top) for about 0.1 mile more, which in fact brings you to the summit—and views. All views are from an extensive rock outcropping that is covered with lichen.

Views from the overlook are commanding, though unidirectional. Because of extensive stands of oak to the east, views in that direction are blocked. However, to the west you can see Skyline Drive threading its way both north and south. You can also see Massanutten Mountain, once a contender for national park status. You can see Hightop to the south. Closer at hand, you invariably see the ever-present vultures circling high overhead, gliding as they search for carrion. Closer yet are stands of laurel, oak, and alder. Equally as important is what you can't see. Below are no towns or cities, and except for Skyline Drive the scene appears very much as it must have appeared in more pristine times.

Continuing from the overlook, in about 100 yards the trail comes to a junction. To complete this hike, turn left, once again on the Frazier Discovery Trail, which leads to another rock outcropping that offers views similar to those just described. Continue on the Frazier Discovery Trail, which drops rather steeply. About 0.2 mile farther the trail comes to a rock outcropping that towers about 100 feet overhead. The trail passes beneath the outcropping, which offers a breath of cool air, refreshing on a hot summer day.

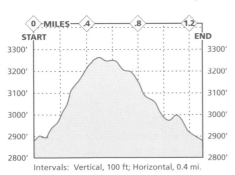

Intervals: Vertical, 100 ft; Horizontal, 0.4 mi.

Finally, just before you reach the trail's end, the forest adds a dense and extensive carpet of ferns to its floor. Several hundred yards later, the trail completes its loop at the fork at the trailhead.

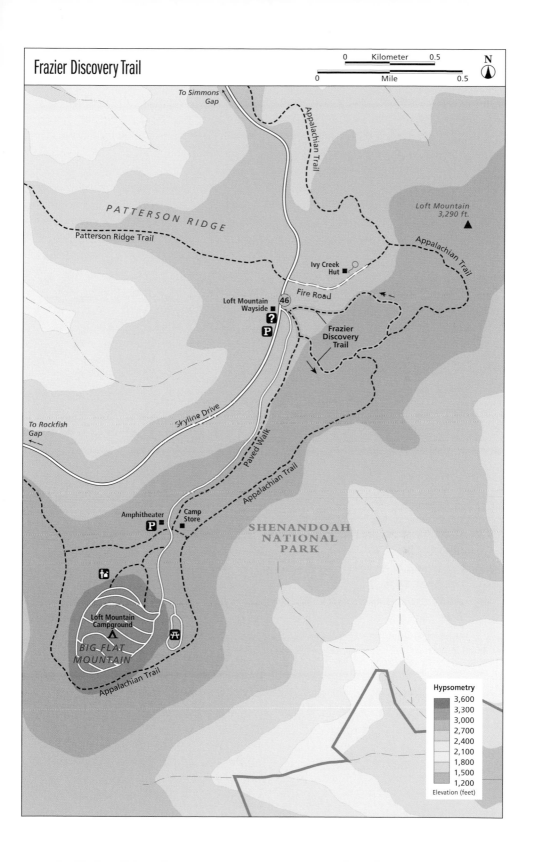

Frazier Discovery Trail

Kilometer
0 0.5

Mile
0 0.5

N

To Simmons Gap

Appalachian Trail

PATTERSON RIDGE

Patterson Ridge Trail

Loft Mountain
3,290 ft.

Appalachian Trail

Ivy Creek Hut

Fire Road

Loft Mountain Wayside

46

?

P

Frazier Discovery Trail

Skyline Drive

To Rockfish Gap

Paved Walk

Appalachian Trail

Amphitheater

P

Camp Store

SHENANDOAH NATIONAL PARK

Loft Mountain Campground

BIG FLAT MOUNTAIN

Appalachian Trail

Hypsometry

	3,600
	3,300
	3,000
	2,700
	2,400
	2,100
	1,800
	1,500
	1,200

Elevation (feet)

The Frazier Discovery Trail offers panoramic views.

Miles and Directions

0.0 Start at the cement post marking Frazier Discovery Trail, on the northern end of the Loft Mountain Wayside parking lot.

0.5 Cement post. Go north (left) onto the Appalachian Trail. Turn onto the left-hand trail for a view from the cliff.

0.6 Loft Mountain overlook and rock outcropping. Cement post. Take the Frazier Discovery Trail to the left.

1.3 Arrive back at the fork at the beginning of the Frazier Discovery Trail. End of loop.

47 Big Flat Mountain Loop

A short flat hike on the Appalachian Trail circles the Loft Mountain Campground, with some views.

Skyline Mile: 79.5
Distance: 1.8-mile loop
Approx. hiking time: 2 to 4 hours
Difficulty: Easy
Trail surface: Dirt and naturally occurring rock
Traffic: Light to moderate

Canine compatibility: Leashed dogs allowed
Maps: National Geographic Trails Illustrated Topographic Map 228; Map 11, Appalachian Trail and Other Trails in Shenandoah National Park, South District (PATC, Inc.)

Finding the trailhead: From the Loft Mountain Wayside at Mile 79.5 on Skyline Drive, take the road east, then south, toward the Loft Mountain Campground. The trailhead is at the amphitheater, which is about 1 mile up the road on the right. Access the trail at the cement post just past the kiosk. GPS: N38 14.974' / W78 40.125'

The Hike

The Loft Mountain Campground, built in 1964, is actually on Big Flat Mountain, an area that was once pastureland. The Appalachian Trail makes almost a complete circle around the campground and offers views, some quite spectacular, at the beginning of the hike.

Making this trek around the campground is a good leg stretcher for the entire family, besides providing an idea of what the area once looked like. Not only do you get great views to the west but also the trail wanders through an open forest and, in places, through forests of ferns, providing parklike settings. The Loft Mountain area was hit hard by the tropical storm of 1996, and evidence of the destruction is well documented in the woods.

Three nice day hike loops are described on the kiosk at the Loft Mountain amphitheater. Study your maps; you'll be able to come up with your own original ideas for longer or shorter hikes in this area. In the meantime, we suggest the following hike.

From the north end of the amphitheater parking lot, take the paved trail toward the amphitheater. After about 30 yards, turn left and go 0.25 mile downhill to a cement post and the junction with the AT. Go left onto the AT and ascend to a saddle. Here you can walk up to the campground, entering at the "A" loop. But stay on the AT; almost immediately, rocky viewpoints are available to the right of the trail. You are looking west and hopefully it is a clear day, because then you can see the Doyles River and watershed. Jones Run is there, too, and both areas contain famous waterfalls.

Continue on the AT through the woods on the soft path, traveling counterclockwise around the campground. The trek becomes a very enjoyable walk in the

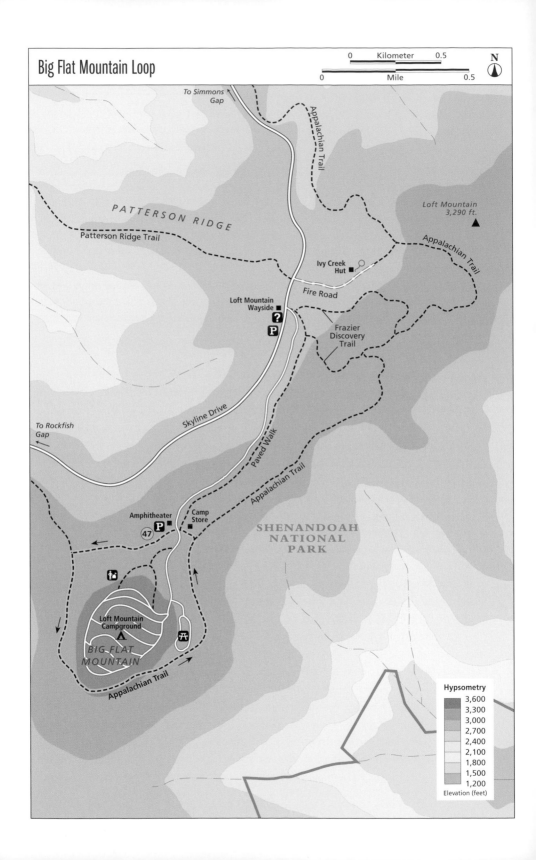

Big Flat Mountain Loop

0   Kilometer   0.5

0   Mile   0.5

N

To Simmons Gap

Appalachian Trail

PATTERSON RIDGE

Loft Mountain
3,290 ft.

Patterson Ridge Trail

Ivy Creek Hut

Appalachian Trail

Fire Road

Loft Mountain Wayside

?

P

Frazier Discovery Trail

Skyline Drive

To Rockfish Gap

Paved Walk

Appalachian Trail

Amphitheater   Camp Store

47   P

SHENANDOAH NATIONAL PARK

Loft Mountain Campground

BIG FLAT MOUNTAIN

Appalachian Trail

Hypsometry

3,600
3,300
3,000
2,700
2,400
2,100
1,800
1,500
1,200
Elevation (feet)

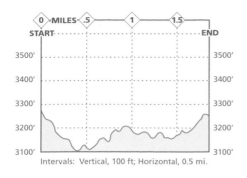

Intervals: Vertical, 100 ft; Horizontal, 0.5 mi.

woods, a walk even young children will find fun. However, many viewpoints are becoming somewhat obscured by the rapid growth of young trees. There are several places to the left where you can once again access the campground, one of which is at a cement post. But stay on the AT north to the second cement post, which is just below the camp store. Turn left at the cement post and walk uphill 70 yards to the store. Go left in front of the store for about 0.1 mile and you're back at the amphitheater parking lot to complete the loop hike.

Obviously, you can begin and end your hike from any of several points in the campground. The hike described above seems to be a good length for those wanting after-breakfast or after-dinner exercise.

Miles and Directions

0.0 Start at Loft Mountain Campground amphitheater.

30 yards Turn left. Descend.

0.25 Cement post and junction with the Appalachian Trail. Go left, up the hill.

0.5 Trail to left to "A" section of campground. To the right begins a series of rocky viewpoints. Continue on the AT, heading south.

1.0 Cement post indicating another path into the campground. Stay on the AT.

1.6 Cement post. Turn left. In 70 yards pass the camp store. Turn left on the paved walkway going uphill toward the amphitheater and campground.

1.8 Arrive back at the end of the loop at the amphitheater.

48 Big Run Loop

A loop trail takes you through the hardwood forest and much park wilderness.

Skyline Mile: 81.1
Distance: 5.8-mile loop
Approx. hiking time: 2 to 4 hours
Difficulty: Easy to moderate
Trail surface: Dirt and naturally occurring rock
Traffic: Light

Canine compatibility: Leashed dogs allowed
Maps: National Geographic Trails Illustrated Topographic Map 228; Map 11, Appalachian Trail and Other Trails in Shenandoah National Park, South District (PATC, Inc.)

Finding the trailhead: Park at the Doyles River parking lot at Mile 81.1 on Skyline Drive, just prior to the Big Run Overlook on the right. Walk across the drive to the Big Run Overlook. Go to the opening in the stone wall—the trail begins to the west. Almost immediately you come to a cement post, indicating you are on Big Run Loop Trail, marked by blue blazes on the trees. GPS: N38 15.222' / W78 41.060'

The Hike

After accessing the trail through the opening in the stone wall at the Big Run Overlook, you come to a sign advising you that fishing is permitted in the Big Run area with a Virginia license.

Follow the blue blazes on the trees and begin descending into the forest. You can still catch views of the Shenandoah Valley to the west. Many young chestnuts flank the trail, as do several species of maples, white pine, sassafras, and mountain laurel.

The descent continues, crossing a tiny, barely running creek at about 1 mile. At 1.5 miles the trail ascends a small knoll between two valleys. Heading downhill once more, at mile 2.2 you reach a second, larger, gurgling stream, a branch of the Big Run. The forest canopy opens. Minnows dart in the stream. This is a great rest or picnic stop, a respite from the summer heat. Dunk your head and soak your feet.

At mile 3.5, you encounter a four-way intersection. You will also find a cement post here, indicating the trail's intersection with the Big Run Loop Trail. Access the trail to the east (left), marked with a blue blaze. The trail to the right is the Rockytop Trail. The Big Run Loop Trail levels as it winds along the ridgetop to the next cement post at a T intersection at mile 4.2. The Appalachian Trail intersects and you turn north (left) onto the AT. Cars on Skyline Drive are easily heard now, as the drive is only 0.3 mile from this point. The hike to the road is level; cross the drive to continue on the AT, which is up the road a very short distance to your left.

Ascend above the road, then descend to a large rock outcropping. In approximately 0.2 mile you encounter the Doyles River Overlook, offering views to the east. Walk the length of the overlook parking lot to continue on the AT at the north end.

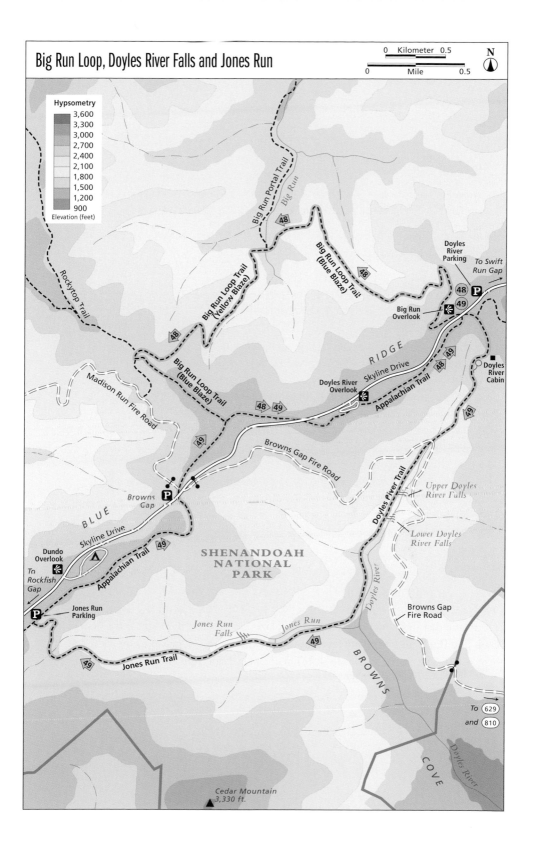

Big Run Loop, Doyles River Falls and Jones Run

Hypsometry

3,600
3,300
3,000
2,700
2,400
2,100
1,800
1,500
1,200
900
Elevation (feet)

0   Kilometer 0.5
0   Mile   0.5

N

Big Run Portal Trail

Big Run

48

Big Run Loop Trail
(Blue Blaze)

48

Doyles
River
Parking

To Swift
Run Gap

Big Run Loop Trail
(Yellow Blaze)

48

48

49

Big Run
Overlook

Rockytop Trail

RIDGE

Skyline Drive

49

48

49

Doyles
River
Cabin

Big Run Loop Trail
(Blue Blaze)

Madison Run Fire Road

Doyles River
Overlook

48   49

Appalachian Trail

49

49

Browns Gap Fire Road

Doyles River Trail

Upper Doyles
River Falls

49

Browns
Gap

P

BLUE

Skyline Drive

Lower Doyles
River Falls

Dundo
Overlook

Appalachian Trail

49

SHENANDOAH
NATIONAL
PARK

Doyles River

To
Rockfish
Gap

P

Jones Run
Parking

Jones Run
Falls

Jones Run

Browns Gap
Fire Road

49

49

Jones Run Trail

BROWNS

To 629
and 810

COVE

Doyles River

Cedar Mountain
3,330 ft.

Intervals: Vertical, 400 ft; Horizontal, 1 mi.

The path continues with gentle ups and downs to the last cement post. Go left for 70 feet to the Doyles River parking lot and your vehicle.

Miles and Directions

0.0 Start at the opening in the stone wall at Big Run Overlook.

1.0 Cross a tiny stream.

2.2 Cross a second, larger stream, a branch of the Big Run. Reach the cement post 100 yards farther on the trail. Access the yellow-blazed trail to your left (west) to stay on the Big Run Loop Trail. Ascend.

3.5 Cement post marking the intersection of the Rockytop Trail with the Big Run Loop Trail. Turn east (left), continuing on the Big Run Loop Trail (yellow blazes).

4.2 Cement post. Junction with the Appalachian Trail. Go north (left) on the AT. Follow the white tree blazes.

4.5 Access Skyline Drive. Cross the road to continue north on the AT.

4.7 Doyles River Overlook with views to the east. Continue to the AT, which picks up at the north end of the overlook.

5.7 Cement post. Turn left onto the Doyles River Trail (blue blazes). Cross Skyline Drive.

5.8 Arrive back at the trailhead and the Doyles River parking lot.

49 Doyles River Falls and Jones Run

This long circuit hike takes you to several of the park's most refreshing waterfalls.

See map on page 181.
Skyline Mile: 81.1
Distance: 7.8-mile loop
Approx. hiking time: 6 to 8 hours
Difficulty: Moderate to strenuous
Trail surface: Dirt and naturally occurring rock

Traffic: Light to moderate
Canine compatibility: Leashed dogs allowed
Maps: National Geographic Trails Illustrated
Topographic Map 228; Map 11, Appalachian
Trail and Other Trails in Shenandoah National
Park, South District (PATC, Inc.)

Finding the trailhead: The trail begins at the Doyles River parking area at Mile 81.1 on Skyline Drive. GPS: N38 15.251' / W78 40.972'

The Hike

Though this trail can at times be strenuous, it is one of our favorites. The trail passes by three distinctive waterfalls, so start early and plan to end late.

From the Doyles River parking lot, the trail descends, crosses the Appalachian Trail, and continues its descent, passing a small spring on the left 0.3 mile from the trailhead. A few hundred yards later, the trail branches. The left fork proceeds to the Doyles River Cabin. Take the right fork, which is the Doyles River Trail.

At about mile 0.9 the trail crosses the Browns Gap Fire Road. Stay on the Doyles River Trail, which soon crosses, then parallels, the Doyles River until it reaches Upper Doyles River Falls 1.3 miles from the trailhead. A spur trail leads to the base of the 28-foot-high falls and is worth the brief effort.

Continue along the trail, which takes you to 63-foot-high Lower Doyles River Falls (1.5 miles from the trailhead). As the trail continues, it parallels the Doyles River, passing more cascades and spillways.

At 2.1 miles the trail forms a junction with the Jones Run Trail, which you now follow. About 0.1 mile later, the trail crosses Jones Run and begins to ascend. At 2.8

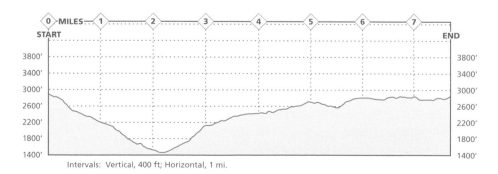

Intervals: Vertical, 400 ft; Horizontal, 1 mi.

miles the trail takes you to Jones Run Falls, a gathering place for many as it has a delightful pool that is readily accessible near its 42-foot drop.

The trail continues to climb, reaching the Jones Run parking area at mile 4.6. To complete this loop, turn right at the AT, which passes the Dundo Picnic Area at mile 5.1. Continue on the AT, passing Browns Gap at mile 5.8. The trail opens to the Doyles River Overlook 1 mile later. After another 1 mile of fairly easy walking, the trail nears its completion, uniting with the Doyles River Trail. Turn left to return to your vehicle.

Option: For a shorter hike to all of the above-mentioned waterfalls, start at the Browns Gap Fire Road (see Miles and Directions below and the hike description above), which pro-

Shenandoah National Park is home to herds of deer, such as this large white-tail buck.

vides a parking lot for about a dozen vehicles. This route reduces the route described above by about 2 miles. The Brown family originally built the road as an old turnpike in the late 1700s, and then used it to take produce from the Shenandoah Valley to Richmond. During the Civil War, Stonewall Jackson used it for troops. Today, it serves as a delightful alternative route that accesses three waterfalls. Like the Doyles River Trail, it descends sharply. It joins with the Doyles River Trail about 0.5 mile above the upper falls. For the remainder of the hike, follow the description provided above, along the Jones Run Trail and back up to the Appalachian Trail, where you really save time by concluding your hike 2 miles from the Doyles River trailhead at Browns Gap.

Miles and Directions

0.0 Start at the Doyles River parking area at Mile 81.1 on Skyline Drive.

0.9 Junction with the Browns Gap Fire Road.

1.3 Upper Doyles River Falls.

1.5 Lower Doyles River Falls.

2.8 Jones Run Falls.

4.6 Jones Run parking. Access the Appalachian Trail heading north.

5.8 Browns Gap. Stay on the AT northbound.

6.8 Doyles River Overlook. Remain on the AT northbound.

7.8 Arrive back at the trailhead and the Doyles River parking lot.

50 Austin Mountain–Furnace Mountain Loop

A strenuous but beautiful hike leads into a rugged wilderness area within the park.

Skyline Mile: 83.0
Distance: 12.4-mile loop
Approx. hiking time: All day
Difficulty: Strenuous
Trail surface: Dirt and naturally occurring rock
Traffic: Light

Canine compatibility: Leashed dogs allowed
Maps: National Geographic Trails Illustrated Topographic Map 228; Map 11, Appalachian Trail and Other Trails in Shenandoah National Park, South District (PATC, Inc.)

Finding the trailhead: Begin at the Browns Gap parking area, 0.1 mile north of Mile 83.0 on Skyline Drive. Follow the road at the yellow chain on the west end of the parking area. Descend on the Madison Run Fire Road. GPS: N38 14.444' / W78 42.658'

The Hike

The Austin Mountain–Furnace Mountain area consists of a huge expanse of land. Fortunately, many trails exist there. This trek offers solitude and views and is geologically interesting. Because of the area's diversity, a number of possibilities exist There are long hikes and several short ones. Time will dictate which alternative you ultimately select. The first part of this narration discusses a long day's hike. We offer another suggestion as an alternative hike.

The long day hike begins 0.1 mile north of Mile 83.0 at the Browns Gap parking lot. Begin by descending the Madison Run Fire Road at the west end of the parking lot. After 0.8 mile you reach a cement post. Leave the road and go right; this is the Madison Run Spur Trail. Ascend through the forest for 0.3 mile to a cement post where you turn left onto Rockytop Trail.

Ascend to a narrow ridgetop that offers splendid views through the trees to both sides. About 0.3 mile later you see a double blue blaze, then a cement post. Go west (left): This is the Austin Mountain Trail. At this point, it is 3.2 miles to the next junction with the Madison Run Fire Road. Along the trail you see prime examples of the damage visited on oaks by the numerous gypsy moths. Because the trees are sparse, lovely vistas open to the southwest. Directly below is Dundo Hollow, and across from it rise numerous mountains, such as Furnace Mountain (2,657 feet).

After about 1.5 miles the descent becomes steep, levels, then drops again and is quite narrow and rocky. Continue to enjoy the great views; just before you drop off the ridge, the farmlands of the Shenandoah Valley come into sight. The trail begins to cross talus slopes. If you look carefully at the rocks you're stepping on, you can see long, indented dark lines, remnants of ancient worms that once bored their way into the sand.

At this point you are passing under the summit of Austin Mountain (2,658 feet). The descent becomes radically steep and very tedious due to the many talus slopes and rocks that cross or litter the trail. Amid this terrain, you come to a double blue blaze; a switchback makes a sharp left, then drops down four rock stairs. In fact, the turn approaches 180 degrees, and soon you cross the lower portion of the talus slopes that you crossed above.

About 0.1 mile from the end of the Austin Mountain Trail, cross a dry feeder stream. Then you pop out onto the Madison Run Fire Road at a cement post. Turn right and follow the Madison Run Fire Road for 0.6 mile—almost to the point where a chain crosses it as the road nears one of the park's western boundaries. At the point where you turn left onto the Furnace Mountain Trail, you'll see the chain about 0.1 mile away.

Almost immediately the Furnace Mountain Trail crosses Madison Run, which even in the summer may be a full, flowing stream. A good campsite lies nearby. The trail swings abruptly to the right, parallels the creek for about 100 yards, then turns left and begins to climb—and it doesn't stop climbing.

At about 7.2 miles from this excursion's beginning, the trail reaches a talus slope and continues its climb. At mile 7.7 the trail reaches a cement post directing you to the left if you wish to climb Furnace Mountain. If you want to see exceptional panoramas of the area, make the 0.5-mile climb to the top.

Return to the trail from the summit. The main trail continues its climb. If you are ascending on a hot summer day, you'll agree that Furnace Mountain is an appropriate name for the mountain whose flank you are climbing. Much of the trail faces southwest, and the length of this excursion makes it difficult to avoid the summer afternoon sun.

The Austin–Furnace Mountain loop is, in fact, one of the park's more difficult treks. As the trail nears a side shoot of Furnace Mountain, it is covered with rock, making summer hiking even more tiring. Only at a point that approximates your 7.9-mile point does the trail level, but the reprieve is a brief one. In just a few tenths of a mile, the trail again begins to climb.

The Furnace Mountain Trail ends at a junction with the Trayfoot Mountain Trail at a cement post at 9.5 miles. If you turn right, the Trayfoot Mountain Trail will take you to the summit of Trayfoot Mountain, 0.2 mile away, but there is no view. Turn left (east) onto the eastbound fork of the Trayfoot Mountain Trail.

At 10.2 miles the Trayfoot Mountain Trail encounters a cement post. If you turn right, the trail will take you to a point that almost reaches spectacular Blackrock Summit, from where you follow signs directing you to the Appalachian Trail. Taking this route would add 0.5 mile to the hike.

To continue on the main route from the 10.2 mile point, continue to the AT on the Trayfoot Mountain Trail. Take the AT north, passing the Blackrock Summit parking lot. The trail climbs, and about 2 miles later the trail returns you to the Browns Gap parking lot and your hike's end.

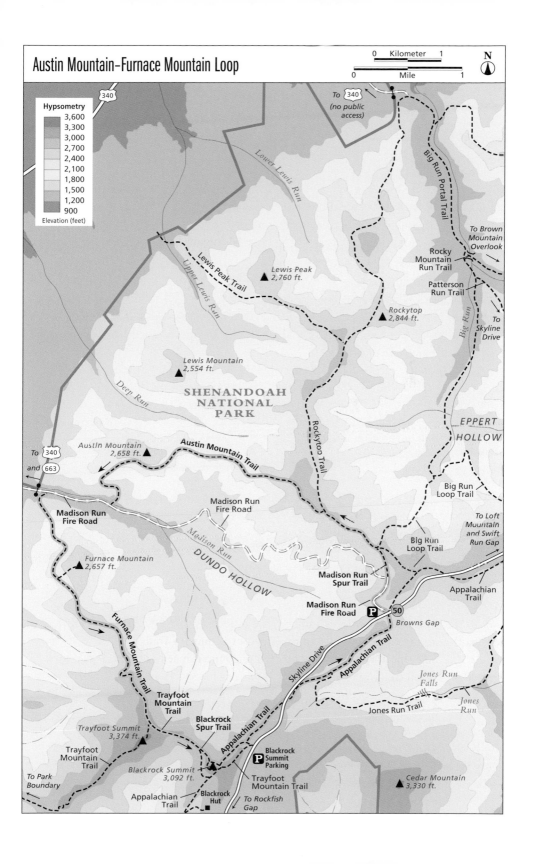

Austin Mountain–Furnace Mountain Loop

To 340
(no public access)

Hypsometry
| 3,600 |
| 3,300 |
| 3,000 |
| 2,700 |
| 2,400 |
| 2,100 |
| 1,800 |
| 1,500 |
| 1,200 |
| 900 |

Elevation (feet)

Kilometer
Mile
N

Lower Lewis Run

Big Run Portal Trail

Rocky Mountain Run Trail

To Brown Mountain Overlook

Lewis Peak Trail

Lewis Peak 2,760 ft.

Patterson Run Trail

Rockytop 2,844 ft.

Upper Lewis Run

To Skyline Drive

Big Run

Lewis Mountain 2,554 ft.

SHENANDOAH NATIONAL PARK

EPPERT HOLLOW

Deep Run

Rockytop Trail

To 340 and 663

Austin Mountain 2,658 ▲

Austin Mountain Trail

Big Run Loop Trail

Madison Run Fire Road

Madison Run Fire Road

Madison Run

DUNDO HOLLOW

Big Run Loop Trail

To Loft Mountain and Swift Run Gap

Furnace Mountain 2,657 ft.

Madison Run Spur Trail

Appalachian Trail

Madison Run Fire Road

P 50

Browns Gap

Furnace Mountain Trail

Jones Run Falls

Skyline Drive

Appalachian Trail

Jones Run

Trayfoot Mountain Trail

Blackrock Spur Trail

Jones Run Trail

Trayfoot Summit 3,374 ft.

Appalachian Trail

Trayfoot Mountain Trail

Blackrock Summit 3,092 ft.

P Blackrock Summit Parking

To Park Boundary

Cedar Mountain 3,330 ft.

Trayfoot Mountain Trail

Appalachian Trail

Blackrock Hut

To Rockfish Gap

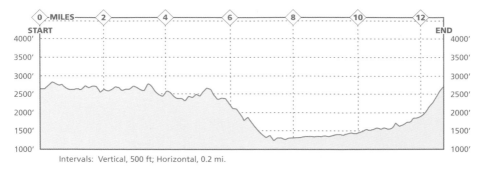

Intervals: Vertical, 500 ft; Horizontal, 0.2 mi.

Option: After hiking near the summit of Austin Mountain, traversing, as you must, the trail's many rocky areas, you may find yourself exhausted or out of time. Fortunately, as you descend onto the Madison Run Fire Road, which you reach at 4.8 miles from your point of origin, you have an option for a 9.1-mile loop. The fire road provides a gradual return to your vehicle along an incline that is fairly gentle. Use the Miles and Directions below to take you to mile 4.8 and the intersection with the Madison Run Fire Road. Be sure to carry plenty of water (at least three quarts) on this hike, particularly on hot, humid summer days.

To complete the shorter loop, turn left onto the Madison Run Fire Road and begin the gradual ascent. Although you are no longer in the wilderness, the boundaries extend to within a stone's throw of both sides of the road. On this part of the hike, we were musing about snakes and bears. Suddenly 30 feet ahead, a large black bear tore from the woods and came to a halt. Jane yelled, "Git," and it got. So much for her fear of bears!

Miles and Directions

0.0 Start at Browns Gap parking area, 0.1 mile north of Mile 83.0 on Skyline Drive.

0.4 At the cement post go north (right) onto the Madison Run Spur Trail, which leads to the Austin Mountain Trail. Ascend.

1.1 Access the Rockytop Trail, at intersection with Big Run Loop Trail.

1.5 Junction with the Austin Mountain Trail and Rockytop Trail. Go west (left) on the Austin Mountain Trail.

4.8 The Austin Mountain Trail joins the Madison Run Fire Road. Turn right.

5.3 Cement post. Turn left (south) off the Madison Run Fire Road and onto the Furnace Mountain Trail.

7.7 Continue straight, or take the optional 0.5-mile spur to the top of Furnace Mountain (worth the detour).

9.5 Cement post. Junction of the Trayfoot Mountain and Furnace Mountain Trails. The Furnace Mountain Trail ends. Bear left (east) onto the eastbound fork of the Trayfoot Mountain Trail.

10.2 At the cement post take the left fork of the Trayfoot Mountain Trail to the Blackrock Summit parking area, bypassing Blackrock Summit (if you wish) and picking up the Appalachian Trail northbound just before the Blackrock Summit parking lot. Continue on the AT for about 2 more miles.

12.4 Arrive back at the trailhead and the Browns Gap parking area. End of loop.

51 Rockytop

This is a ruggedly beautiful all-day hike (or backpack) on Rockytop's ridges, crossing Big Run many times.

Skyline Mile: 83.0
Distance: 14.7-mile loop
Approx. hiking time: All day or overnight back-pack (backcountry permits required)
Difficulty: Strenuous
Trail surface: Dirt and naturally occurring rock

Traffic: Light
Canine compatibility: Leashed dogs allowed
Maps: National Geographic Trails Illustrated Topographic Map 228; Map 11, Appalachian Trail and Other Trails in Shenandoah National Park, South District (PATC, Inc.).

Finding the trailhead: The trailhead is at Browns Gap parking area, 0.1 mile north of Mile 83.0 on Skyline Drive. Take the Madison Run Fire Road, at the chain in the parking lot. GPS: N38 14.444' / W78 42.658'

The Hike

Rockytop and the country through which this hike courses can best be appreciated by driving to the overlook at Mile 81.2 (Big Run Overlook) and studying the interpretive sign at the overview. The sign summarizes the significance of the watershed, which really is a detail of the topography over which the trail progresses. Note Rockytop Ridge. Note Big Run and Big Run Portal. Note as well the magnitude of the country. That's where the trail courses for 14.7 miles. That's where the trail drops from Rockytop Ridge down toward Big Run Portal and then back up through Big Run. Along Big Run the trail crosses back and forth over several creeks no fewer than half a dozen times.

Waters that course along these streams provide some of the park's best trout fishing. These creeks flow generally toward the east and then north, where they collect to form the South Fork of the Shenandoah River. That river flows on a northern course, eventually merging with other waters to form the Potomac. The South Fork flows around the northern portion of Shenandoah National Park, where it joins the North Fork of the Shenandoah just north of Front Royal. The Shenandoah River joins the Potomac River at Harpers Ferry, West Virginia, where the combination then flows southeastwardly, eventually into the Chesapeake Bay at a point about midway between Washington, DC, and Norfolk, Virginia. As the sign says, the waters of the Shenandoah may be the least appreciated of all the park's features.

Over the course of our trek past Rockytop and down into the land of the Big Run Portal, thunder gods growled at one another along Rockytop Ridge while rain beat out a staccato rhythm on the walls of our tent. During our two-day venture, more than a dozen deer watched from the trail's edge as our muffled footfalls carried us past them.

Much of the area has been designated as wilderness, and in places camping opportunities abound. If you can afford the time, make this a multiday backpacking trip.

Though some prefer to hop onto the Appalachian Trail immediately at the Browns Gap parking lot, to minimize repetition almost completely, we opted to begin our trek by descending the Madison Run Fire Road. From the parking lot, descend this road for 0.8 mile to the Madison Run Spur Trail. Turn right onto the spur trail, which climbs to the Rockytop Trail, which you stay on for the next 0.3 mile. After accessing the Rockytop Trail, watch for trails to Austin Mountain and for the Lewis Peak Trail. Stay on the Rockytop Trail.

Hiking the ridge to Rockytop is inspiring. The trail courses back and forth across Rockytop Ridge, sometimes offering northerly views, sometimes southerly. Because the density of vegetation changes, sometimes the views only hint at the area's grandeur, though often they make bold statements. At mile 3.7 the trail passes the Lewis Peak Trail.

Rockytop is 6.3 miles from the trailhead, but things start to happen before reaching the summit. Along the way, the land becomes more rocky and, frequently, talus slopes course down the hill, cutting wide swaths across the trail. Considering the size of the boulders, trail maintenance is excellent and originally must have demanded much ingenuity on the part of the old Civilian Conservation Corps boys. In places, the trail has been fortified on the downhill side with boulders intended to restrain the downward progression of other rocks and boulders.

Near the summit of Rockytop, a long talus slope becomes part of the trail. The slope stretches for close to 100 yards. Rocks here, and along much of the way, are sandstone in origin, and it is here that the ancient sea worm once made its home.

At places along the ridge crest (near Rockytop), trees may have toppled. Imagine what the wind can do here, and then you know why the trails may not be as clear as elsewhere in the park. Just below Rockytop, the berries can be as thick as the filling in Grandma's blueberry pie. The black bears know it, and should you encounter one dining on nature's bounty, the prevailing advice regarding these bears is to stand your ground. They generally retreat.

The trail passes through the patch and quickly begins a descent of approximately 2.5 miles. Shortly thereafter the trail passes onto an old fire road and about 1 mile later (at 8.8 miles from the trailhead), the old fire road crosses an old steel bridge. On the other side of the bridge, a cement post resides where you must turn right to stay on the Big Run Portal Trail. The trail crosses and recrosses Big Run and several other creeks no fewer than half a dozen times. These crossings are made over the course of the next 4 miles.

When we made our first creek crossing, rain poured, but all along Big Run large oak trees offered shelter. There are also good campsites throughout the area, so if your weather pattern duplicates ours, consider pitching your tent. Just remember to camp out of sight of others, and that you can't build a campfire. Big Run is the very area in which a camper inadvertently started the infamous Big Run Fire of 1986. The fire started in Big Run, spread up the flanks of Rockytop and Rocky Mountain, then

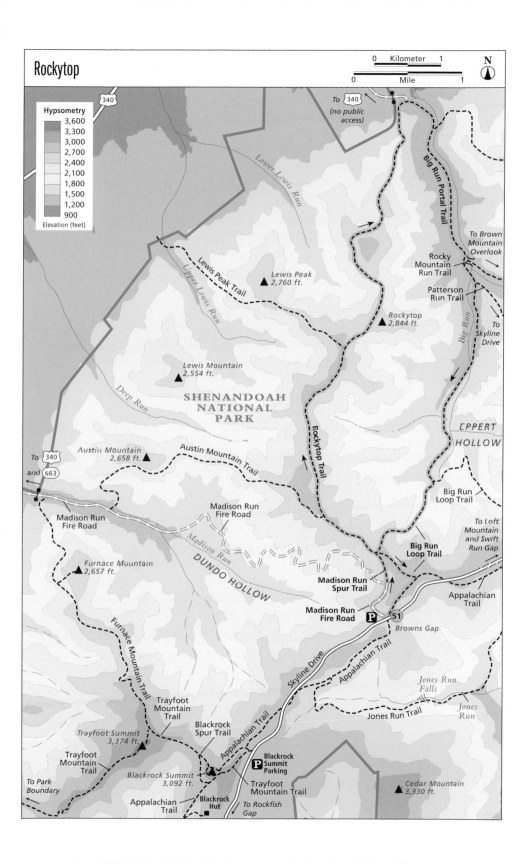

Rockytop

Kilometer
0　1

Mile
0　1

N

Hypsometry

Elevation (feet)
3,600
3,300
3,000
2,700
2,400
2,100
1,800
1,500
1,200
900

340

To 340
(no public access)

Lower Lewis Run

Big Run Portal Trail

To Brown Mountain Overlook

Rocky Mountain Run Trail

Lewis Peak Trail

Upper Lewis Run

▲ *Lewis Peak 2,760 ft.*

Patterson Run Trail

▲ *Rockytop 2,844 ft.*

To Skyline Drive

Big Run

▲ *Lewis Mountain 2,554 ft.*

SHENANDOAH NATIONAL PARK

Deep Run

Rockytop Trail

EPPERT HOLLOW

To 340
and 663

Austin Mountain ▲ 2,658 ft.

Austin Mountain Trail

Big Run Loop Trail

Madison Run Fire Road

Madison Run

DUNDO HOLLOW

To Loft Mountain and Swift Run Gap

Big Run Loop Trail

Madison Run Fire Road

Madison Run Spur Trail

Madison Run Fire Road

P

▲ *Furnace Mountain 2,657 ft.*

51

Browns Gap

Appalachian Trail

Furnace Mountain Trail

Skyline Drive

Appalachian Trail

Jones Run Falls

Jones Run

Trayfoot Mountain Trail

Blackrock Spur Trail

Jones Run Trail

▲ *Trayfoot Summit 3,374 ft.*

P **Blackrock Summit Parking**

Trayfoot Mountain Trail

▲ *Blackrock Summit 3,092 ft.*

Appalachian Trail

To Park Boundary

Appalachian Trail

■ Blackrock Hut

Trayfoot Mountain Trail

To Rockfish Gap

▲ *Cedar Mountain 3,330 ft.*

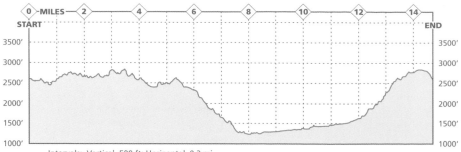

Intervals: Vertical, 500 ft; Horizontal, 0.2 mi.

ran along Patterson Ridge. Eventually, the fire burned 4,475 acres. More than 500 firefighters battled the blaze. Another fire occurred in June and July of 2001.

At mile 12.4 the Big Run Portal Trail joins the Big Run Loop Trail and the easy going is over. The trail ascends almost all the way back to the trailhead at Browns Gap. There's no way to avoid it, though perhaps your load is now easier, for presumably you've eaten most of your food and drunk most of your water. So start chugging.

At 13.4 miles, the trail intersects once again with the Rockytop Trail. Turn left and hike 0.7 mile to the AT. At the AT turn south (right) and walk the final 0.6 mile to the trailhead. Much of this is downhill.

Miles and Directions

0.0   Start at Browns Gap parking area, 0.1 mile north of Mile 83.0 on Skyline Drive.

0.8   Cement post. Turn right onto the Madison Run Spur Trail.

1.1   Cement post. Junction of the Rockytop and Big Run Loop Trails. Go left onto the Rockytop Trail.

1.5   Cement post. Austin Mountain Trail junction. Stay right on the Rockytop Trail.

3.7   Cement post. Junction with the Lewis Peak Trail. Stay right on the Rockytop Trail.

6.3   Approach Rockytop (2,844 feet).

8.3   Cement post. Junction. Go right onto the Big Run Portal Trail. (There is a private road to your left. No public access.)

8.8   Old steel bridge and, on the far side of the bridge, junction of the Big Run Portal Trail and the Brown Mountain Trail. Stay on the Big Run Portal Trail.

11.2   Cement post noting it is 2.3 miles to the Big Run Loop Trail. Intersection with Rocky Mountain Run Trail.

11.4   Cement post noting intersection with the Patterson Run Trail.

12.4   Junction of the Big Run Portal Trail with the Big Run Loop Trail, which comes in from the left and which you now follow.

13.4   Crossroads of the Big Run Loop Trail, the Rockytop Trail, and the Madison Run Spur Trail. Turn left onto the spur trail for 0.7 mile to the Appalachian Trail. (You will recognize this junction as the one leading from the Madison Run Fire Road and the spur you took from it.)

14.1   Junction with the AT. Go south (right), following the white blazes.

14.7   Arrive back at the trailhead and the Browns Gap parking lot.

52 Blackrock Summit

A short loop hike climbs to a rocky summit with a short boulder scramble at the top.

Skyline Mile: 84.8
Distance: 1-mile loop
Approx. hiking time: 1 to 1.5 hours
Difficulty: Easy
Trail surface: Dirt and naturally occurring rock
Traffic: Moderate to heavy

Canine compatibility: Leashed dogs allowed
Maps: National Geographic Trails Illustrated Topographic Map 228; Map 11, Appalachian Trail and Other Trails in Shenandoah National Park, South District (PATC, Inc.)

Finding the trailhead: The trail begins at Mile 84.8 on Skyline Drive, at the Blackrock Summit parking lot on the west side of the drive. Cross the chain and access the old fire road (Trayfoot Mountain Trail), heading uphill. GPS: N38 13.0938' / W78° 44.009'

The Hike

Once Blackrock was a huge cliff, which cracked thousands of years ago. It tumbled down the mountain's slopes to become the incredible jumble of rocks that awaits you atop the summit. The uneven surfaces are actually the cliff's top. The rocks of Hampton quartzite are covered with dark patches of rock tripe, a variety of lichen.

In 1781 Thomas Jefferson apparently expressed concern about the safety of Virginia's great seal and the state's archives. Accordingly, Jefferson gave them to a friend who hid them in a cave at Blackrock until the war's end.

The trailhead is located at a sign that interprets the mountain's geology. After acquainting yourself with the area's geology, head uphill for 0.1 mile on the Trayfoot Mountain Trail to the junction with the Appalachian Trail. Take the AT south, following the white blazes. The AT remains level almost all the way to the top—a distance from the junction of about 0.4 mile.

The sight at the summit, which greets you as you leave the forest canopy, is commanding. Huge jumbles of rocks fall away to form a talus slope on the right of the trail. Meanwhile, more boulders rise sharply to the summit. The trail stops just short of the summit, and to reach it you must scramble a short distance over a maze of boulders. Occasionally, hikers report seeing rattlesnakes sunning themselves on the boulders, so watch where you step.

From the summit you can see Trayfoot Mountain, Horsehead Mountain,

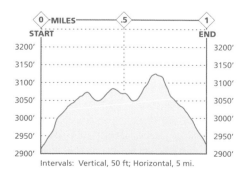

Intervals: Vertical, 50 ft; Horizontal, 5 mi.

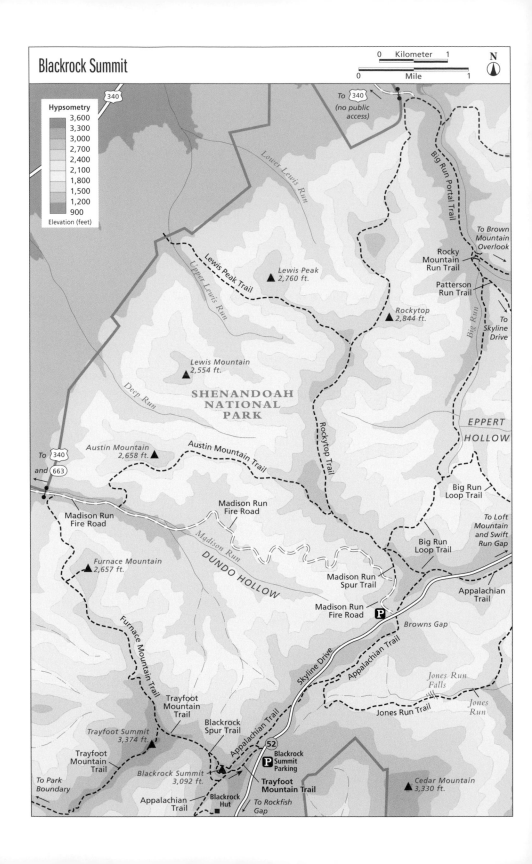

Blackrock Summit

Hypsometry

3,600
3,300
3,000
2,700
2,400
2,100
1,800
1,500
1,200
900

Elevation (feet)

0 Kilometer 1
0 Mile 1

N

To 340
(no public access)

Lower Lewis Run

Big Run Portal Trail

To Brown Mountain Overlook

Rocky Mountain Run Trail

Patterson Run Trail

Lewis Peak Trail

Lewis Peak
2,760 ft.

Rockytop
2,844 ft.

To Skyline Drive

Upper Lewis Run

Big Run

Lewis Mountain
2,554 ft.

Deep Run

SHENANDOAH NATIONAL PARK

EPPERT HOLLOW

Rockytop Trail

Austin Mountain
2,658 ft.

Austin Mountain Trail

To 340
and 663

Madison Run Fire Road

Big Run Loop Trail

Madison Run Fire Road

To Loft Mountain and Swift Run Gap

Madison Run

DUNDO HOLLOW

Big Run Loop Trail

Furnace Mountain
2,657 ft.

Madison Run Spur Trail

Appalachian Trail

Furnace Mountain Trail

Madison Run Fire Road

P

Browns Gap

Jones Run Falls

Trayfoot Mountain Trail

Blackrock Spur Trail

Skyline Drive

Appalachian Trail

Jones Run

Trayfoot Summit
3,374 ft.

Appalachian Trail

Blackrock Summit Parking

Jones Run Trail

Trayfoot Mountain Trail

52

To Park Boundary

Blackrock Summit
3,092 ft.

Blackrock Summit Parking

P

Cedar Mountain
3,330 ft.

Appalachian Trail

Blackrock Hut

Trayfoot Mountain Trail

To Rockfish Gap

Buzzard Rock, and Furnace Mountain. On a very clear day, try to locate Hightop. From the summit, you can access Trayfoot Summit, another 0.7 mile one way. The trail is easy and the remains of an old fire tower greet you, but you get no view.

On our hike, we watched biology in action. Toward the end of the trail segment circling Blackrock Summit, a wasp was burrowing into the web spun by a moth, where it began feeding on larvae.

The trail continues following the AT south around the peak to another cement post at mile 0.6. On the post an arrow points left to the old road (Trayfoot Mountain Trail), which leads back to the trailhead and the parking lot.

Miles and Directions

0.0 Start near Mile 84.8 on Skyline Drive, at the Blackrock Summit parking lot on the west side of the Skyline Drive.

0.1 Cement post. Intersect with the Appalachian Trail; take the AT south, following the white blazes.

0.5 Blackrock. Scramble up rocks and boulders to the peak. At the cement post the AT intersects with the Blackrock Spur Trail. Continue circling the summit.

0.6 Cement post. Junction of the Blackrock Spur Trail with the AT. Turn left to return to the parking lot via Trayfoot Mountain Trail.

1.0 Arrive back at the trailhead. End of hike.

53 Trayfoot Mountain–Paine Run Loop

This wilderness loop hike passes by Blackrock Summit, ascends Trayfoot Mountain, and crosses a number of beautiful creeks.

Skyline Mile: 87.4
Distance: 9.6-mile loop
Approx. hiking time: 6 to 10 hours
Difficulty: Strenuous
Trail surface: Dirt and naturally occurring rock
Traffic: Light

Canine compatibility: Leashed dogs allowed
Maps: National Geographic Trails Illustrated Topographic Map 228; Map 11, Appalachian Trail and Other Trails in Shenandoah National Park, South District (PATC, Inc.)

Finding the trailhead: The trail begins at Blackrock Gap, Mile 87.4 on Skyline Drive. Access the Appalachian Trail north. GPS: N38 12.387' / W78 44.986'

The Hike

This is one of our favorite hikes because it threads through such a variety of land features. Take plenty of water for this hike, particularly if it's a warm day.

This hike begins at Blackrock Gap and climbs to reach Blackrock at 1.3 miles, where it skirts the jumble of rocks forming this spectacular mountain. Views from here are beautiful. At 1.4 miles the trail meets the Trayfoot Mountain Trail and dips between piles of boulders, where it levels for a short distance but quickly begins to climb to the summit of Trayfoot Mountain. After passing the summit of Trayfoot, the trail, which is generally level for about 0.2 mile, progresses along a ridge. The trail begins a sharp descent, passing back and forth across the ridge. About a mile from the summit (3.5 miles from the trailhead), the trail passes by a series of interesting rock outcroppings, then continues its general downhill course.

At 6.2 miles the trail reaches the base of the Trayfoot Mountain Trail, where you encounter a cement post noting the trail's intersection with the Paine Run Trail. Almost immediately you cross Paine Run and begin a gradual ascent, crossing a

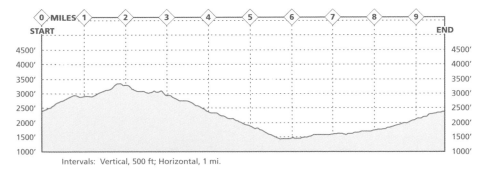

Intervals: Vertical, 500 ft; Horizontal, 1 mi.

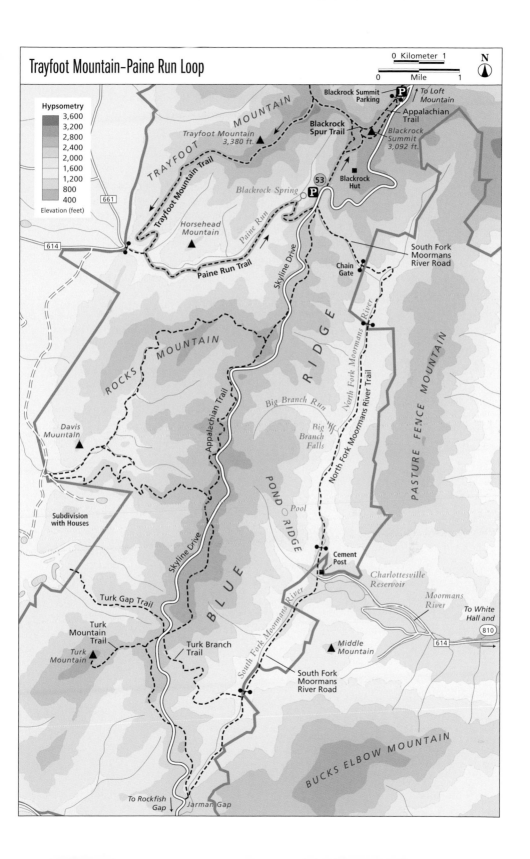

Trayfoot Mountain–Paine Run Loop

Hypsometry

	3,600
	3,200
	2,800
	2,400
	2,000
	1,600
	1,200
	800
	400

Elevation (feet)

0 Kilometer 1

0 Mile 1

N

TRAYFOOT MOUNTAIN

Trayfoot Mountain 3,380 ft.

Blackrock Spur Trail

Blackrock Summit Parking

P

To Loft Mountain

Appalachian Trail

Blackrock Summit 3,092 ft.

Trayfoot Mountain Trail

661

Blackrock Spring

53

P

Blackrock Hut

Horsehead Mountain

Paine Run

614

Paine Run Trail

Skyline Drive

South Fork Moormans River Road

Chain Gate

ROCKS MOUNTAIN

North Fork Moormans River

BLUE RIDGE

North Fork Moormans River Trail

PASTURE FENCE MOUNTAIN

Davis Mountain

Appalachian Trail

Big Branch Run

Big Branch Falls

POND RIDGE

Pool

Subdivision with Houses

Cement Post

Charlottesville Reservoir

Moormans River

To White Hall and

810

Skyline Drive

Turk Gap Trail

Turk Mountain Trail

Turk Mountain

Turk Branch Trail

South Fork Moormans River

South Fork Moormans River Road

Middle Mountain

614

BLUE

BUCKS ELBOW MOUNTAIN

To Rockfish Gap

Jarman Gap

number of feeder streams as you go. At 8.7 miles the trail passes a spur that leads to Blackrock Spring. Often the trail is overgrown and seems to offer a haven for snakes. Bypass the spur and continue climbing along what quickly becomes an obvious road-bed and remains such almost until you reach the trailhead at 9.6 miles.

Miles and Directions

0.0 Start at Blackrock Gap, Mile 87.4 on Skyline Drive.

0.6 Spur to the Blackrock Hut on the right, off the Appalachian Trail heading north.

1.1 Begin skirting Blackrock Summit.

1.2 At cement post halfway around the summit, go left onto the Blackrock Spur Trail.

1.4 Junction with the Trayfoot Mountain Trail. Turn left onto the Trayfoot Mountain Trail.

2.2 Cement post. Go left (southwest) on the Trayfoot Mountain Trail at the junction with the Furnace Mountain Trail, which goes to the right. Ascend summit of Trayfoot Mountain 0.2 mile farther.

2.4 Summit of Trayfoot. Begin descent of about 3.0 miles.

6.2 Cement post indicating the park boundary is 0.3 mile to the west. Turn left onto the Paine Run Trail. Cross creek immediately.

6.4 Cross creek again.

8.7 Intersection with spur trail to Blackrock Spring. Keep right on Paine Run Trail; ascend.

9.6 Arrive back at the trailhead at Blackrock Gap.

54 Moormans River

A fascinating hike departs from Skyline Drive and descends past homesteads to an area at one time ravaged by a "once-in-2,000-years storm."

Skyline Mile: 87.4
Distance: 9.4 miles one way; shuttle required
Approx. hiking time: 6 to 10 hours
Difficulty: Strenuous
Trail surface: Dirt and naturally occurring rock
Traffic: Light

Canine compatibility: Leashed dogs allowed
Maps: National Geographic Trails Illustrated Topographic Map 228; Map 11, Appalachian Trail and Other Trails in Shenandoah National Park, South District (PATC, Inc.)

Finding the trailhead: The route begins at the Blackrock Gap parking lot at Mile 87.4 on the west side of Skyline Drive. Cross to the east side of the drive to the cement post, and access the North Fork Moormans River Trail (fire road). GPS: N38 12.403' / W78 44.960'

The Hike

In 1995 the clouds opened and in a twenty-four-hour period dumped more than 30 inches of rain on portions of Shenandoah National Park. The sudden flood of water over the Moormans River area affected lives and property. The waters took the lives of eight people and caused millions of dollars in property damage. The effects were felt as well in Shenandoah National Park. Water permeated the ground and saturated the soil, which then began to slough. When it did, it carried entire forests, tossing them about like so many matchsticks, and great walls of stone and mud from the hilltops came down like avalanche chutes. Even the trout fishing was adversely affected.

Still, the Moormans River remains an area of much intrigue, perhaps because the damage was caused by nature, not by humans. Park trail crews have invested many hours in restoring the trails. The area is slowly revegetating itself. Though the storm uprooted whole stands of trees, large sycamores still grow along the river. Moormans River is one of the few park areas where this species proliferates.

The trail begins across from the Blackrock Gap parking area and immediately begins to descend along the North Fork Moormans River Trail. What will later become a substantial river is simply a small, almost inconspicuous stream. Within a mile the stream grows, in part from the several small feeder streams that you must cross. In slightly over a mile, barbed wire begins to flank both sides of the road, suggestive of the considerable private land the fire road parallels. Around mile 1.1, you see posted signs indicating that you're leaving the park. At mile 1.5 you will see a cattle-loading chute on your left; it's still in use. A hundred yards later, a gate designates private property and a stream comes in from your left. The trail courses through some private property.

Hunters sometimes use this old school bus, which hikers can see by descending the Moormans River Trail.

At mile 2.1 a chain gate announces your return to Shenandoah National Park. Immediately, the trail crosses a small stream. The trail is obviously still a fire road, but one that is not used as much as the upper portion. The trail soon crosses a bridge that may have been washed out by the flood. Just a short distance farther, at about mile 2.3, you encounter your first exposed area of devastation. Above you trees are uprooted in a dramatic fashion—all by a stream that in the summer can at times be dry. At about mile 2.9 the scene repeats itself: Another small stream has significantly altered the landscape. At approximately 3.5 miles cross Big Branch Run, with its 40-foot waterfall and pools 200 yards above the trail.

Just past mile 3.5 the North Fork Moormans River begins to swell substantially. No longer is it a trickle; rather it is a significant stream. Almost at the same point, you see an extensive range of cliffs that rise above the river's far bank, which is off to your left.

At 4.7 miles the trail crosses the river and the trail becomes indistinct. You must follow a series of rock cairns that lead you downriver to the trail. About 0.3 mile farther, you encounter another cement post and a sign advising you that you are leaving the park.

At mile 5.7 a cement post marks the Charlottesville Reservoir parking area. To find the trail, you must rock hop across the stream and climb the bank to the other side of the river.

Your trail continues outside the park, following the South Fork Moormans River Road. As you hike you cross several small streams. At mile 6.35 you wade or rock hop across the South Fork Moormans River, now to your right. At mile 7.3 you'll see a well-preserved rock foundation of an old home.

Not until mile 7.5 do you reenter the park. Shortly thereafter, you see an old rock wall that stands 5 feet high in places and is 70 to 75 yards wide.

At mile 7.7 you see a cement post that notes the distance to Turk Gap. Continue straight to Jarman Gap, crossing several small feeder streams and passing both a sign warning of the presence of an underground pipeline and another rock wall. At 9.4 miles from your point of origin, the Appalachian Trail crosses your route. Continue straight, concluding your hike at Jarman Gap.

Moormans Overlook hints at the beauty hikers into this drainage might see.

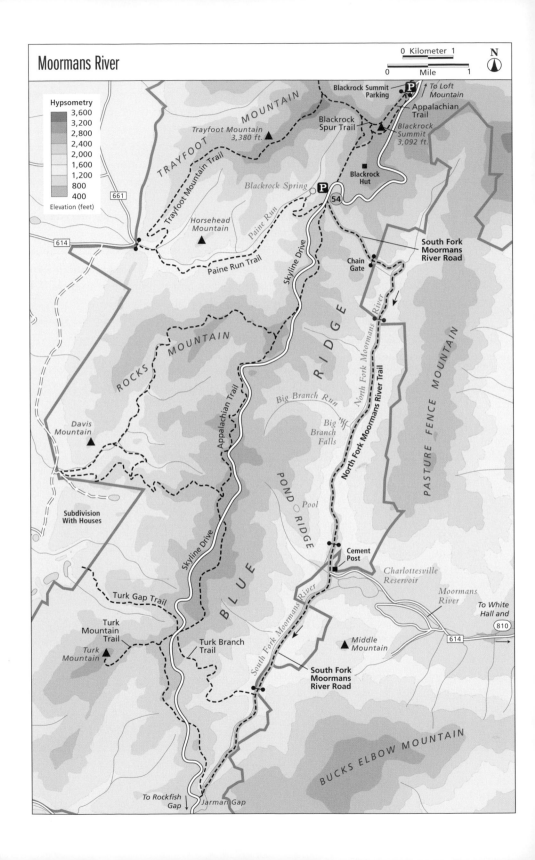

Moormans River

Hypsometry

3,600
3,200
2,800
2,400
2,000
1,600
1,200
800
400

Elevation (feet)

TRAYFOOT   MOUNTAIN

Trayfoot Mountain
3,380 ft.

Blackrock Summit
Parking

To Loft
Mountain

Appalachian
Trail

Blackrock
Spur Trail

Blackrock
Summit
3,092 ft.

661

Trayfoot Mountain Trail

Blackrock Spring

Blackrock
Hut

P

54

Horsehead
Mountain

Paine Run

South Fork
Moormans
River Road

614

Paine Run Trail

Chain
Gate

ROCKS   MOUNTAIN

North Fork Moormans River

B L U E   R I D G E

Skyline Drive

North Fork Moormans River Trail

PASTURE FENCE MOUNTAIN

Davis
Mountain

Big Branch Run

Big
Branch
Falls

Appalachian Trail

Subdivision
With Houses

Pool

POND   RIDGE

Cement
Post

Charlottesville
Reservoir

Moormans
River

To White
Hall and

Skyline Drive

Turk Gap Trail

South Fork Moormans River

Middle
Mountain

810

614

Turk
Mountain
Trail

Turk Branch
Trail

Turk
Mountain

South Fork Moormans River

South Fork
Moormans
River Road

BUCKS ELBOW   MOUNTAIN

To Rockfish
Gap

Jarman Gap

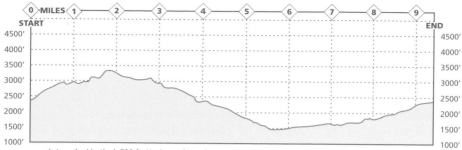

Intervals: Vertical, 500 ft; Horizontal, 1 mi.

Miles and Directions

0.0 Start near Blackrock Gap parking lot at Mile 87.4 on the west side of Skyline Drive.

1.1 Cement post. Cross chain gate. Leave Shenandoah National Park.

1.4 Cement post. Turn right and cross North Fork Moormans River.

2.2 Cross chain gate and note sign announcing entry to Shenandoah National Park. Now on the North Fork Moormans River Trail.

2.3 Area of huge devastation from 1995 rains.

3.5 Cross Big Branch Run.

4.7 Cross the stream and follow rock cairns for a short distance.

5.0 Cross the stream, which is now on the right.

5.1 Beautiful cliffs on the left. On the downstream side of the cliffs, the trail crosses the stream.

5.7 Cement post at center of parking lot. Trail approaches the Charlottesville Reservoir.

6.3 Cross the stream. Next, wade the South Fork Moormans River, now to the right (usually quite shallow except in the spring).

7.2 Beautiful pool.

7.3 Cross the feeder stream. Well-preserved rock foundation of an old home.

7.5 Cement post signifying return to the park.

7.6 Imposing old rock wall.

7.7 Cement post noting the Turk Branch Trail. Stay straight on South Fork of Moormans River Road.

9.4 Cement post noting crossing of the Appalachian Trail. Stay straight on the old road to Jarman Gap and the end of the hike.

55 Riprap Trail

This series of trails crosses some of the park's more strenuous, pristine, and inspiring features.

Skyline Mile: 90.0
Distance: 9.3-mile loop (or 6.7 miles one way/shuttle to Wildcat Ridge parking area)
Approx. hiking time: 10 hours or overnight (backcountry permit required)
Difficulty: Moderately strenuous
Trail surface: Dirt and naturally occurring rock

Traffic: Light to moderate
Canine compatibility: Leashed dogs allowed
Maps: National Geographic Trails Illustrated Topographic Map 228; Map 11, Appalachian Trail and Other Trails in Shenandoah National Park, South District (PATC, Inc.)

Finding the trailhead: The trail begins at Mile 90.0 on Skyline Drive at the Riprap parking lot on the west side of the drive. At the parking lot take a 50-foot-long connecting trail uphill to the AT. Turn right on the AT and continue north for 0.4 mile until it intersects with the Riprap Trail, where you turn left. GPS: N38 10.670' / W78 45.911'

The Hike

Wilderness is the theme of the trails here. It begins the moment you hit the Riprap Trail, just 0.4 mile from the trailhead. It stays with you the entire distance, except for the last mile of the Riprap Trail, where a fingerlike projection of the trail was removed. You quickly reclaim the wilderness as soon as you access the Wildcat Ridge Trail at about mile 4, leaving the wilderness once again when you access the Appalachian Trail at mile 6.7.

Wilderness includes those areas where all permanent evidence of human manipulation of the environment has been removed. When Shenandoah's wilderness was established in 1976, and to comply with the mandates of the 1964 Wilderness Act, one trail shelter was removed. "Today," as the act specifies, "the area contains no permanent evidence that people may once have inhabited the area."

Natural features include ancient quartzite rocks and lofty overlooks from areas where ancient worms once burrowed. As you progress into the wilderness, the area includes long runs created by beautiful streams. It also includes the park's largest pool, where hikers have long made a tradition of overnight treks to bathe and swim on hot summer days.

Many who venture into the area opt to make this an overnight backpacking excursion. The trip is a long one, but well worth every minute you might care to spend. Even if you can't spend days, the trip is well worth the time. The entire loop hike can certainly be made in one day or broken into smaller segments.

This 9.3-mile loop via three trails is a moderate to strenuous hike, but one of the prettiest in the park. Within 0.4 mile, after reaching the Riprap Trail, you travel not only in the backcountry but also in designated wilderness for most of the trip. Fishing is permitted with a Virginia license, and you discover backcountry camping spots after the first few miles.

From the end of the parking lot, take the Appalachian Trail north (white blazes), ascending for 0.4 mile under a canopy of oak, maple, and sassafras, to the cement post junction for the Riprap Trail. Go west (left), following the blue blazes. The trail, lined with blueberry bushes, makes a switchback descent, then ascends to a knoll. You come suddenly upon a jumble of lichen-covered rocks and boulders—a jumble known as riprap. At about 0.7 mile you reach a saddle, which provides great views of the Paine Run watershed. The striated boulders

Striated blocks of Erwin quartzite hug the trail at Calvary Rocks.

are Erwin quartzite, as are the rocks at Calvary Rocks and Chimney Rock, not far ahead. Follow the ridgetop up and down to Calvary Rocks, at mile 1.4 with a northwest view. Continue another 0.2 mile to Chimney Rock for another view. Iron pegs embedded in the rock are part of an old bridge. For a shorter hike (3.2 miles round-trip) retrace your steps from here.

The narrow trail levels, with a couple more small lookout points. It begins a gentle descent off the ridge back into the forest; the downhill trek becomes steeper and rockier.

A tiny, sometimes dry, stream enters from the left but soon becomes wider, flowing freely over rocks. A brown signpost with an arrow indicates that you must stay to the right. It's obvious that the trail has been rerouted here for a short distance. It

Generations of hikers have enjoyed the view near Chimney Rock.

drops steeply with some rough, rocky parts but is stabilized on the downhill side with rock piles.

At approximately 3.3 miles you must ford the stream by hopping rocks. About 100 yards farther, there's a delightful (and popular) swimming hole on the right. The swimming hole provides a lovely rest and picnic spot. The stream flows in from a wide, gentle incline, and trout inhabit the waters. Across the stream, an old path leads to the former site of the old Riprap Shelter, now removed because of the area's wilderness designation.

Continue down the trail, ford the stream, and arrive at a cement post that provides mileages. Continue on the level but rough and rocky trail, with talus slopes on the right.

At the next cement post, at mile 4, turn left (southeast) onto the Wildcat Ridge Trail (blue blazes). Cross another stream almost immediately and parallel it to your left. Cross the stream two more times, then begin the steep ascent to Wildcat Ridge. As you chug ever upward, where the trees begin to thin, you get some sparse views of the ridges to the west.

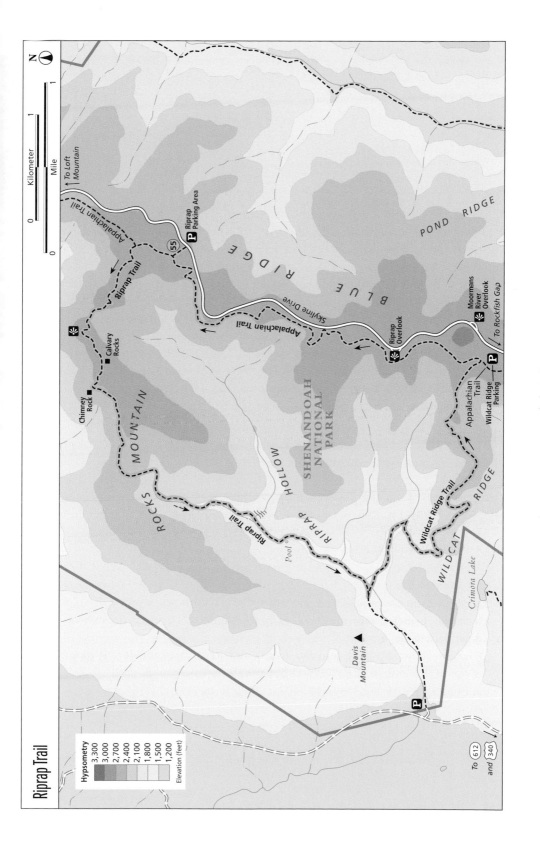

Riprap Trail

Hypsometry

3,300
3,000
2,700
2,400
2,100
1,800
1,500
1,200

Elevation (feet)

N

Kilometer

Mile

ROCKS MOUNTAIN

Chimney Rock

Calvary Rocks

Appalachian Trail

Riprap Trail

Riprap Parking Area

To Loft Mountain

55

Riprap Trail

Appalachian Trail

Skyline Drive

BLUE RIDGE

POND RIDGE

Riprap Overlook

Moormans River Overlook

To Rockfish Gap

Appalachian Trail

Wildcat Ridge Parking

WILDCAT RIDGE

Wildcat Ridge Trail

SHENANDOAH NATIONAL PARK

RIPRAP HOLLOW

Pool

Riprap Trail

Davis Mountain

Crimora Lake

To 612 and 340

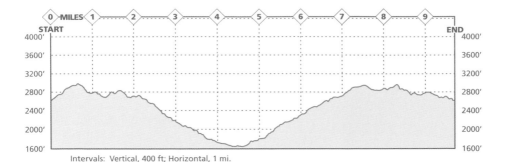

Intervals: Vertical, 400 ft; Horizontal, 1 mi.

The trail basically climbs to the next cement post at 6.6 miles. Here you have a choice: If you have two vehicles and have left one (or you have arranged a pickup) at the Wildcat Ridge parking area, head straight east, following the blue blazes for 0.1 mile to the parking lot, making the entire hike a journey of 6.7 miles. If your vehicle is at the Riprap trailhead, you must access the AT at the 6.6-mile cement post and head north (left) for 2.7 more miles, making a hike total of 9.3 miles.

The final 2.7 miles along the AT are not particularly strenuous. The trail combines level hiking with some uphill and some downhill. The AT swings well away from the Skyline Drive, and offers occasional views to the west. You see sweeps of rock along the way, areas that the forest is attempting to reclaim. The very last part of the trek swings you around one brief switchback; then you're home.

Miles and Directions

0.0 Start near the rear Riprap parking lot at Mile 90.0 on Skyline Drive on the west side of the drive.

0.4 Join the Riprap Trail from the Appalachian Trail at the cement post. Go west (left, following blue blazes).

0.7 Saddle, talus slope.

1.4 Calvary Rocks, views to northwest.

1.6 Chimney Rock.

3.3 Swimming hole.

3.4 Cement post with mileages. No trail change.

4.0 Cement post. Go southeast (left) onto the Wildcat Ridge Trail.

6.6 Junction with the AT. Go north (left) on the AT to the Riprap Trailhead to complete the loop.

6.7 End of the one-way hike at the Wildcat Ridge parking lot, and junction with the AT. Go left on the AT if you don't have a vehicle parked here.

9.3 Arrive back at the Riprap Trailhead and your vehicle by way of the AT to complete the loop.

56 Turk Mountain

An ascent to the inspiring summit of Turk Mountain is followed by a descent along the same trail.

Skyline Mile: 94.1
Distance: 2.2 miles out and back
Approx. hiking time: 2 to 4 hours
Difficulty: Moderate
Trail surface: Dirt and naturally occurring rock
Traffic: Light to moderate, depending on the day of the week

Canine compatibility: Leashed dogs allowed
Maps: National Geographic Trails Illustrated Topographic Map 228; Map 11, Appalachian Trail and Other Trails in Shenandoah National Park, South District (PATC, Inc.)

Finding the trailhead: The trail begins at Mile 94.1 on the west side of Skyline Drive, across the road from the Turk Gap parking area. Take the Appalachian Trail south (left), following the white blazes, to begin. GPS: N38 07.756' / W78 47.091'

The Hike

The trail up Turk Mountain begins across the road from the Turk Gap parking lot, at which point you immediately access the Appalachian Trail south. Continue along the AT for 0.1 mile and turn right onto the Turk Mountain Trail, which follows a brief downhill course, dropping through a saddle. At about 0.4 mile the trail begins to ascend abruptly and continues to do so throughout the climb. Near the top, the trail switchbacks several times, culminating approximately 1.1 miles later at an elevation of 2,981 feet.

Upon reaching what is essentially the trail's end, if you want good views you must scramble over rocks for a short distance. Mountain laurel is edging onto the rocks, but for the most part the scramble is free of slippery vegetation and is well worth the time, not only for the views but also for the geology.

The rocks forming the summit contain mostly quartzite, which the eons and the erosional forces of freezing and thawing have worn down. It is obvious that cataclysmic forces have been at work, for the fractured rocks composing the talus slope spread downward and out for hundreds of yards.

Views from Turk Mountain range across the southwestern portion of the

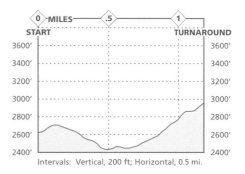

Intervals: Vertical, 200 ft; Horizontal, 0.5 mi.

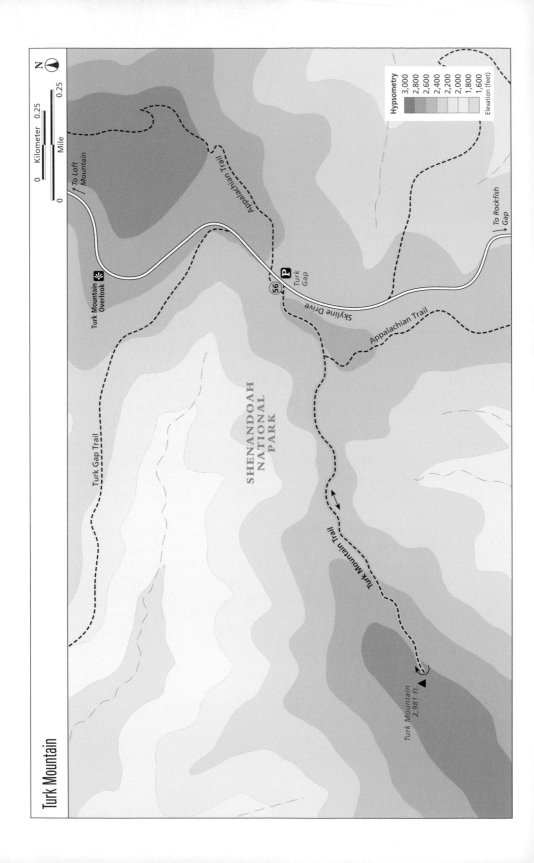

Turk Mountain

N

0   Kilometer   0.25
0   Mile   0.25

To Loft
Mountain

Turk Mountain
Overlook

Appalachian Trail

56

Turk
Gap

Skyline Drive

Appalachian Trail

To Rockfish
Gap

Turk Gap Trail

SHENANDOAH
NATIONAL
PARK

Turk Mountain Trail

Turk Mountain
2,981 ft

Hypsometry
3,000
2,800
2,600
2,400
2,200
2,000
1,800
1,600
Elevation (feet)

horizon. In the distance you can see the Shenandoah Valley and, a bit to the south, Sawmill Ridge and Scott Mountain.

The fortunate part of an uphill hike is that the return is downhill. So it is with the rest of this hike.

Miles and Directions

0.0 Start near Mile 94.1 on the west side of Skyline Drive, across the road from the Turk Gap parking area.

0.1 Cement post. Take the Turk Mountain Trail to the right. The AT continues straight.

1.1 Turk Mountain summit and viewpoint. Retrace your steps.

2.2 Arrive back at the trailhead. End of hike.

A glimpse of the spectacular views in store for hikers on the trail.

57 Jarman Gap to Beagle Gap

A one-way excursion leads past reminders of mountain people to the summit of Calf Mountain.

Skyline Mile: 96.8
Distance: 2.7 miles one way; shuttle required
Approx. hiking time: 2 to 4 hours
Difficulty: Moderate
Trail surface: Dirt and naturally occurring rock
Traffic: Light

Canine compatibility: Leashed dogs allowed
Maps: National Geographic Trails Illustrated Topographic Map 228; Map 11, Appalachian Trail and Other Trails in Shenandoah National Park, South District (PATC, Inc.)

Finding the trailhead: The trail begins at Jarman Gap, on Skyline Drive at Mile 96.8. Access the fire road to the right, on the east side of the drive. Go 0.1 mile to the cement post and the Appalachian Trail junction. GPS: N38 05.886' / W78 46.861'

The Hike

From the trailhead, hike 0.1 mile along an old fire road to the Appalachian Trail. Turn right at the cement post onto the AT southbound and begin a gradual climb. One of the rewards of hiking this trail is the vegetation. As you proceed along the first 0.1 mile, look for the large stands of tulip poplar that grace the woods. You'll recognize the trees by the large leaves with main veins that end in a notch. The tips appear to be cut off.

After picking up the AT, the trail climbs gradually. Within 0.5 mile the trail passes another old fire road, where we found artifacts from an old cabin—old bed springs eroded by the forces of nature. As the park service points out, what once was garbage now serves as pieces in a huge puzzle that cultural anthropologists are still assembling.

Continue on the AT, which soon passes a spring that may be dry in summer. A little farther along, a sign greets you and informs that you are hiking the AT and that it is maintained by the Potomac Appalachian Trail Club. Yet a short distance farther, the trail passes beneath a power line. At 1 mile the trail passes a spur trail that AT hikers often use. The spur provides access to the Calf Mountain Shelter and a spring, located respectively at 0.3 and 0.2 mile along the spur.

As you approach the summit of Calf Mountain, the trail increases in steepness. At one point it switches back and forth and then provides you with a

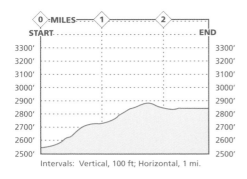

Intervals: Vertical, 100 ft; Horizontal, 1 mi.

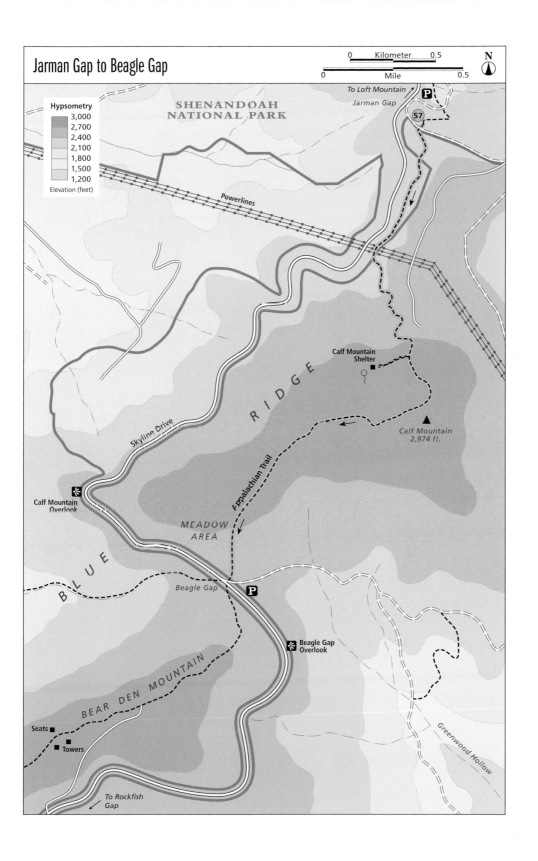

Jarman Gap to Beagle Gap

Hypsometry

3,000
2,700
2,400
2,100
1,800
1,500
1,200

Elevation (feet)

0   Kilometer   0.5

0   Mile   0.5

N

SHENANDOAH
NATIONAL PARK

To Loft Mountain

Jarman Gap

P

57

Powerlines

Calf Mountain
Shelter

R I D G E

Skyline Drive

Appalachian Trail

Calf Mountain
2,974 ft.

Calf Mountain
Overlook

MEADOW
AREA

B L U E

Beagle Gap

P

Beagle Gap
Overlook

BEAR DEN MOUNTAIN

Greenwood Hollow

Seats

Towers

To Rockfish
Gap

series of wood and stone steps. The rather abrupt incline, however, is short, and within 0.1 mile the trail levels along the summit of Calf Mountain.

The summit of Calf Mountain once served as pastureland, and it's obvious that vegetation is reclaiming the clearing. The trail opens into a parklike setting, and the vegetation consists of sumac, mint, some thistle, and much young pine. In August the raspberries that also flank the trail are ripe.

The trail soon descends, and within 0.1 mile you see more evidence of former human activity: An old stone wall with a width of about 25 yards cuts across the trail. The descent continues through the pasture setting, and as you near the trail's end, an old apple orchard still puts forth a fall harvest. This one-way hike ends on the AT at Beagle Gap.

Miles and Directions

0.0 Start adjacent to Jarman Gap, on Skyline Drive at Mile 96.8.

0.1 Cement post. Appalachian Trail junction. Go south on the AT (white blazes).

1.0 Cement post. Calf Mountain Shelter and spring on right.

1.7 Calf Mountain summit.

2.7 Cement post. Arrive at the trailhead at Beagle Gap, Mile 99.5. End of one-way hike.

58 Bear Den Mountain

A leg stretcher to the Bear Den Mountain summit (2,885 feet), offering spectacular views.

Skyline Mile: 99.5
Distance: 1.2 miles out and back
Approx. hiking time: 1 hour
Difficulty: Easy
Trail surface: Dirt and naturally occurring rock
Traffic: Light

Canine compatibility: Leashed dogs allowed
Maps: National Geographic Trails Illustrated Topographic Map 228; Map 11, Appalachian Trail and Other Trails in Shenandoah National Park, South District (PATC, Inc.)

Finding the trailhead: The trail begins at Mile 99.5 on the west side of Skyline Drive, across from the Beagle Gap parking area. Go through an iron gate with a white blaze (designating the AT) on a wood post. GPS: N38 04.374' / W78 47.619'

Witch hazel, as seen along trail to summit of Bear Den Mountain.

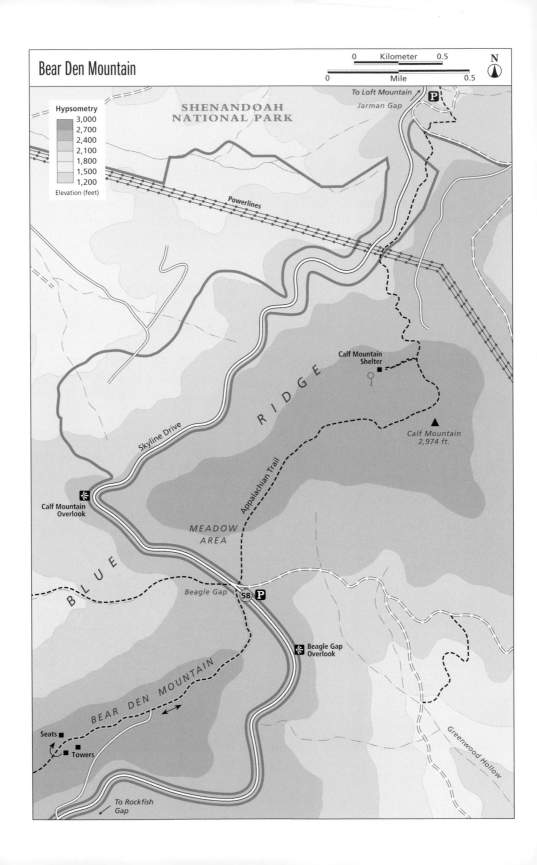

Bear Den Mountain

Hypsometry

3,000
2,700
2,400
2,100
1,800
1,500
1,200
Elevation (feet)

SHENANDOAH
NATIONAL PARK

To Loft Mountain

Jarman Gap

P

Powerlines

Calf Mountain
Shelter

R I D G E

Skyline Drive

Calf Mountain
2,974 ft.

Appalachian Trail

Calf Mountain
Overlook

MEADOW
AREA

B L U E

Beagle Gap

58 P

Beagle Gap
Overlook

BEAR DEN MOUNTAIN

Seats

Towers

Greenwood Hollow

To Rockfish
Gap

The Hike

Walk directly across Skyline Drive (west) from the Beagle Gap parking lot, and proceed through the opening in the iron gate with a white blaze on a wood post. Look northwest for views of the Shenandoah Valley.

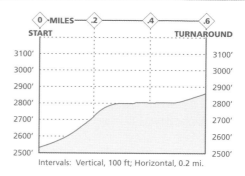

Following the Appalachian Trail (blazed on rocks), the trail ascends gently through an old meadow. After about 0.2 mile a road intersects the AT; cross it and follow the AT. The ascent leads 353 feet to the summit of Bear Den Mountain. If the day is clear, panoramic views open in all directions. Best of all, seven old tractor seats have been inserted by their posts into the ground, offering thrones on which to perch. The landscape below offers scenery fit for a king or queen.

If you want a slightly longer walk, hike the ridge over to the second set of communication towers. The views are not necessarily better, just slightly different. Retrace the AT back to the parking lot.

Miles and Directions

0.0 Start at the iron gate with a white blaze directly across from the Beagle Gap parking area at Mile 99.5, on the west side of Skyline Drive.

0.6 Summit of Bear Den Mountain. Retrace steps.

1.2 Arrive back at the trailhead and the Beagle Gap parking lot.

Bear Den's trails offer good views and plenty of opportunities to study the surrounding vegetation.

59 Calf Mountain

A pleasant hike to the top of Calf Mountain winds through old pastures and some new-growth trees.

Skyline Mile: 99.5
Distance: 2 miles out and back
Approx. hiking time: 1 to 2 hours
Difficulty: Easy
Trail surface: Dirt and naturally occurring rock
Traffic: Light

Canine compatibility: Leashed dogs allowed
Maps: National Geographic Trails Illustrated Topographic Map 228; Map 11, Appalachian Trail and Other Trails in Shenandoah National Park, South District (PATC, Inc.)

Finding the trailhead: The hike begins at Mile 99.5, at the Beagle Gap parking area on the east side of Skyline Drive. Walk through the opening in the wire fence with a white blaze on it. GPS: N38 04.391' / W78 47.592'

The Hike

This short jaunt up to Calf Mountain is a delightful one, partly because it winds through old meadows and is not a hike through woods. The trail is good for the entire distance, consisting generally of soft dirt rather than rock. In the summer—if it's hot and humid—you might want to make this one early or late in the day. It's also a good walk for frisky children.

Walk through the V opening in the wire fence and ascend through a meadow filled with wildflowers and berry bushes. Entering a small stand of new-growth trees and bushes, the trail quickly becomes a bit steeper for about 0.2 mile. Then you again hike out on the level, and into meadows, and come upon a large stand of old, still-bearing, apple trees.

At about 0.7 mile views open to the east. This is not the summit; the top is about 0.3 mile farther. You'll know you have gone over the top when you begin a descent on logs and rocks placed across the trail. From the top, retrace your route and enjoy, once again, the area's openness, its lush vegetation, and its introduced apple orchard.

Miles and Directions

0.0 Beagle Gap parking lot; walk through opening in fence.

0.7 Viewpoint.

1.0 Reach the summit of Calf Mountain. Retrace the Appalachian Trail back to the parking lot.

2.0 Arrive back at the trailhead at the Beagle Gap parking lot.

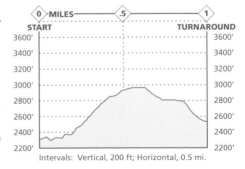

Intervals: Vertical, 200 ft; Horizontal, 0.5 mi.

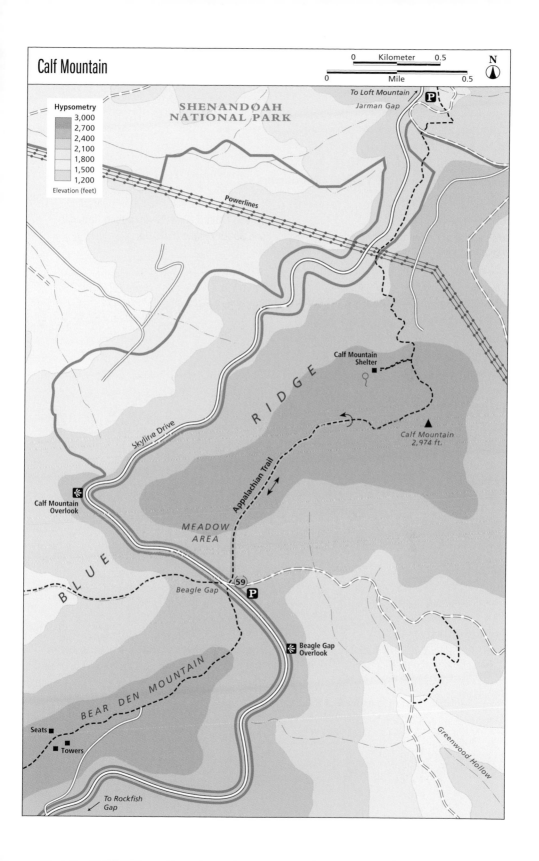

Calf Mountain

Kilometer 0.5

Mile 0.5

N

Hypsometry

3,000
2,700
2,400
2,100
1,800
1,500
1,200

Elevation (feet)

SHENANDOAH
NATIONAL PARK

To Loft Mountain

Jarman Gap

P

Powerlines

R   I   D   G   E

Calf Mountain
Shelter

Skyline Drive

Calf Mountain
2,974 ft.

Appalachian Trail

Calf Mountain
Overlook

MEADOW
AREA

B L U E

59

Beagle Gap

P

Beagle Gap
Overlook

BEAR DEN MOUNTAIN

Seats

Towers

Greenwood Hollow

To Rockfish
Gap

Appendix A: For More Information

The following are excellent sources for hiking and backpacking information, maps, camping and reservations information, books, and other materials concerning Shenandoah National Park.

Shenandoah National Park Headquarters
3655 US 211 East
Luray, VA 22835
(540) 999-3500 (nonemergencies)
For emergencies in the park: (800) 732-0911
www.nps.gov/shen

Shenandoah National Park Association
3655 US 211 East
Luray, VA 22835-9036
(540) 999-3581
www.snpbooks.org

Dickey Ridge Visitor Center
Mile 4.7, Skyline Drive
Information, maps, permits, restrooms, water, books, films, exhibits

Harry F. Byrd Sr. Visitor Center
Mile 51.0 at north entrance to Big Meadows
Information, maps, permits, restrooms, water, food, ranger programs, films, books, exhibits

Potomac Appalachian Trail Club (PATC, Inc.)
118 Park St. SE
Vienna, VA 22180
General information: (703) 242-0315
Fax: (703) 242-0968
www.patc.net
Office hours: Mon through Thurs from 7 to 9 p.m. and Thurs through Fri from noon to 2 p.m.

Appalachian Trail Conference (ATC)
Washington & Jackson Streets
PO Box 807
Harpers Ferry, WV 25425
(303) 535-6331

Ranger Stations within the Park
North District: Mile 22.1
Central District: Mile 51.0 at Big Meadows (just before maintenance area)
South District: Mile 73.2 at Simmons Gap (east side of Skyline Drive)

The park has four entrance stations. Upon entering, you must purchase either an annual pass, a seven-day pass, or a National Parks pass. Fees vary from year to year.
Mile 0.6: Front Royal Entrance Station, just off US 340
Mile 31.5: Thornton Gap Entrance Station, US 211 interchange
Mile 65.5: Swift Run Gap Entrance Station, US 33 interchange
Mile 104.6: Rockfish Gap Entrance Station, I-64 and US 250 interchange

Finding Maps

Several types of maps are available for the Shenandoah National Park hiker and can be obtained at the visitor centers, the waysides, and at sporting goods stores throughout the area, as well as by writing or calling the map publishers. Map types include topographical maps, descriptive trail booklets, and free map handouts. All provide excellent information. However, the topographical maps are probably the most accurate. You would be wise to carry these, especially on extended trips, along with a good compass.

Providing completely accurate mileages of trails is difficult, however, so bear in mind that the trails may be slightly shorter or longer than indicated. In addition, the trail lengths on the maps sometimes differ from what is posted on the trail signs. Often more important than the actual length is the difficulty rating. A very strenuous trail of 2 miles often does take longer to hike than an easy one of 5 miles.

Free copies of some trail maps are available from the visitor centers and through the Shenandoah National Park website. The booklets for three short hikes can be obtained at the visitor centers, from the Shenandoah National Park Association, and in boxes at the trailheads. A minimal fee is charged for these booklets.

Quad and topographical maps may be purchased from the following sources:

Shenandoah National Park Association (see above)

Shenandoah National Park Visitor Centers (see above)

Trails Illustrated
Division of National Geographic Maps
PO Box 4357
Evergreen, CO 80437-4357
(800) 962-1643 or (303) 670-3457
www.natgeomaps.com/ti_228
Topographical Map 228 covers Shenandoah National Park.

Potomac Appalachian Trail Club (PATC, Inc.)
118 Park St. SE
Vienna, VA 22180
(703) 242-0315
www.patc.us/store/snp.htm
Three PATC topographical maps (numbers 9, 10, and 11) cover Shenandoah National Park.

Waysides within Shenandoah National Park. Three waysides provide gas, oil, air, water, groceries, and camping and RV supplies and equipment. Hours of operation vary with the seasons. None of these waysides provide repairs. Elkwallow has a snack bar; Loft Mountain has breakfast and lunch; and Big Meadows has a restaurant.
Mile 24.0: Elkwallow Wayside
Mile 51.2: Big Meadows Wayside
Mile 79.5: Loft Mountain Wayside

US Geological Survey (USGS)
National Mapping Division
12201 Sunrise Valley Dr., Mail Stop 809
Reston, VA 22092
(703) 648-7070
www.usgs.gov

US Geological Survey (USGS)
Branch of Distribution
Federal Center
Denver, CO 80225
Customer service: (800) 435-7627 or (303) 202-4200
The USGS provides 1969 quad maps that do not contain current information such as trail modifications.

Appendix B: Further Reading

The Shenandoah National Park Association makes available a wonderful selection of books for all ages. The visitor centers in the park also stock a great inventory of books for sale, as do the ARAMARK facilities along Skyline Drive. Topics available from these outlets include natural history, human history, mountain lore, hiking and backpacking, maps, children's books, and coloring books. The list of available resources is extensive.

Many of the following books were helpful as we prepared this book. Others make fascinating reading.

Amberson, Joanne. *Easy Hikes on the Appalachian National Scenic Trail in Shenandoah National Park.* Luray, Va.: Shenandoah National Park Association, 2003.

————. *Hikes to Peaks & Vistas in Shenandoah National Park.* Luray, Va.: Shenandoah National Park Association, 2002.

————. *Hikes to Waterfalls in Shenandoah National Park.* Luray, Va.: Shenandoah National Park Association, 1997.

————. *Short Hikes in Shenandoah National Park.* Luray, Va.: Shenandoah National Park Association, rev. 2004

Bell, C. Ritchie, and Anne H. Lindsey. *Fall Color and Woodland Harvests.* Chapel Hill, N.C.: Laurel Hill Press, 1990.

Crandall, Hugh, and Reed Engle. *Shenandoah: The Story Behind the Scenery.* Las Vegas: KC Publications, Inc., rev. 1997.

Engle, Reed. *Everything Was Wonderful: A Pictorial History of the Civilian Conservation Corps in Shenandoah National Park.* Luray, Va.: Shenandoah National Park Association, 1999.

————. *In the Light of the Mountain Moon: An Illustrated History of Skyland.* Luray, Va.: Shenandoah National Park Association, 2003.

Fletcher, Colin, and Chip Rawlins. *The Complete Walker.* New York: Alfred A. Knopf, 1971.

Harmon, Will. *Leave No Trace.* Helena, Mont.: Falcon, 1997.

————. *Wild Country Companion.* Helena, Mont.: Falcon, 1994.

Horning, Audrey. *In the Shadow of Ragged Mountain: Historical Archaeology of Nicholson, Corbin & Weakley Hollows.* Luray, Va.: Shenandoah National Park Association, 2004.

Lambert, Darwin. *The Undying Past of Shenandoah National Park.* Boulder, Colo.: Roberts Rinehart Publishers, 1989.

Reeder, Carolyn, and Jack Reeder. *Shenandoah Secrets: The Story of the Park's Hidden Past.* Vienna, Va.: Potomac Appalachian Trail Club, 1991.

Schneider, Bill. *Bear Aware.* Guilford, Conn.: The Globe Pequot Press, 2004.

Stupka, Arthur. *Wildflowers in Color.* New York: HarperCollins, 1994.

Watts, May Theilgaard. *Tree Finder: A Manual for the Identification of Trees by Their Leaves.* Rochester, N.Y.: Nature Study Guild, 1991.

Appendix C: Hike Finder

Easy Day Hikes
Hike 2: Fox Hollow Trail
Hike 3: Snead Farm–Dickey Ridge Trail Loop
Hike 4: Lands Run Falls
Hike 5: Fort Windham Rocks–Indian Run Spring
Hike 10: Traces Trail
Hike 14: Byrds Nest Summit and Byrds Nest Shelter No. 4
Hike 22: Stony Man Trail
Hike 23: Millers Head
Hike 24: Limberlost
Hike 29: Story of the Forest Trail
Hike 30: Big Meadows
Hike 32: Blackrock
Hike 35: Lewis Mountain Trail
Hike 36: Pocosin Trail
Hike 41: Simmons Gap
Hike 45: Loft Mountain Loop
Hike 47: Big Flat Mountain Loop
Hike 52: Blackrock Summit
Hike 57: Jarman Gap to Beagle Gap
Hike 58: Bear Den Mountain
Hike 59: Calf Mountain

Hikes with Children
Hike 2: Fox Hollow Trail
Hike 3: Snead Farm–Dickey Ridge Trail Loop
Hike 5: Fort Windham Rocks
Hike 7: Mount Marshall Trail and Beyond
Hike 10: Traces Trail
Hike 22: Stony Man Trail
Hike 24: Limberlost
Hike 26: Hawksbill Summit
Hike 28: Dark Hollow Falls (with in-shape kids)
Hike 29: Story of the Forest Trail
Hike 30: Big Meadows
Hike 31: Lewis Spring Falls Trail (alternative route)
Hike 35: Lewis Mountain Trail
Hike 36: Pocosin Trail
Hikes 45/46/47: Loft Mountain area hikes
Hike 52: Blackrock Summit

Hike 51: Rockytop
Hike 55: Riprap Trail

Hikes with Great Views
Hike 7: Mount Marshall Trail and Beyond
Hike 9: Sugarloaf–Keyser Run Fire Road–Hogback Mountain Loop
Hike 16: Old Rag
Hike 17: Marys Rock North
Hike 18: Marys Rock South
Hike 26: Hawksbill Summit
Hike 34: Bearfence Mountain
Hike 40: Powell Gap
Hike 52: Blackrock Summit
Hike 58: Bear Den Mountain

History Hikes
Hike 2: Fox Hollow Trail
Hike 3: Snead Farm–Dickey Ridge Trail Loop
Hike 10: Traces Trail
Hike 20: Corbin Cabin Cutoff–Nicholson Hollow–Appalachian Trail Loop
Hike 30: Big Meadows
Hike 36: Pocosin Trail

Hikes to See Waterfalls

Hike	Falls	Height in Feet	Skyline Mile
Hike 11	Overall Run Falls, upper falls	29	22.2
Hike 11	Overall Run Falls	93	22.2
Hike 25	Cedar Run Falls	34	45.6
Hike 25	Whiteoak Falls No. 1	86	45.6
Hike 25	Whiteoak Falls No. 2	62	45.6
Hike 25	Whiteoak Falls No. 3	35	45.6
Hike 25	Whiteoak Falls No. 4	41	45.6
Hike 25	Whiteoak Falls No. 5	49	45.6
Hike 25	Whiteoak Falls No. 6	60	45.6
Hike 27	Rose River Falls	67	49.4
Hike 28	Dark Hollow Falls	70	50.7
Hike 31	Lewis Spring Falls	81	51.2
Hike 38	South River Falls	83	62.8
Hike 49	Doyles River Falls No. 1	28	81.1
Hike 49	Doyles River Falls No. 2	63	81.1
Hike 49	Jones Run Falls	42	81.1

Appendix D: Where to Stay

Campgrounds

Four campgrounds are available in Shenandoah National Park, and they range from those with RV/camper spaces to tent sites, some of which are walk-in tent spaces. Trailer hookups are not available in any of the campgrounds. However, all but Lewis Mountain have a disposal area. Obviously there is something for everyone. Big Meadows Campground requires reservations, so it's a good idea to call ahead, especially during the busier summer months. For those unable to plan ahead who find themselves in need of a campsite, it seems that unreserved sites become available early in the mornings as others pull out.

Backcountry or wilderness camping is allowed in most areas of the park. Those areas that are off-limits are listed for you in the handouts you acquire with the required backcountry camping permit, which can be obtained from the visitor centers or ranger stations.

From Skyline Drive, north to south, the campgrounds are as follows:

Mile 22.2: Mathews Arm Campground (179 sites). Flush toilets. Some sites are reserved. Call (877) 444-6777 or visit www.recreation.gov.

Mile 51.2: Big Meadows Campground (230 sites). Reservations system May through Oct. Can camp without reservations if the campground is not full. To reserve a site, talk with the folks at the campground entrance gate or call (800) 365-2267. You can also call (877) 444-6777 or visit www.recreation.gov. Showers, camp store, laundry, water.

Mile 57.5: Lewis Mountain Campground (32 sites). First-come, first-served basis, tent and vehicle pull-in sites. Showers, camp store, water, laundry.

Mile 79.5: Loft Mountain Campground (219 sites). Tent sites, RV sites, vehicle pull-ins. Some sites reserved. Call (877) 444-6777 or visit www.recreation.gov. Showers, laundry, camp store, water.

Lodging Units

Lodging units for rent (best to make reservations) can be found at Skyland Resort (Mile 41.7) and Big Meadows (Mile 51.2). At Lewis Mountain (Mile 57.5), several cabins are available for rent. Remember that summer and fall are crowded, so call early (800-999-4714) to reserve. These are operated by ARAMARK, the official park concessioner. The lodging complexes have dining rooms and/or food service. Visit www.visitshenandoah.com/accommodations.aspx.

Shelters

Five shelters exist in the park. They are for day use and emergency shelter only. Byrds Nest Shelter No. 4 is in the North District, while Byrds Nest Shelters No. 1, 2, and 3 and the Old Rag Shelter are in the Central District.

Huts

The Potomac Appalachian Trail Club (PATC) provides seven three-sided huts along the Appalachian Trail; these are intended mostly for Appalachian Trail long-distance hikers and are spaced about a day's hike (8 to 10 miles) apart. In emergencies other hikers may use the huts if they are not full. Otherwise, you must camp out of sight of the hut unless different regulations are posted at the hut sites.

Cabins

The PATC also owns and maintains six cabins scattered throughout the park. Information on renting them and what is supplied may be obtained by contacting the PATC office at 118 Park St. SE, Vienna, VA 22180; general information: (703) 242-0315; fax: (703) 242-0968; www.patc.net/PublicView/Custom/PATC_Cabins/Cabins.aspx.

A hiker taking a rest and enjoying the views at Bear Den.

Hike Index

About the Authors

Bert Gildart has been writing about the outdoors for more than forty years. For thirteen summers he served as a backcountry ranger in Glacier National Park. He has written more than 300 magazine articles for such publications as *Smithsonian, Travel + Leisure, Modern Maturity, Field & Stream,* and *National Wildlife.* Together, Bert and his wife, Janie, have hiked hundreds of miles throughout many wilderness and backcountry areas of the country. They have collaborated on several other FalconGuides including: *Best Easy Day Hikes Shenandoah National Park, A FalconGuide to Death Valley National Park, A FalconGuide to Dinosaur National Monument, Best Easy Day Hikes Black Hills Country,* and *Hiking the Black Hills Country.* Bert is also the author of a Globe Pequot Press book of essays on and images of Glacier National Park. He has won awards from the Montana Press Association and from the Outdoor Writers Association of America.

American Hiking Society

Because you hike.
We're with you every step of the way

As a national voice for hikers, **American Hiking Society** works every day:

- Building and maintaining hiking trails
- Educating and supporting hikers by providing information and resources
- Supporting hiking and trail organizations nationwide
- Speaking for hikers in the halls of Congress and with federal land managers

Whether you're a casual hiker or a seasoned backpacker, become a member of American Hiking Society and join the national hiking community! You'll enjoy great member benefits and help preserve the nation's hiking trails, so tomorrow's hike is even better than today's. We invite you to join us now!

American Hiking Society